To L

MW00473331

Frank Church, D.C., & Me

Frank Church, D.C., & Me

Bill Hall

Foreword by LeRoy Ashby

WSU
PRESS

Washington State University Press
Pullman, Washington

Washington State University Press, Pullman, Washington 99164-5910
© 1995 by the Board of Regents of Washington State University
All rights reserved

First printing 1995

Printed and bound in the United States of America on pH neutral, acid-free paper. No part of this book may be reproduced or transmitted in any form or by any means, electronic or mechanical, including recording, photocopying, or by any information storage or retrieval system, without permission in writing from the publisher.

Cover photography by Robert Hubner

Library of Congress Cataloging-in-Publication Data
Hall, Bill, 1937-
    Frank Church, D.C., and me / by Bill Hall ; with a foreword by LeRoy Ashby.
      p. cm.
    ISBN 0-87422-119-6 (pbk. : acid-free paper)
    1. Church, Frank. 2. Legislators—United States—Biography.
3. United States. Congress. Senate—Biography. 4. Hall, Bill,
1937- . I. Title.
E840.8.C49H34   1995
328.73'092—dc20
[B]   95-6505
                                      CIP

Washington State University Press
Pullman, Washington 99164-5910
Phone: 800-354-7360
Fax: 509-335-8568

For Don Watkins, Myrna Sasser,
Cherie Coleman Slayton, and Debbie Herbst.

Contents

Foreword

Idaho's Frank Church was one of modern America's premier U.S. Senators. From 1957 to 1981—years of enormous national stress and tumult—he distinguished himself as a decent and honorable politician, deeply embroiled in the major issues and debates of his day. During his four terms he became an articulate critic of America's cold war foreign policies, a leading advocate of legislation to protect the environment and the elderly, and a staunch defender of democratic principles against a national security state built on secrecy, spying, and executive privilege. In the mid-1970s he presided over several of the most important investigations in modern American history, and during his last two years in office he chaired the prestigious Senate Committee on Foreign Relations. He set a standard for political honesty.

Church built his brilliant career despite formidable physical and political odds. Born in 1924 of modest origins in Boise, Idaho, he suffered from frequent bronchial infections. His parents sometimes feared that he would not last the night. Although never very healthy, he was extremely intelligent and self-assured. As a fourteen-year-old in 1939, he wrote to a Boise newspaper about why the United States should not get involved in what was quickly becoming World War II; the editor was so impressed with the letter that he published it on the front page. Early on, Church also won recognition for his superior speaking abilities. In 1941 he prevailed over 108,000 contestants to capture the American Legion National High School Oratorical championship. The Legion scholarship allowed him to enroll briefly at Stanford University before entering the armed forces in 1942. As a military intelligence officer in the China-Burma-India theater he received a Bronze Star.

Following the war he married Bethine Clark, his high school sweetheart. The daughter of a former Idaho governor and federal judge, she became one of the most influential people in Church's life. Their relationship constituted what one friend described as "history's longest running high school romance." Gregarious, energetic, and politically shrewd, she was Church's trusted advisor as well as his closest friend. In 1949 she also helped to pull him through a terrifyingly close brush with death.

Church was completing his law degree at Stanford when he learned that he had testicular cancer and would probably die within six months. With massive radiation treatments he survived, but doctors estimated that his battle against cancer had shortened his life considerably. Certain that he existed on "borrowed time," he concluded that "the only way to live . . . is by taking great chances."

In that spirit, he took a huge political gamble in 1956 by running for the United States Senate. He won decisively, even though he was only 32, had never before held elective office, and faced a tough, red-baiting Republican incumbent. Six years younger than any of his colleagues, whose average age was 58, he took office as the "baby" senator and the "Boy Orator of the Snake."

For the next 24 years Church continued to battle formidable political obstacles. No previous Idaho Democrat had served more than one term; he served four and narrowly missed a fifth. And he did so despite a liberal reputation in a state with strongly conservative leanings. His success reflected his ability to keep close contact with the grassroots, to look out for his constituents, to pick his fights carefully, and to identify himself with the state's hallowed tradition of independence and individual courage. Honest to the core, he also earned respect for his integrity and avoided even a hint of scandal.

From the moment Church entered the Senate he was determined to be a major political figure. Within six months after taking office he played a pivotal role in the passage of the 1957 Civil Rights Act, the first legislation of its kind in almost a century. By 1959 he had elevated himself over several more senior senators to gain a seat on the Foreign Relations Committee. In 1960 he delivered the keynote address at the national Democratic convention and aligned himself with the forces of John Kennedy. During the 1960s he was one of the earliest and most articulate opponents of the Vietnam war. Initially, he questioned the war on practical grounds, believing it a tragic mistake; but more and more he attacked it as immoral, a threat to America's ideals, and proof that cold war ideologies damaged America abroad and threatened democratic principles at home.

Despite his growing outrage at the war, Church nevertheless remained a believer in the American political system, its give-and-take, and its dependence on coalitions and compromises. Although he sometimes opened himself to criticism for being too quick to compromise, he was convinced that change in a democracy comes incrementally, via a respect for other opinions and an appreciation of the need to gather votes.

Church thus worked to build an anti-war coalition that crossed party boundaries. Among his chief allies was Kentucky's Republican senator John Sherman Cooper. The landmark Cooper-Church amendment in 1970, in response to the "incursion" of U.S. troops into Cambodia, represented the first time in American history that the Senate exercised its constitutional powers over the purse to limit a war's expansion.

By the middle 1970s the Idaho senator's eloquent opposition to American interventionism in Vietnam and elsewhere had helped to make him a national political figure. His support of environmental legislation was also significant. By fighting for laws to protect wilderness areas, for example, he demonstrated that a mountain and desert state politician could build grassroots constituencies around ecological issues. And, as chair of the Senate Special Committee on Aging, he became a leading champion of elderly citizens, who honored him again and again.

His role in the mid-Seventies as chair of two startling investigations added to his reputation as "a rising star," in the words of columnist George Will. One investigation probed the influence of multinational corporations on U.S. foreign policy; the other exposed abuses of power by the Central Intelligence Agency, Federal Bureau of Investigation, and other intelligence-gathering agencies. The highly publicized inquiries revealed shocking malpractice at the highest levels of government and business. Federal agencies had invaded the rights of American citizens; the C.I.A. and the International Telephone and Telegraph Corporation had been instrumental in the overthrow of the legally elected Salvador Allende government in Chile; corporations such as Lockheed and Gulf Oil had paid bribes to foreign governments. The list of corporate and governmental crimes went on and on.

In 1976, at the conclusion of the Intelligence Committee's controversial investigation, Church entered the Democratic presidential primaries as a "late, late candidate." In stunning upsets, he defeated frontrunner Jimmy Carter in Nebraska and Oregon. But after four quick primary victories, Church's presidential bid fell victim to a lack of time and money, Carter's big lead, and the appearance of an even later candidate, California governor Jerry Brown.

Although Church and the Carter administration were anything but close, the Idaho senator was a crucial ally in the narrow passage of the critical 1978 Panama Canal treaties. He paid a high political price, however, for managing the floor debate over the treaties, which opponents portrayed as emblematic of America's global decline. The ratification fight, as much as anything, hindered his pursuit of a fifth term. In 1979 he finally reached his goal of chairing the Committee on Foreign Relations, but by then his political fortunes were ebbing. Targeted by New Right groups across the nation, he struggled for reelection against a tide of innuendo, falsehoods, and sleazy tactics. Amazingly, he almost won, losing to arch-conservative Steve Symms by less than 1 percent of the vote.

Three years later, while practicing law with a large firm in Washington, D.C., Church learned that he again had cancer. This time, there was no treatment. He died on April 7, 1984, at the age of fifty-nine.

A major strength of Bill Hall's immensely readable *Frank Church, D.C., and Me* is its inside view of one of the most important and exciting periods in Church's notable career. In 1975-76, Hall served as the senator's press secretary. During that memorable time Church chaired the investigations of multinational corporations and the intelligence community, and launched his belated presidential candidacy.

Hall's book contains an informative behind-the-scenes look at a presidential primary campaign. The reader learns about the contending factions, and the infighting, within Church's camp. Hall also supplies many insights into Church himself. The senator in these pages bears little resemblance to the person some observers regarded as aloof, overly earnest, prudish, even "prissy"—"Senator Cathedral," as some critics dubbed him. Church's wit, informality, and lack of pomposity are clear in Hall's narrative.

But Hall does more than offer significant perspectives on Frank Church the senator and presidential candidate. He also provides a funny, even hilarious, account of life inside the Beltway. Very cleverly, Hall taps a rich vein of American comedy in which he resembles memorable naifs ranging from Silas Dogood to Buster Keaton, Laurel and Hardy, and Alfred E. Neuman—guileless innocents who bumble along, seemingly oblivious to the scowls and embarrassment of their urbane and sophisticated "betters." Like Neil Simon's hapless "Out-of-Towners," Hall emerges as a rube in the big city. And by portraying himself as a country yokel inside the circles of government, he solidifies his place as a leading Pacific Northwest humorist.

Hall is less the political innocent than his narrative suggests, however. Born in southeastern Idaho in 1937, he has long been a self-described "political junkie." Moreover, before joining Church's staff, he covered state politics as a journalist and editorial writer for almost two decades. By the mid-Seventies he was a major political commentator for the *Lewiston Tribune*, one of the state's leading newspapers.

At first glance, Hall and Frank Church were in many respects an unlikely combination. For years Hall had delighted in lampooning elected officials and other "big shots," including Church. In 1974, for example, he wrote an editorial so critical of the senator's "lame" position on one issue that Church's Republican challenger reprinted it.

Less than a year later Church nevertheless asked Hall to be his press secretary, replacing the very capable Cleve Corlett, who had recently joined Senator Joe Biden's staff. Like other major politicians, Church was well aware that the media's growing influence required knowledgeable press aides who could effectively get out news releases, arrange press appearances, and handle the print, radio, and television outlets. Indeed, when the senator won his first election in 1956, he had displayed an early and acute appreciation of the role of TV in politics. With Corlett's departure in 1975, Church needed a press secretary who knew Idaho and the media, and who would speak with candor. He turned to Hall. Although Hall was an avid political watcher who found the prospects of a ringside seat in the nation's capital alluring, he was not anxious to give up his journalistic independence nor move from northern Idaho to

Washington, D.C. He knew that press secretaries in some senators' offices played very restricted roles, doing "little more than
carrying the boss's ashtray," as one Senate aide has observed.
Corlett's experience indicated that Church viewed his press secretary as a valued adviser, not merely as some "spin control" artist,
but Hall was hardly predisposed to jump from an editor's desk to a
senator's staff.

If he were going to make that leap, however, it would be for
Church. On political issues the two men were usually in agreement.
They also both prized the art of friendly persuasion and placed great
value on the power of words. Church, moreover, unquestionably
sensed that Hall's apparent cynicism about politics masked a deeply
felt idealism. Hall's moralistic nature fused nicely with a similar
dimension in Church, whose emphasis on right conduct—personal
and national—prompted some people to call him a Boy Scout. Hall
applauded, for example, Church's belief that the lessons of foreign
policy are really quite simple: treat other countries as you would
want them to treat your own. This golden rule of politics was only
one of many ideas that Church and Hall shared. As civil libertar-
ians, they believed in the marketplace of ideas. Both also had strong
democratic impulses. And both resented elite snobbery.

According to one piece of wisdom, bosses are seldom heroes
to their valets or servants. But Bill Hall's respect and admiration
for Frank Church grew during Hall's months working for the senator. That growing appreciation tells the reader much about Church.
Hall does not allow his memoir to turn maudlin, however. He never
lets the reader forget that his story is also about a rustic's awkward
adventures in the nation's political mecca, Washington, D.C.

LeRoy Ashby
Pullman, Washington
May 1995

Chapter One
"Welcome to Washington, You Clumsy Oaf"

In 16 months as press secretary to a presidential candidate, I think I am proudest that I kept my orange tennis shoes and never wore a pin-striped suit.

When you become press secretary to what the Cold Warriors used to call the Next Leader of the Free World, there are prestigious pressures to discard your old orange tennis shoes.

I didn't.

That doesn't mean I wore orange tennis shoes in the Senate offices, except on weekends. Nor does it mean that I wore them to Washington cocktail parties, except on that one occasion which was all a misunderstanding. But I did wear those orange tennis shoes in casual moments no matter how the disapproving sniffed or snickered.

And not once did I wear a pin-striped suit, though it is the uniform of the Senate. Administrative assistants wear pin-striped suits. Legislative assistants wear pin-striped suits. Interns can't get in the door without a pin-striped suit. Even network correspondents wear pin-striped suits—tailored, of course.

Oh, I'll admit I wanted to. When you move to Washington from some unstarched place like Idaho, a pin-striped suit can be appealing. As you stand there in front of the shop window, the latest outlander wanting to work his way up in Washington, you get the message on how those threads became the uniform. A pin-striped suit singles out its occupant as significant but sincere, magnetic but not flashy, a humble heavyweight.

Except how can you be singled out by the same suit everybody else is wearing? Away from the shop window, the perspective is sobering. When you work in the Senate every day, and you see everyone sporting the uniform, and you have doubts about all this to begin with, a line must be drawn. To a person making the uneasy transition from working newspaperman to politician's flack, the commitment to the republic must be tempered. The heart and mind and soul may have been given over to the government, but the body will resist the uniform for a few more months, in case the heart and mind and soul—and the very cold feet—have made a terrible mistake.

* * *

It was in the prophetic chill of February, 1975—months before I would be held prisoner inside a presidential campaign headquarters—that I took leave of Lewiston, Idaho. I left behind a community that tolerated me, a prolific vegetable garden that reciprocated my love, and a lusty little western daily that printed and cherished five thousand of my words each week.

In return, I acquired Washington, D.C., which neither tolerated nor loved nor cherished me or my words. For 16 months, D.C. was indifferent.

I am inclined to blame the Republicans for those months in Washington, although it was a Democrat who drew me there. The Republicans teach small town boys like Richard Nixon and me to feel guilty if we enjoy a modest life, give some useful service to a few kind souls around us, and then decline an opportunity to move upward and grasp the levers of power. The Republicans condition us to equate comfort with complacency and minor usefulness with major sloth. The Republicans command us to grasp those levers of power during the time or two in our lives when they may come within our reach.

The levers came within my reach unexpectedly. Senator Frank Church of Idaho was throwing less cold water than usual on the perennial rumors he might run for president. Church, after 19 years in the Senate and with some national following for his early opposition to the Vietnam war, had been the subject of presidential speculation before. And senators so mentioned are rarely adamant in their denials. They always keep the door open a crack, just to let the rumors circulate. It doesn't hurt a senator's standing among the home folks to be mentioned for the presidency. It doesn't do his ego any damage either. And his mother likes to read it.

Until 1974, Church's denials had always been conventional: "Naturally, I am flattered at the speculation, and I suppose one never knows, but I am content in the proud calling of serving the people of Idaho and could aspire to no higher honor than that."

Now, you could read a lot into that and say the man was just being coy. After all, it wasn't a flat no.

It never is. A senator in that position is saying that, though he would give his left ventricle to be president, he realizes the prize probably isn't in the cards this year. So let the rumors roam, in case he is mistaken. But he's not really running for president.

The fall of 1974 was different. Church answered the speculation about his candidacy with the standard no-greater-honor-than-serving-Idaho line, but then added that he would make no final decision about the possibilities for his candidacy until he had more fully explored them.

That was an eyebrow raiser. He was, if not a candidate, at least an explorer. Explorers usually become candidates.

At that intriguing point I decided to explore the possibilities of joining him. We had known each other, professionally, for years. A presidential campaign sounded like fun in a sadomasochistic sort of way. Like a drama critic who had always believed he could write a play himself, I had come to believe, after 15 years as a political critic, that I just might make a pretty fair country strategist if ever placed at the elbow of a presidential contender.

Such vanity—to believe you are ready for the majors because of a few years' involvement in the politics of a state that never produces a president.

Of course, there were other pushy rustics with similar delusions during that period. As I recall, they were from Georgia. (They would be succeeded some years later by audacious hicks from Arkansas, of all places.)

So I called Church, volunteering as an advance man, speechwriter, groupie cuddler—wherever he thought I might fit in.

He wanted me as his press secretary—within the month. But there was a complication: Church had just been named chairman of the new Senate Intelligence Committee, charged with uncovering all manner of mischief in the CIA, the FBI, the IRS, and practically every other agency of government that had ever dabbled in constitutionally kinky techniques. I would be the press secretary for Church and his new committee. The presidential candidacy had been pushed onto the back burner for the duration of the investigation. But I was heading for Washington.

The family was excited. The relatives were proud. The neighbors began showing some respect: Their dogs stopped crapping on my lawn.

But the press secretary to the Next Leader of the Free World came down with a case of the qualms. Suddenly, every instinct I had told me I would be miserable in that role—leaving lovely Idaho for steamy Washington, trailing in someone else's shadow, living another man's career, crossing over from professional iconoclast to genuflecting press agent. I would break the news to Church that I had been impulsive.

But there were dissenters. Friends and family, their Republican instincts rising, had counted on following me, vicariously, all the way to the White House. Surely I could endure a few months of anything. And if I didn't go, I might kick myself for years—especially if Church went all the way and someone else went with him as press secretary.

It was an incompetent argument, based on the premise that I had an urge to follow in the footsteps of Richard Nixon's press secretary or some other tiny tower of integrity. But I took the job. I left for Washington and crossed over to the flack side of the press table, with my misgivings intact. Many cross over, but few return. I might be an image butler for the rest of my days. I had never realized what a snob I was about press secretaries until I became one.

Oddly enough, for all my apprehension, I was an overnight success in Washington. From the day I started, reporters were beating down the door for interviews with Frank Church.

As a matter of fact, reporters were beating down the door for three weeks before I arrived in the capital. Church's chairmanship of the Senate Intelligence Committee (with a potential run for the Rose Garden on the horizon) was the hottest story in town. You would think Washington reporters might have been satiated so soon after Watergate. But there was a whole new crop of would-be Woodwards and budding Bernsteins. Perhaps obsession is the norm in Washington, but as I arrived, the town had big-story fever. From the first day on the job, I couldn't do anything but answer the telephone—as many as 70 or 80 calls a day. It didn't take many days of life with a phone glued to my head before a call from a famous figure in journalism became, not another thrill, but just another pain in the ear.

After two days of that meat grinder, the Senate Press Gallery informed me, to my horror, that Senate press secretaries invariably list their home telephones with the gallery. Any of the several thousand reporters in the city—foreign and domestic, professional and faker, affable and antagonistic, drunk or sober—would receive my home number.

I thought they were putting me on. Surely the press secretary to the Next Leader of the Free World could not be expected to hand over his home number to that legion of faunching animals. Surely the close personal adviser to he who would soon purge the CIA of its KGB tendencies could not be expected to submit to a nightly wave of phone calls. Helping Church bring the brownshirts to heel would require a clear head. Think of my need for sleep. Think of the republic.

I was informed that it was my job to think of the reporters. Occasionally they would need to check a detail or obtain a comment on some breaking news. The reporters grudgingly accepted an unlisted number for a senator. But in a crunch, they had to have some way to get in touch with him. The way developed, after years of experience going back long before What'shisname rolled in from Idaho, is to provide the reporters with the home numbers of press secretaries. That's why they call them "press" secretaries. When someone has a stroke, a doctor is called—through an answering service. At night, I would be Church's answering service. The reporters would have a stroke if I didn't cough up the number.

Having a little stroke myself, I coughed.

To my astonishment, few of the thousands of reporters in Washington abused the privilege. I rarely received more than a half dozen calls a week at home, and hardly any in the middle of the night.

Correspondent Daniel Schorr of CBS (later defrocked by network brass and eventually finding his way to National Public Radio) did get me out of bed on a couple of occasions with early-morning questions. But Schorr, who never seemed to sleep himself (it must have taken three people with bionic aggressiveness to replace him on the network) always apologized, somewhat insincerely. He reminded me that any press secretary worth his federal pension would already be awake and preparing to savor the "CBS Morning News."

I would later learn the loneliness of fighting for scraps of attention while others feasted in the spotlight. But in the beginning, the feast was ours, and the diet was rich. In the beginning, my job was not to solicit stories from the reporters, but to screen the countless pleas for interviews. For a few months, during the crucial learning period when they could easily have mashed my potato, I had the bastards at my mercy.

In the beginning, most of the callers were simply seeking background information on the new Intelligence Committee chairman. They would rather have had it from the horse's mouth. But they knew the interview load was heavy, so they would accept a briefing from the horse's mouthpiece. Nevertheless, 30 or 40 reporters each week pressed for personal interviews with Church. Thirty or 40 interviews a week couldn't readily be fit into the schedule of any senator—with the possible exception of former Senator and Vice President Hubert Humphrey, who had apparently been granted extra hours in each day by a God who found him as affable as everyone else did.

I was envious of Humphrey because I was able to slip only about half a dozen face-to-face interviews into Church's schedule each week. But that, plus his frequent press conferences following closed sessions of the committee, was usually enough. After all, he was giving a going over to "The Company," or "the spooks," as the CIA was known in Washington. That was news. The reporters would use almost everything they could get from Church, however they got it. His kisser was all over the tube every night, and his words all over the papers. In 19 years in the Senate, he had never known such attention.

And it all began about the time he hired a new press secretary.

Church, his wife Bethine, and veteran members of his personal staff began to tease me about what a terrific press secretary I was—about how I joined the team and all of a sudden Idaho's senior senator had been snatched from the lap of oblivion.

What worried me was that sometimes I wasn't sure they were kidding. That could be a problem, given the way Washington works. If you start getting credit for gratuitous attention, then you might also get the blame if press attention withers and the fickle report-ers go chasing after some other pretty face.

So I protested. I really had very little to do with all that lime-light, I insisted. But the more I protested my incompetence, the more Church and staff seemed to believe I was not only one hell of a press secretary but an uncommonly modest one besides.

And true to my misgivings, there would come a time when the intelligence investigation would fade, before Church had won his spurs as a presidential candidate. Members of the national cam-paign staff would avert their eyes in the presence of a leper and ask why the press didn't give our leader more coverage—meaning, what the hell did I do for a living anyway?

Neither Frank nor Bethine Church ever said a word about the drought. But I often wondered what they were thinking. After all, they had been among those who flashed that you-modest-rascal-you smile back when I was insisting on my inadequacy as a press secretary.

*   *   *

There is, as anyone who has ever yanked up his roots knows, a sense of dislocation, a feeling of floating in some inhospitable new womb, when you change communities. The discomfort is ampli-fied when you make a move at mid-life as radical as from Lewiston, Idaho, to Washington, D.C. The discomfort approaches pain when you switch not only communities, but roles as well.

After spending the first half of my life at what I considered productive work, I was suddenly going through occupational meno-pause. Worse, I was undergoing a reverse metamorphosis, from political analyst to political flack, from butterfly to worm, from small-time media heavy, secure in his role, to big-time lightweight with-out clamor or fans.

The state capitals—the Boises and Omahas, the Manchesters and the Jacksons—have their miniature versions of the Washing-ton heavies, their grassroots byline writers who generate letters to the editor, public attacks by bush-league Nixons and Quayles, plus invitations to appear on the local imitation of "Meet The Press." And it's a small matter that those shows are on one station rather than on the network; to a ham, an audience is an audience.

The smaller the community, the more inflated the media egos. There is, from his vantage, no celebrity more awesome than a 23-year-old anchorman with his pimples powdered over and his hair freshly teased.

Balding, middle-aged editorial writers are too proud to preen, but they have been known to strut. There is so little competition in the underpopulated states that the rise to sagehood can be rapid and the reign prolonged. Washington, by contrast, has more political analysts than it does hookers. In Idaho, pundits are rare, and therefore stunning. The leading lights of the Washington media all shine about the same. They have competition to keep them humble. The herd is in Washington. The stars are in the sticks.

When you leave all that, accept a servile role to a politician, and move outside your element into an urban anthill where you are known to neither reader nor viewer, you can come to believe that your mettle has been debased.

Few Washington reporters treated me like a prostituted newsman; they were neither condescending nor judgmental. Occasionally a young reporter seemed to regard me as a high-priced call girl, but they always treated me like a lady in public. Nevertheless, in the beginning, the reporters knew I was green and easy and not yet graceful at parrying the subtle probing of seasoned interrogators.

Two reporters from *The New York Times* invited me to dinner one Friday night. Church's administrative assistant, Verda Barnes, who had been in Washington since shortly after Franklin Roosevelt arrived, was uneasy that a virgin press secretary would be dining with two old hands from all the news that's fit to print. Verda believed that some news of government offices, though perhaps fit to print, is better not whispered to reporters, lest the little rascals sometimes stray over the line and print the occasional news that isn't fit. Indeed, she considered it tacky to tempt such people. Or to put it more precisely, she gave the new press secretary the fisheye and warned, "Don't get drunk and spill every secret in the office."

I retorted that I had been around a few years. Just maybe, I said scathingly, I could handle myself in a tight corner with reporters. I was, after all, aware that they weren't inviting me to dinner because they admired my press releases and hoped to pick up a few writing tips.

The dinner and the wine were exceptional. The restaurant was decorated in a confidential style. The Washington insiders sat whispering all around us.

The press secretary spilled his guts somewhere between the entree and the second bottle of Bordeaux.

But there was no harm done. The second bottle of Bordeaux had the same effect on my companions. One of them called the next day to make certain I understood, after his rather unfortunate words about a superior, that off-the-record conversations are a two-way street. He was so concerned over his own indiscretions that he had forgotten a couple of matters I had stupidly discussed.

I reassured him. After all, any normally cautious person could have done the same thing, given the excellence of the Bordeaux.

He was relieved. And that's how I learned, quite by accident, the Washington maxim, that he who has you by the short hairs must be seized in similar fashion. It keeps everyone friendly—and attentive.

* * *

In the beginning, the hardest part of being a reporter-turned-press secretary is keeping your trap shut—not just about office secrets, but especially during news conferences and interviews. After a lifetime of joining the pack in grilling one politician after another, my reporter's reflexes kept planting questions in my head and my mouth kept wanting to utter the crucial question. I had to fight it. Neither a senator nor a reporter likes having a press secretary butt in.

But I had a larger urge more hazardous than simply wanting to join in the interview. I imagine it goes without saying that not every reporter in Washington is a mental giant. More than once, when a dull reporter stumbled past an unusual opening, I restrained myself just in time. I almost blurted out the central question—the question Church hoped to avoid. I sometimes wish I had slipped just once to see the reaction:

> SENATOR: And so we may never know whether Nixon actually ordered the assassination of Allende.
> REPORTER: That's a shame, senator.
> PRESS SECRETARY: Why don't you subpoena the bastard and ask him under oath?

> SENATOR: Well . . . ah . . . I think maybe we'd better let our
> guest ask the questions.
> REPORTER: That's right, fella; I'll do the questioning here.
> PRESS SECRETARY: Sorry, old man. . . . Could I freshen your
> drink?

As a general rule, Church relished tough questioning. Most politicians without a great deal to hide do. They know they come off best under fire. It is the difference between playing tennis against a weak or a strong opponent. And a politician is rarely at his best in a silly, worshipful interview:

> REPORTER: Senator, do you like music?
> SENATOR: Yes, I'm very fond of music.
> REPORTER: What kind of music do you like, Senator?
> SENATOR: I like all kinds of music.
> REPORTER: Do you ever sing, Senator?
> SENATOR: Yes, I sing often—in the shower.
>   WASHINGTON—Sen. Frank Church, who is expected to
> announce shortly his intention to become the next leader of
> the free world, asserted today that he likes all kinds of music.
>   Church admitted in a candid interview that he often sings.
> And the senior senator from Idaho revealed for the first time
> that he prefers a shower to a bath.

*   *   *

It is true that a press secretary, accorded the high honor and personal privilege of daily contact with a presidential candidate, is among that select handful close enough to become an intimate and trusted adviser. It is also true that a press secretary is among that select handful close enough to become an intimate and trusted flunky. However, Church was to learn that I couldn't be trusted as a flunky.

In some respects, the relationship was normal for a personal aide to a senator. I counseled him on how best to ensure the future of humankind—while lighting his cigars. That is the usual dual role in the Senate, and I suspect also in the White House:

> If I were in your shoes, Mr. President, I would. . . . Whoops!
> We've got a piece of lint on our lapel, haven't we? There, that's
> got it. . . . Now then, if I were in your shoes, I would nuke the
> Norwegians.

The theory behind all this stooping and fetching is that a major politician has his head full of momentous matters. He needs backup on the trivia. The personal aides serving a leading politician are expected to spare his fretting over humdrum details like remembering where he left his car keys. You relieve that crucial mind of its normal human allotment of nitty gritty and conserve its use for full focus on preserving the republic. Where would we all be now, these political valets will ask, if Churchill had been abandoned by an insolent staff to fetch his own brandy?

And when the vainglorious rationales won't suffice, you do the flunky chores simply because you feel sorry for the poor bastard and the pace he is maintaining. You treat him in the fashion once reserved for pregnant queens, rushing forward with a chair, a glass of sherry, any little touch that might ease the burden—the awesome burden, as it is known in the White House and in the breast of any pampered senator who covets the White House.

Anyone who "serves" a senator must understand from the beginning that one who serves is a servant. It comes with the territory.

But there is a complication: The servant half of the servant-adviser role isn't fit work for a grownup. Consequently, youth is the norm among Senate campaign aides. Most are in their twenties. Middle-aged men who have spent their prior lives as newspaper mavericks adjust with great awkwardness.

Church and I discovered during those first few weeks—both to our horror—that, as a political valet, I was accident prone. If I lighted a cigar, I singed the noble eyebrows. If I poured a glass of iced tea, I fumbled ice cubes onto the thick carpet. I was especially dangerous when flinging open doors in the grand manner of someone making way for the mighty.

Church was the least of the Senate's many prima donnas. Nonetheless, he was so accustomed to being waited on after 19 years in office that he had come to accept the routine attentions of a staff member without even noticing.

I changed that. He soon came to stare in disbelief, and I think eventually with prudent alarm, as I crashed into him rushing to open a door or menaced him in a rainstorm with his own umbrella.

I served as his driver only once. On the way to a television interview, I got us lost somewhere in suburban Virginia. We were set straight by a service station attendant who kept staring at my familiar-looking passenger who was drumming his fingers on his knees. Driving Church home from the interview, I couldn't get the range of the freeway exits. It was dark. The signs didn't pop into view until the last instant, and I was always in the wrong lane. Five or six times, I whipped across several lanes of traffic, the horns of other cars cursing us. Church's little car was on two wheels and his nerves on edge as we bluffed our way through the racing pack and sped onto the exit ramp.

He never let me drive again. For months thereafter—until the Secret Service came aboard and took the wheel—I may have been the only aide in Washington regularly chauffeured about the city by a United States senator.

Of course, we also had our problems when others drove. Early in 1976, I accompanied Frank and Bethine Church to No. 10 Downing in London where the senator had a private chat with Prime Minister Harold Wilson. Their conversation finished, Wilson—a twinkling, grandfatherly man more in the mold of an unpretentious Idaho governor than of the Queen's first minister—walked us to the front door. His casual manner put me off my guard. I almost expected to saunter out onto an Idaho porch and get into our pickup truck—Harold leaning his elbows on the window ledge telling us to come again—before we drove off into a western sunset.

Harold, patting Frank on the elbow, did tell us to come again. And then the front door to No. 10 Downing flew open on London and a limousine and the glare of television lights. There was no pickup truck.

I came to my senses and moved into action. Blinded by the lights, I positioned myself at the door of the limousine, popping it open. As the last shadowy figure entered, I popped the door shut, stopping just short of clicking my heels and tossing a small salute. The watching world's opinion of the probable president would depend in part on the precision of the staff. I dashed to the other side of the limo and crashed into Frank Church, trying to struggle into the vehicle from the same side. What I had thought was two shadowy figures entering on the other side had been Bethine alone.

As we motored away from No. 10 Downing, Church fixed me with that why-are-you-doing-this-to-me gaze he used to get when I was especially dangerous. He had known me all my adult life, but I think there were times when he wondered whether I might be a CIA plant.

I was not accustomed to stuffing the correct number of dignitaries into the television side of a limousine, but it was plain that Church, so poorly conditioned by driving me about Washington, needed a lot of work on his role as well. I vowed that before the presidential campaign began, Church and I would drive off to some secluded street for a few hours of limousine lessons.

Doors were a constant headache. I couldn't get the hang of them. At one time or another I botched getting Church through car doors, room doors, and revolving doors. The revolving door was the worst. It was my second week on the job. Church and I returned to the Senate Courtyard, a large, roofless garden where senators park their personal automobiles. As we got out of the car, I dutifully grabbed his briefcase and followed a respectful step behind. He rushed into the revolving door of the building.

I quickly did the same.

Too quickly. In my haste to remain at his heel, I jumped into the same cramped section of the revolving door with the senator. The momentum of the heavy door repeatedly slapped me and the briefcase into Church. I goosed a U.S. senator with his own briefcase all the way around a revolving door.

The door finally ejected us, quick-stepping in unison like some vaudeville act, into the presence of an amazed building guard who pretended not to notice.

Church stopped and turned with that look of a man wondering how the CIA had ever found me.

"I'm sorry, Senator. I was trying to keep up with you."

He snatched the disrespectful briefcase from my hand with the strong, swift reflex of a tough cop disarming a psychopath. Finally, he managed a weak smile.

"You're a very friendly press secretary," he said, turning on his heel and striding toward the office, occasionally glancing over his shoulder to make certain he maintained a safe distance.

Nor did Bethine Church miss the fun of breaking in an awkward new Senate aide so thoroughly out of his element.

She invited me to breakfast in the Senate dining room one day following her appearance on ABC's "Good Morning, America." It was a memorable occasion for both of us.

Visiting constituents are often treated by their senators to lunch in the ornate Senate dining room on the first floor of the Capitol. The room is only pseudo-plush and relatively commonplace by comparison with the rest of that extraordinary building. The second most striking feature of the Senate Dining Room is a melodramatic stained glass rendition of George Washington.

The most striking feature of the room is the senators themselves, and appropriately so; the stars should always outshine the set. If your senator takes you to lunch in the Senate Dining Room, you will see all about you other senators at other tables on the same constituent-wooing mission. On signal, the senators sometimes do a bit of table hopping, allegedly dropping by to greet Frank, but in reality coming over to thrill the tittering constituent whom Frank had just noticed was slavering in that direction. To a constituent fascinated by politics it is an experience akin to inviting a movie fan to lunch at a studio commissary.

I don't say that cynically. As a reporter from Idaho, I had relished the dining room treatment myself. As a matter of fact, I enjoyed senator watching throughout my months in that institution. After all, they are a fascinating conglomeration of style and character, the most fascinating anywhere in American politics—and all the more so when you get close enough to see the warts.

Lunch is showtime. Breakfast is far different. At breakfast, the Senate Dining Room is only a dining room, not a political zoo. The animals are eating, but they are not on display. The senators are scattered about the room, fueling up for another day, often with a newspaper as their only companion, much as any other American at breakfast. When a colleague enters, they look up and nod, but they mostly leave each other alone. It is the quiet time, the private time, the last privacy these very public people will have for the remainder of another long day.

Bethine Church could shatter the repose of a monastery. And the monks would welcome the intrusion. She is a bubbly, unpretentious woman, her upbringing on an Idaho ranch apparent. She feels useless if she isn't mothering someone. One harmless sneeze is worth a five-minute lecture on vitamins, regular meals, and wearing sweaters. I have seen her scold complete strangers for not taking care of themselves. To Bethine, there are no strangers. The reporters who were to come aboard the campaign plane had never been so fussed over. She gets close to the nagging line, but rarely offends. You don't know whether to be irritated or touched and you usually come down on the side of the latter. She'll scold and coddle you whether you like it or not, so you might as well relax and enjoy it.

Bethine was a particular favorite of the senators, most of whom enjoyed the novelty of being treated like helpless small boys by a woman who is oblivious to the awe with which others regarded them. As we entered the dining room that morning, she made a quick tour of the room, pecking cheeks, patting weary shoulders, and scolding those who, in her judgment, had ordered inadequate breakfasts. As we ate, late arrivals trooped by, one by one, for some stroking. Senator John Stennis of Mississippi was the last to spot her and drop over to our table.

Bethine introduced the new nothing from Idaho. In similar situations, other senators had given me the reflex handshake of veteran campaigners and a perfunctory "Good ta see ya," before turning quickly to others in the endless blur of faces. Stennis actually uttered a few coherent sentences, kindly welcomed me to the Senate as an equal, and gave me a courtly bow. He chatted with us for a few moments and then, as he was leaving, again reached across the table, shaking my hand and bowing once more with great dignity.

I might be from Idaho, but I catch on fast. I returned the bow— no longer the shuffling nod of a minor Senate aide, but a courtly southern bow, the bow one distinguished gentleman of the Senate establishment reserves for another.

I was smashing—except that, on the final bow (I gave him three or four, just to get the hang of it), my necktie dipped into my coffee cup. As I sat down, the sodden tie fell dripping into the crotch of my light gray suit.

Neither Bethine nor the courtly southern senator noticed. Nor did I until my courtly southern privates began to glow with the spreading warmth of Senate coffee.

"Well," Bethine sighed as Stennis left, "I guess we'd better let you get to work."

"I'm afraid," I ventured, "we're going to have to wait a few minutes—until my pants dry."

Her eyebrows lifted. She hesitated, saying nothing, and then bluntly leaned over—in the middle of the Senate Dining Room, for

God's sake—and stared at the damning location of the fresh, wet coffee stain on the crotch of my trousers.

She threw back her head and laughed like the mother of an outrageous child. In my opinion, she was drawing more attention to the situation than necessary.

But she saved my bacon. We wouldn't have to wait for my pants to dry. She had a better idea. She strolled around the table and backed up to my chair. I stood up tight behind her in what I have come to think of as the revolving door formation. In lockstep, we made our exit, Bethine waving blithely to all the senators and all the senators waving back, wondering about that strange man so loyal and close—so very close—to Bethine Church. Like a vaudeville team doing the buck and wing, waving our straw hats and moving in unison toward the wings, we never missed a step. Thank God, we both have natural rhythm.

As we exited into the outer room, Bethine marched us straight to the rack where my raincoat hung. Draping the coat nonchalantly over my arm and holding it in the strategic location, I bid the still-giggling Bethine good-bye.

And then the press secretary to the Next Leader of the Free World went home and changed his pants.

*   *   *

Early in my new career, Church summoned me to assist him in hosting a dozen reporters for a social interview session. Many of the reporters of Washington have banded together to form interview groups. Individually, they might have some difficulty getting appointments with the leading lights of Washington. However, by joining together, they represent a combined circulation in the millions. When they invite Washington notables to appear at a breakfast or luncheon to be interviewed, the invitation is often rather quickly accepted.

The day in question involved only a dozen or so reporters in one of the smallest groups. But they still represented a substantial circulation scattered clear across that great big country we hoped would learn to love Frank Church as much as Bethine did. Because they were only a dozen or so, they asked to interview Church on his turf. We invited them to his Capitol office.

It is one of the ill-kept secrets of the Senate that members are assigned, in addition to a suite of public rooms in one of the Senate office buildings across Constitution Avenue from the Capitol, a small private office in the Capitol itself. The latter offices are known as hideaways.

Church's hideaway was well-appointed, but its best feature was location—only a few steps off the Senate floor. There he could literally hide away and do some work between roll calls, rather than hang around the cloakroom or make the three-block trip to his public suite in the Russell Senate Office Building—the Russell S.O.B., as it is known. (Next door was the Dirksen S.O.B. The little carts pushed through the hallways to deliver the mail are all stenciled "S.O.B.," causing doubletakes among tourists.)

As the reporters congregated in Church's Capitol hideaway, I learned that another little wall had been erected between me and my former colleagues. In my former life, I would have gathered around Church with the other reporters and joined in the warm-up quips.

In my new life, I was a butler. I met each reporter at the door, introduced him or her to Church, took an order for a drink, delivered the drink, and then met the next arrival at the door. Church and I were both astonished—Church because I didn't hurt any reporters with the door, and I because I seemed to have some unwanted knack for being a butler. I was actually adept at remembering the names and the drinks, and at remaining in the background where a press secretary belongs. I was adept, but I didn't enjoy it.

The feeling of social demotion was not altogether my imagination. Months later, A. Robert Smith, an old friend and a correspondent for several Northwest newspapers, suddenly interrupted my line of campaign propaganda: "When are you going to get out of this bullshit and go back to the work you were good at?"

I told him I had just served notice.

"Thank God," he kindly said. "I'll never forget that day in Church's hideaway. I kept thinking, 'There's a good editorial writer pouring drinks for a bunch of reporters.'"

A dear friend and former newspaperman, who either did not remember what it had been like on the other side or never suffered my bouts of snobbishness, bought me my first year's dues in the Senate Press Secretaries Association. I attended the very next meeting. It was also my last meeting. The room was filled with lobbyists and retired press secretaries, almost all of whom had been working reporters. Men and women who had once made politicians tremble now clustered together in the fiscal security of serving senators. They talked about books they had always meant to write, and about the day Senator A shouted an obscenity at Senator B during a committee hearing, and about how nasty some columnists could be.

They were an engaging group, and they seemed to enjoy each other's company. But there was an underlying sadness. They were no longer the young reporters they had once been, minds sprinting, manner brassy, their conversations salted with the premeditated irreverence of professional iconoclasts. These former political agnostics had discovered gods.

Thereafter, I spent my time with working reporters, or with other Senate aides, but not with press secretaries.

During that same period of dislocation and almost terminal anonymity, a stranger kept aggravating my discomfort by calling in the middle of the night. The calls came off and on for a month, always at three in the morning, from a man speaking thick black English, a man more embarrassed each time he dialed the wrong number.

I finally pieced together what was happening. My given name is Wilbert. It's a popular name in the black community for reasons as incomprehensible as its popularity in my family.

I checked the phone book. Sure enough, there was another Wilbert Hall a few blocks away in my mostly black neighborhood. The calls were a natural mistake for a sleepy man, fumbling with the phone book in the middle of the night and trying to rouse his buddy for some gawdawful shift.

But the calls served to underscore the feeling that nobody knew me, because the one soul in that city who thought he did know and called to prove it had the wrong Wilbert.

A few days later, Paul Wieck, who writes for *The New Republic* and other publications, saved me from total self pity. I accompanied Church to an editorial board luncheon of that magazine. Paul, who had made western politics his specialty, was my seat mate.

"Are you the Bill Hall who used to write a political column in Idaho?" he asked.

I really like that Paul Wieck.

And so a certain social confidence began to return. With it came an invitation to an honest-to-God Washington cocktail party. An Idaho legislator was in town. Washington friends from the days when she served as an intern to Church were giving a party in her honor and invited Church's new press secretary. It was my chance to break out of the doldrums, into the Washington scene, and to cure my recent siege of Woody-Allenitis by proving I could still operate gracefully in that kind of crowd. But I took no chances.

Would it be in order to bring something, some wine perhaps?

No, but it was kind of me to ask.

And was I correct in assuming it would be black tie?

No, of course not. It would simply be a little party for a few of her old friends. "Strictly informal."

Washington was more like Idaho than I had imagined. In Idaho, if the gathering is no big deal, the hostess always specifies the informal picnic clothes that permit everyone to relax and have a good time. We don't go overboard on a simple little party in Idaho either. Except in Washington, I learned, informal doesn't mean picnic clothes. In Washington, it means an informal suit and tie as opposed to a formal tuxedo.

I was the only one at the party wearing orange tennis shoes.

Chapter Two
"If You Don't Love Me or Fear Me, Then At Least Notice Me"

Four and a half centuries before I hit Washington, Niccolo Machiavelli debunked the notion that popularity is power in a political city. "It is far safer," he wrote, "to be feared than loved."

I knew that, of course. But as I arrived, I discovered that some fool on Church's staff had neglected to put out the word to Washington that I was on the way. So my potential for power went unrecognized. Indeed, I was not recognized. Hence I was not feared—at first.

Nor was I loved. I would have settled for that.

Being neither feared nor loved, I found I wasn't safe in Washington. Not that the power people threatened me. They didn't seem to realize who the hell I was. But there were others.

Perhaps it is not generally known that there are many dangerous people in Washington who don't work for the government. They are called criminals. They can be unpleasant if it has never been explained to them that, considering your high position, it would be prudent for them to either fear or love you, take their choice. But I never blamed those who menaced me on the streets of Washington. It wasn't their fault. No one had told them how important I was.

I admit I wasn't quite ready for crime in Washington. Life in Idaho is meager conditioning for life in America's most conspicuous failure in the war on crime.

In Idaho, many residents lock neither their homes nor their cars. Murder is rare. Armed robbery is rare. I can't remember the last mugging; I'm not sure anybody in Idaho knows how to mug someone. Penny-ante burglary is about the only crime approaching the commonplace.

Reported instances of rape are also relatively rare. How rare is best gauged by what happened not long after I moved to Lewiston.

Not to make light of the crime, but the events of that period sound like one of those my-home-town-is-so-small routines. With 50,000 people in this valley, eastern imaginations to the contrary, we have far more than one town drunk. And as a chronic observer of city politics, I can testify personally to an epidemic of village idiots. But my home town is so small that when three rapes were reported in as many weeks, talk swept the community about "the town rapist," or "the Lewiston rapist," as he came to be more notoriously known.

Before the panic had run its course, it was the men in town who had reason to be fearful. Lewiston has one of those call-in radio shows where people go on the air to exchange recipes, meeting notices, and right-wing misconceptions about the Constitution. For two weeks, the program was overrun with gruff women calling in to advertise that they had an arsenal in the closet and damn well knew how to use it. And they do. Idaho is gun country. I suppose it was defensive bluster, but their tone was harsh and their words threatening.

During one of those programs, the callers digressed into the accusation that judges concern themselves more with the rights of criminals than with the safety of the community. The callers cautioned each other against shooting the Lewiston rapist on the sidewalk. Judges have been known, they said, to award damages to the relatives of criminals shot approaching the house. To be legally safe, one caller counseled her colleagues, it would be prudent, having plugged a suspected rapist, to drag him up on the porch before the police arrive.

Unfortunately, that Lewiston rapist was never caught, or shot. But I'm still surprised, given the climate and the advice, that no one plugged a door-to-door salesman by mistake. As a matter of fact, I'm a little disappointed that no one plugged a door-to-door salesman deliberately. Idaho may be below its quota of criminals, but we have an overabundance of twits banging on your door while you're trying to eat dinner or take a nap. Nevertheless, if somebody had snuffed a salesman, there would have been no lawsuits. The body, one hand frozen on a sample case, would have been dragged onto the porch and declared the Lewiston rapist.

Naturally, after such limited skirmishes in Idaho, I was ill prepared for the great war in Washington, though I thought I was ready. After a lifetime of covering politicians, Washington's powerful movers and shakers held no special terrors. I grasped the hand of the Secretary of State at the White House correspondents dinner with the unwavering camaraderie of the inner circle. I accepted a fatherly pat on the arm from the Prime Minister of England without flinching. Grace under pressure came naturally as, one by one, I met the creaking clout of the Senate's ancient dukes. I was only slightly shaken as I met their respective wives.

But after a lifetime of living in Idaho, the theoretically powerless rank and file criminals of Washington found it simple to intimidate me with their avarice and their guns. And my initial choice of a D.C. neighborhood was unfortunate for a physical coward. I was not prepared for my instructions in survival as a new resident of Capitol Hill. My tutor was Verda Barnes, the Washington-wise senior Senate aide who had been conditioned in caution by a young man who hadn't heard how influential she was. So he went right ahead and knocked her down and stole her purse. Thereafter, she felt socially obliged to educate greenhorns.

She was aghast at my choice of an apartment—only a block and a half from the Senate office buildings, and on the fringe of a criminal no-man's land in northeast D.C.

"First," she warned, just as I congratulated myself on having found an apartment right on Capitol Hill so I could walk everywhere, "don't walk around Capitol Hill after dark. If you must go someplace, take a taxi, even for a short distance. Taxis are inexpensive in Washington."

"But I'm just down the street from the police station," I protested.

"So is the Capitol, and there were two young women murdered on the Capitol grounds two years ago. However, if you are crazy enough to walk around Capitol Hill, don't carry more money than you can afford to lose. . . . But don't carry too little money either."

"Come again?"

"Sometimes muggers will get mad if you have only a couple of dollars. Then they'll hurt you. Always try to carry about $20. Just hand it over when they ask, and you might be all right."

"You mean a mugger is going to get mad at me if I'm not carrying as much money as he thinks I should be?"

"It has happened."

So I followed Verda's advice—for a time. Before long, I got to the point where I would rather be mugged than sit in the back of one more cab while the driver shook his head over another rich idiot too lazy to walk three blocks.

My reaction to the foreign environment that would be my neighborhood for the first six months was similar to that reported by Dr. Hunter S. Thompson, the gonzo journalist, when he moved into a Capitol Hill apartment some years earlier—fear. But my remedy was different. He sent for another Doberman. I tried to avoid trouble rather than confront it. I hid out during the day in the well-guarded Senate Office Building, during the night in my apartment. And I walked the short distance between them as swiftly as I could and, whenever possible, before dark. The tourists may think all those people striding so breathlessly around Capitol Hill are workaholics, young men and women in a hurry to get to the top. Some are. But others are greenhorns, fresh from the boondocks, trying to spend as little time as possible on the public streets where they are most vulnerable to real and imagined muggers. In Washington, what makes Sammy run is not ambition alone.

I suppose Doctor Thompson would not approve of my passive approach, but during those early weeks I was like an eastern dude around an Idaho campfire, scanning the provocative forest shadows at the edge of the fire's glow. This was their forest, their jungle, and I was ill equipped. I had spent my life in western frame houses, with sprawling grass yards, beneath Joyce Kilmer trees, in crime-free neighborhoods where we usually forgot to lock our doors.

In Washington I always locked my door. Small-city residents, unfamiliar with the security arrangements of large-city apartment living, will think I am exaggerating. Inner city veterans, accustomed to the precautions, will wonder what was so remarkable about the safety arrangements in my D.C. apartment building.

The answer is nothing. Indeed, mine was a minimum security building by Washington standards.

The main door to the building is locked at all times. Each resident must carry a main building key. That first line of defense is easily breached. In the first place, residents have the keys duplicated and scatter them like popcorn among reliable and sleazy friends. But a front-door key is unnecessary anyway. More than once I visited friends in similar crackerboxes and breezed through the front door as a resident entered or left. Apartment dwellers don't often get to know each other. For all they knew, I belonged there.

Once inside a minimum security building, you can head directly for the last line of defense, the apartment door. In maximum security buildings, which are more expensive, there is a guard. You cannot pass until the guard calls the person you're visiting, describes you, and affirms that you are, indeed, welcome in the building. And some buildings have such added precautions as closed circuit television and elevators that will function only with a key carried by each resident.

My building had the standard minimum security arrangement—a buzzer system. You would stand outside and push the button next to my name—a cryptic "B. Hall," the unisex designation adopted to frustrate rapists—or, it occurred to me, to encourage bisexuals with a venturesome spirit.

Hearing the buzz inside, I would push the talk-listen button and inquire as to your identity. If you didn't answer, "Chester Thug, and I've come to rob and hurt you," I would push the button which would signal you with a jarring buzz that the door was unlocked for the duration of the buzzing.

Of course, that precaution is also child's play. If a thief is in a real frenzy to rob someone and doesn't want to stand around and wait for a resident entering or leaving the building to let him in, he can buzz anyone in the building, professing to be a resident who has forgotten his key, and ask them to buzz open the door. Building managers constantly lecture tenants about that practice, but it normally takes only a buzz or two to find an unwitting sponsor for a criminal entry to the building.

Once at my door, further progress became only a little more difficult. There was a steel door with a snap-lock on the doorknob and one of those chain locks that lets you open the door just far enough for the person on the other side to get a gun through.

That was the extent of my security—duck soup for a beginning burglar with a tool or two.

From my vantage, the worst complication of the security arrangements was the spring hinges on the apartment door. The door closed itself—heavily—so there would be no risk of your accidentally leaving it ajar. But that also meant you couldn't leave your apartment without the key if you wanted to step out in the hallway in your bathrobe and check your mailbox. The manager of my building was too smart to live there herself. If you locked yourself out, wearing a bathrobe and without a key, you had to call the manager at home. But I never kept change for the pay phone in my bathrobe. It is a problem without a solution. If you rap on another apartment door, stand there in your bathrobe with your hairy legs hanging out and say, "Hi, there, I wonder if I might use your telephone or maybe borrow a quarter," people are not going to be friendly about it, and they may hurt you. People in Washington are real excitable about that sort of thing.

The most intimidating feature of my apartment was the heavy steel bars on the windows. The apartment was on the ground floor so the bars were necessary. But they were an unpleasant reminder of lost freedom. Sometimes an urge would sweep over me to rake a tin cup across the bars and demand a lawyer.

Those were my security arrangements. It was the wall between us and them. It was a flimsy wall by Washington standards, but I was grateful for it. Each evening, as darkness fell, I did what was expected of people like me. I got off the streets and locked myself in this little room with a steel door and bars on the windows.

In Washington, they call that an apartment. In Idaho, they call it a jail. Washington had made me my own jailer.

My situation reminded me of the sardonic question—whether it is truly the insane who are locked inside mental institutions, or whether society is so unbalanced that the few sane people remaining live inside those institutions voluntarily and have locked out the rest of humanity for their own protection.

Washington and crime are like that. In Washington, the lawful are jailed each night, albeit by their own hand. In Washington, the lawless residents stroll the streets on a summer evening while their more prudent victims languish behind bars.

In daylight, the neighborhood offered no relief from the nightly impression that you could get hurt out there. Indeed, the impression was strengthened by the daytime habits of some of my neighbors.

One morning, shortly after my arrival on Capitol Hill, I took that suit with the coffee-stained trousers to the cleaners on the next corner and found the business open but the door locked. Through the glass in the door, I could see a worn and exhausted woman giving me the once over. Behind the counter was a large German shepherd barking his lungs out.

I looked honest. The worn woman pushed a button like the one to my apartment and the door in front of me buzzed, telling me it was momentarily unlocked. But I was still too new to such systems. I wasn't ready. By the time I gave the door a jerk, she had decided I was the jerk and stopped buzzing. Seeing me still tugging futilely at the door, she buzzed briefly again—just as I gave up. The embarrassment of being exposed as a greenhorn in the big city finally focused my mind. I placed my hand on the door-knob, nodded, and the by-now furious woman buzzed a third time. We finally got together. I pulled, the door opened, and I entered.

"When I push the buzzer," she screamed over the barking of the dog, "you pull the door."

"I'm sorry," I yelled back above the barking, "I'm new in town."

She didn't care. I had been uncommonly stupid. I had made another lousy day even more trying. She would cut me no slack. She repelled the smile I offered and fixed me with a tough, tense, suspicious stare, saying nothing and waiting for me to explain my intrusion into her shop.

I was to learn that her manner was not uncommon in many of the little shops of Washington which are the frequent victims of armed robbers. The cold eyes and the taut bearing of the shop-keepers are, of course, a defense. They are adhering to the code of the terrorized merchant:

> "Assume everybody who comes to the counter intends to rob you. Be nasty. Be tough. Erect a rude shield between you and them. Let them know with your manner, just in case the crimi-nal is about to whip out a gun, that it is suicide to mess with you. Never forget that courtesy is carelessness, warmth is weak-ness and a smile can get you killed."

She didn't know whether I was one of them or not. She was posing. The dog was sincere. He wanted to rip my throat out. He only had eyes for me. Between the two of them, they had achieved the desired effect. I felt like a criminal.

Nevertheless, I tried one more time to crack through the woman's practiced hostility. Handing over the money for the suit, I shouted sympathetically above the barking, "You must have had a robbery."

That took her by surprise. But she hesitated for only a moment before resenting it. Why would I belabor the obvious? Of course, she had had a robbery. She eyed me with the look of a woman debating with herself whether to unleash the dog. Then she thought better of it. I was probably as dumb as I sounded.

"Four times in two years," she snapped, dismissing me with the presentation of the claim check.

Thereafter, I took my business to another cleaning establishment across Massachusetts Avenue from my apartment. I was to learn that the new shop held its own reminders of D.C. violence, but at least it didn't have a deafening dog coveting my throat.

The proprietor was a remarkable young man, a Czechoslovakian refugee in his early twenties who was building a small chain of cleaning shops. He did not practice the code of the terrorized merchant. He risked some warmth on his customers. And appropriately for a Capitol Hill merchant, he was an able politician. In a city where a newcomer can feel faceless, he called me by name the second time I entered his shop.

I was surprised, therefore, when I stopped by one morning with another suit I had spilled something on and encountered that same young man—Milan Ganik—in a grim and uncommunicative mood. But then I noticed his hands were trembling. And a policeman was present taking notes.

Milan Ganik had just been robbed. It was 8:30—a.m.!

Ten minutes earlier he had been face down on the floor, a pistol at the back of his neck. As soon as the bandits left, so did his counter clerk. She quit. It was one robbery too much. As I arrived, he was trying to wait on customers and answer the policeman's questions at the same time.

"You're a little late," he said, finally finding a smile. "Ten minutes earlier and you could have been on the floor with me and the other customers."

That experience didn't do my shaky courage any good. But I continued trading with him. You might get shot, but at least your corpse would hit the floor next to the remains of one of Washington's few genial shopkeepers. And no loud-mouthed dog would bark over your body.

On that same day Jay Shelledy, an editor of my Lewiston newspaper, visited from Idaho. In a typical western gesture, he invited the young shopkeeper to dinner, as a kind of compensation on be-half of decent society for the expense and trauma of the robbery.

Ganik told us that night over dinner that the robbers had been caught. But he had been advised by friends not to identify them for the police. He had been warned that their colleagues would retali-ate. Ganik identified them anyway, not in angry retaliation, but . . . well, he just felt he should. Nevertheless, he wondered that night if his friends would prove to be right, if he would perhaps be shot in the inevitable next robbery.

He wasn't. Months later, after I had returned to my Idaho home, the young merchant from Washington took a first drive across his adopted land and visited Jay and me. He reported that the robbers had never gone to trial. The D.C. courts had freed them on a legal technicality, so he assumed they had no grudge against him.

Some years later, Milan Ganik went back to school and be-came a lawyer.

*   *   *

I was never mugged in my neighborhood, but I was repeatedly robbed, although without a gun. The accusation that central city markets will rip off their customers is true in most instances. The prices are higher and the service worse than in the suburban stores around the District. I suppose the rationale is that each individual store, rather than the entire chain, must underwrite its own rob-beries and shoplifting. The stores with the largest losses have the highest prices. The honest customers get to pick up the tab for the crooked ones. Thus it is the customers, rather than the store own-ers, who are robbed each time—free enterprise's version of group punishment. The prices in those markets are a rather effective re-buttal to the shoplifters and robbers who rationalize that they are stealing only from the wealthy store owners. To the contrary, the thieves and the store owners are business partners, stealing from thee and me.

There were times when I was inclined to conclude, if you can't lick 'em, join 'em. But I was never sure, if I did decide to start steal-ing from the people, whether I should become a shoplifter or a grocery store stockholder.

Capitol Hill had what masqueraded as a supermarket. It was the smallest supermarket, with the largest volume of customers, I have ever seen. I do not doubt Capitol Hill folklore that it was the most profitable outlet in the nation for that chain. And that little supermarket made a fetish of Washington's principal pastime—standing in line. Thanks to three million residents of the region, plus an annual flood of tourists, the lines form everywhere—at the cafeteria in the Senate Office Building, at the Bill of Rights in the National Archives, at the National Zoo's panda cage where the tourists cluster with their children in hopes of a rare glimpse of the beasts breeding, and in the aisles of the Capitol Hill outlet of a national supermarket chain where you can routinely watch a national corporation screw the public.

You stand in line in that store to get a shopping basket. You stand in line at the head of each aisle while shopping. And of course, you stand in line—forever—at the checkstands. Count on an hour to buy a dozen items.

That got to me. Standing in line for the Bill of Rights is worth it. I even considered it worthwhile the day I waited my turn at the panda cage and the female panda had a headache. But waiting your turn to paw through a chain store's wilted lettuce struck me as a waste of time. That's part of the reason I finally left Washington. I kept thinking, if I had wanted to spend the rest of my life standing in line, I would have joined the army.

Incredibly, there was on the Senate side of Capitol Hill an even more expensive, cramped, and unsavory food store than the infamous chain store outlet I usually frequented. Yuckorama Food Central, as we will call it, was not so much a food store as it was a defiant repudiation of the pure food and drug laws. And naturally, the Yuckorama was the handy store only a half block from my apartment. I swore never to trade there, except when I needed a last-minute item, which, for a busy person living alone, was most of the time. For better or for worse, it was my neighborhood store.

The specialty of the house was dirt. The muddy vegetables were wilted. The floor was coated with what looked like dried slobber from the winos who worked the aisles for handouts, surreptitiously wolfing down half-rotted apples from the produce bins. Caked dirt, not just dust, coated the tops of slow-moving canned goods. I used to buy vacuum-packed peanuts and wash the cans before opening them. Worst of all, the checkout clerks seemed to be sweating all the time. They were pungent.

But the Yuckorama, in addition to being the only market in the neighborhood, was open late. That was convenient both to the customers and to the robbers who occasionally knocked it over, to the cheers of the customers.

The store was periodically segregated. The neighborhood is mixed, both racially and economically. Located in a gray area between economic worlds, the business counted among its victim-customers poor black families, affluent Capitol Hill employees who preferred townhouses in risky neighborhoods to commuting from the distant suburbs, plus a multiracial assortment of Senate interns and other beginning congressional employees who populated the apartments in that section of the city. Before dark, the Yuckorama customers were an assortment of races and economic types. After dark, I assume for reasons of white fear, nearly all were black. Some were weary working mothers with odd-hour jobs just getting home. And a lot of young studs stopped by to pick up six-packs of beer.

I had been warned not to enter the market after dark, and never to flash the twenty I always carried to avoid angering muggers. But there were times when liberal guilt or late hours at the office made it impossible to heed the warning. On those occasions, the other shoppers in the store, though black, were just as edgy as I at being caught having to walk the streets after dark.

One of the first nights I walked to the Yuckorama in darkness, I stumbled into a sticky situation. As I approached the store, half a dozen young toughs from the neighborhood were loitering outside, blocking the door and more or less daring anyone to run the risk of being jostled while pushing through them. And there was nothing bigoted about them. They were equally rowdy with black or white, and especially active in their pushing and grabbing as young women ran the gauntlet.

I had heard about such gangs, made up of the unemployed and unoccupied young men with which we have blessed our core cities. In that particular neighborhood, they had been responsible for numerous muggings. And there had been a couple of murders nearby just before I moved to town.

And so there I came down the street, fresh from Idaho, clopping along in my bedroom slippers. The walk to the store was so short that I hadn't bothered to put on my shoes. By the time I spotted the young toughs, there was no turning back without loss of face. So I risked loss of my rear end as well and plunged on. I feigned an absent-minded look, as if I didn't realize they were there. I didn't want to show fear in the hope they were like other young people who don't enjoy tormenting some tweedy old duffer if they get no reaction from him. I tried very hard to be no fun at all.

Maybe it worked because, as I clopped up to the entrance, the black sea parted. Laughing at their game, they let me pass. And they only hooted a little when I left the store a few minutes later.

Thereafter, I gave more attention to my Washington warfare costume. It occurred to me that, at 150 pounds and slight of build, bedroom slippers was asking for it. I was determined to look forbidding. On subsequent night missions to the Yuckorama, I dressed for the occasion. In the closet, largely for nostalgic purposes, were my cowboy boots from Idaho. That would add a couple of inches of height and would perhaps give me the look of a mean dude who enjoyed stomping people. I added a puffy ski jacket which gave me more bulk in the chest and shoulders. And of course, I removed my glasses. The final touch was a lighted cigarette (a habit I abandoned shortly after I abandoned Washington). I let the burning weed droop nonchalantly from one snarling corner of my mouth with the added benefit of the smoke wafting up, forcing me to squint my eyes until they became mean little slits. Or so I calculated. For good measure, as I approached the Yuckorama, I would slip into a John Wayne stride, loping along slightly sideways, my hands curled into iron fists at the ends of sinewy arms. I kept hoping they had seen a lot of movies. On reflection, I was probably safer in the bedroom slippers—too pathetic to bother with.

Moreover, even if the costume did work, even if one ominous night someone lurking in a doorway blanched and let me pass, it may have been for the wrong reason. There is no one more likely to be left alone in a big city than a wacko. There was, for instance, a man in a stocking cap who used to stand on a corner near the National Gallery of Art, rushing up to people to shout the words of Jesus in their faces. You could look down that sidewalk and see a stream of pedestrians crossing the street through heavy traffic to avoid the guy. They'd rather get hit by a cab than have some fruitcake bellowing the Bible at them.

Perhaps that is why I was never bothered again by the young toughs around the Yuckorama or by any muggers. They may have melted into the night when they looked down the street and saw some skinny guy headed their way walking slightly sideways like a runty John Wayne and wearing cowboy boots and a pastel orange jacket.

*   *   *

It all gets to you after a time—the muggers, the street gangs, the multiple locks on steel doors, the bars on the windows, the barking guard dogs, the robberies across the street, the police helicopters sweeping the neighborhood with high intensity lights, and the incessant sirens in the night, the sirens singing of another misfortune. To make matters worse, some of the fear in the capital is manufactured. And there is no larger fear factory than the local television stations. Their newscasts are drenched in violence.

For naive reasons, I had been looking forward to Washington television. I had imagined that Washington, a political capital and a breeding ground for many of the major political reporters on the network, would focus on the city's principal industry and provide a nightly feast of news on politics and government.

Not so. The feast is fear. The nightly diet on the television stations of the principal political capital of the western world is the same provincial fascination with street crime found on any other television station in America. Washington television loves rape and robbery and, most of all, murder. The stations don't just mention murder, they milk it—especially the murder of children, preferably by perverts.

They begin with footage of the murder scene and, if the camera crew got lucky, a shot of the body being carted out. The voice-over is an interview with the investigating officer. He explains what happened in language so clinical, so detached, that the mess under the blanket on the stretcher might be a dead carp. The footage is pseudo-artistic, shot from inside the ambulance as they load the mess aboard. You can almost hear the glee in the control room.

Next comes the school picture of the kid who was wasted, with an antiseptic anchor person on the voice-over explaining that the youngster loved the Washington Redskins and his mother.

Dissolve to the crying mother who tries to explain that he always looked over his younger brothers and sisters. But it's too much for her. She can't go on. The camera can and does. It inches a little tighter, devouring the moment as she collapses on the shoulder of the boy's father, who has that angry, why-did-we-ever-agree-to-this-goddam-interview look on his face.

Dissolve to the pervert getting into a police car, trying to keep his face away from the camera. Apparently he has a mother, too. As he turns, his hands cuffed behind him, to swing into the car, the monster shows his face. The camera rockets in for a freeze-frame close-up to let everyone out there in Televisionland savor a few seconds of hate and fear.

The following night, after reports of a couple of new murders, the anchor person discloses that the pervert has entered a not-guilty plea, which is the story peg for rehashing some of the first night story.

And on the third night comes the funeral footage. The camera remains at what Washington television considers a tasteful distance from the mourners. Framing the aching mother in nearby head-stones, the zoom lens creeps forward, reverently, barely getting close enough to show the reddened, sleepless eyes before the shat-tered woman faints once more in the arms of her husband.

After a time, I became slightly jaded, along with the rest of Washington. But in the beginning, sitting alone in a foreign neigh-borhood, in my barred and bolted cell, the nightly fare on the tele-vision news was not a big help. In fact, it occurred to me that outside those barred windows and that bolted door one hell of a lot of people were getting themselves killed.

*   *   *

To my knowledge, the only killers I encountered during my stay in Washington had worked with our government. The Senate Intelli-gence Committee, which Frank Church chaired, heard testimony one day from John Rosselli, a Mafia figure. Approximately a year after he testified, his body was found in a barrel bobbing in the sea. During that same summer of 1975, when Rosselli went before the committee, his Mafia and CIA colleague, Sam Giancana, was also scheduled to appear. But at the last minute, Sam couldn't make it. He turned up full of holes in Chicago.

Some say both murders were a coincidence, that they were routine gangland revenge for assorted, long-standing transgres-sions against their brothers in crime. Chicago reporters told me they weren't so sure. No one knows for certain.

The Intelligence Committee called Rosselli because the investigators wanted to know if it was actually true that Rosselli and Giancana had worked with the American government—specifically the CIA—in attempts to assassinate Cuban Premier Fidel Castro.

Of course, they had, Rosselli answered proudly. After all, he boasted, he was a patriot.

It was a surrealistic experience. At night I cowered in my apartment because of the organized and unorganized criminals outside on the street. By day, I kept the waiting reporters company while a Mafia goon inside a closed session of the Senate committee boasted about his patriotic work in trying to help our government snuff the leader of another country. Hiding in that apartment and standing in the Capitol corridor, patriotism and crime and right and wrong all seemed to get a little fuzzy.

A few nights after Rosselli testified, I took in a performance by Mark Russell, the mischievous satirist who has long been a staple of Washington humor. He was similarly stricken with the irony of it all.

"And what do you do for a living?" asked Russell in his pose as a Senate investigator.

"I'm a notorious gangster and hit man."

"And how long have you worked for the government?"

During that same period of the committee's sessions on the Mafia and the CIA, I came down with a slightly different strain of Washington apartment paranoia. Early in the Church committee's investigation, several reporters had taken me aside and warned that one should be careful when investigating the American intelligence community. The CIA has ways of making life unpleasant for those who make life unpleasant for the CIA, they whispered.

My initial reaction was to laugh off their warnings as the delusions of melodramatic reporters. I really doubted that my government would go that far. After all, I'm as patriotic as John Rosselli. And patriots trust their government. Still, it was something to think about during long evenings locked in that apartment. The CIA had virtually admitted some pretty rough action abroad, so who is to say how far they might go to protect themselves at home against what they considered dangerous idealists?

It was during those evenings of toying with such disgraceful doubts that I first noticed the footsteps in the overhead apartment.

It sank in slowly at first, but a pattern began to emerge. As soon as I got out of bed in the morning, the feet above would also get out of bed and begin walking on the other side of my ceiling. If I arose at 6 a.m., the feet would arise at 6 a.m. If I slept in until 8 a.m., so did the feet. The pattern was the same at night. The feet wouldn't go to bed until I did. If I turned in at 10 p.m. or at 2 in the morning, so did the feet.

But there was a shade of difference at night. Before going to bed, the feet would take a bath. I would pop into bed and turn off the light. Immediately, the feet would creak to the bathroom and begin drawing water. After a few minutes, there would be some sloshing about, followed by water being emptied from the tub, and then the clean feet would pad off to bed.

I was pretty sure it was an agent, but the bath puzzled me. I know a lot of clean people personally, and, among the men, it is the general practice to take a shower every morning. Among women, a nightly bath is more common. What kind of a man in that CIA macho factory would take a bath every night rather than a manly shower in the morning?

Suddenly it hit me: The bastards had sent a woman—a big woman, judging from the heavy footsteps—a big woman trained in karate and capable of breaking my feet with her bare hands if I gave her any trouble when she finally came downstairs to compromise me and the investigation.

But another thing puzzled me: Agents usually work in teams, spelling each other on the bugging equipment. I might be from Idaho, but I knew that much; I'd been to the movies. Why would they assign only one person—even a big, strong, probably vicious woman—to watch over me? Surely my government had enough respect for me to know that, when provoked, I could be more trouble than one woman could handle.

But there was no doubt about it. I knew those footsteps well. Day after day, she was the only one up there. Except that one night toward the end. Suddenly one night, there were two pairs of feet up there. Long before I went to bed, and without taking a bath, the feet stopped walking. Before long, the bedsprings were squeaking.

My God, I thought, they're screwing on government time! Wait until I tell the committee about this!

Of course, I never told the committee. I noticed the feet for a period of only about six weeks. On more rational reflection, it seemed possible that, on the nights when the feet went to bed at a different time, I forgot about the situation and didn't notice. It seemed possible that I noticed only on the mornings when the feet and I arose at the same time, and on the nights when we went to bed together, so to speak.

But during those adventuresome evenings when I may have read too much into the habits of the upstairs feet and assumed they were official, I never fully resented the surveillance. After all, the feet were simply doing their job. And though misguided in their mission, the feet, during those lonely first weeks in Washington, were my only companion.

*   *   *

After a time, the sirens, the neighborhood robberies, the television news, and the locks and bars began to fade from attention. You can't live in constant fear, even when the fear may be well placed. After a time, I became like most D.C. residents, a little hardened to it all, shrugging off the risks and not really stopping to think about crime all that often.

But you can also go overboard on being fatalistic. There is a middle ground between hiding in a locked apartment and using no discretion at all. As the months wore on and I no longer really heard the sirens or paid much attention to the nightly murder report on television, I did a stupid thing one day and lived to tell about it.

As a further extension of the Washington practice of treating everyone like a crook—just in case—it was damn near impossible to cash a check in that city. And this was just before bank cash machines came along. Paradoxically, in the city where it was most dangerous to carry large amounts of money, it was almost essential to carry considerable cash if you wanted to buy anything. So it became my habit to save myself frequent trips to the bank. Whenever I stopped by the bank, I would write a rather large check for enough cash to last a week or two. Normally, I would squirrel away most of the money in a hiding place (none of your business) taking with me each morning only enough bucks for that day's activities—including, of course, at least $20 for cranky muggers.

One day, while looking for an address in a section of D.C. known for daylight muggings, the chilling thought struck that I had neglected to leave the excess cash in my hiding place. I was walking around the streets of Washington carrying a wallet bloated with $190.

I suddenly remembered the money because I could hear footsteps behind me. They seemed to be keeping in step, trying not to be heard. I followed what I assume is the usual practice of those being stalked in the streets of the nation's capital. I checked him out. Without turning around, I simply speeded up a little.

He speeded up a little.

I slowed my pace a trifle.

He slowed his pace a trifle.

I immediately speeded up again, and he did too.

That didn't leave much doubt.

My next move was instinctive. If there is a saving grace to my cowardice, it is that, when convinced I am a goner anyway, I decide I might as well die like a gentleman. The British blood wells up in me. For instance, I don't fly well, not well at all. When there is a little pitching and swaying of the plane, I often become convinced that I am doomed. And whenever I am convinced that I am doomed, I sit up nice and tall, cross my legs nonchalantly and act like a big boy. I will die if I must, but I won't snivel. It is only when there might be a way out that I sometimes snivel.

And so, with the mugger now certain to pounce, I vowed that I would at least choose the moment. Lighting my last cigarette and mentally crossing my legs, I would turn and face the villain squarely. With luck, he would take the money and not my life. At worst, the awful waiting would be over.

And so I quickly turned.

Too quickly. I scared the hell out of a tourist.

Thereafter, I used better judgment about the amount of cash I carried. But the incident was a turning point. For the first time, someone on the streets of Washington had been afraid of me.

It was not the last time. On the night Frank Church won the Nebraska primary, in the spring of 1976, I was driving home from the celebration in the middle of the night and ran a blinking light. This time, the siren was for me.

The prowl car pulled in behind as I sat at the wheel waiting for my ticket. I watched in the side mirror of the car as the lone officer

walked uneasily toward me, wondering if I was a fleeing felon willing to kill to avoid detection. As he neared the car, he unsnapped
his holster and placed a hand on the butt of his gun. He was scared
to death.

He relaxed slightly when he got a look at me and at my Idaho
driver's license. But the gun was ready in case I was meaner than I
looked. He wasn't going to spend any more time with me than necessary. He gave me a quick verbal warning and retreated to the
prowl car.

As I pulled away from the curb, I couldn't get over that hand
on the gun. He had really been frightened—of me! After all those
sweaty months, the shoe was on the other foot. After only a year in
politics, I was feared.

Machiavelli was right. If one must choose, it is far safer—
in the middle of the night in Washington, D.C.—to be feared
than loved.

Chapter Three
The Senator and the Naked Ladies

It is perhaps the measure of a modest life that I had never had any direct contact with Senator Barry Goldwater or with *Penthouse* magazine until I became press secretary to the Senate Intelligence Committee.

Previously, I had seen both only from afar—*Penthouse* waving its perfect nipples from the newsstand and Goldwater waving his peculiar nostrums from the platform of the 1964 Republican National Convention where he was nominated for the dubious honor of being slaughtered at the polls by Lyndon Johnson. I never bought the nipples or the nostrums. But I had a good look at both before the Intelligence Committee had finished probing.

The Intelligence Committee, formed in the wake of newspaper disclosures about the excesses of the CIA and the FBI, had no press secretary of its own during its first few months. It made do (reluctantly, in most cases) with Chairman Frank Church's personal press secretary—me. Consequently, I was accustomed to fielding press calls on the investigation. But I wasn't prepared for the day the receptionist announced that a gentleman from (tee hee) *Penthouse* was in the outer office waiting to see me. He wanted Frank Church to write a letter—for publication—congratulating the magazine on its CIA series.

Some skin magazines have a complex. They fill their pages with breasts, and just because of that some people jump to the conclusion that they aren't serious magazines. It is the mark of such magazines that they reach a point where they no longer want to be treated like sex objects. They want to be admired for their intellect. Hence *Penthouse* was exposing not only breasts but also the Central Intelligence Agency.

Penthouse wanted respect. And the man from *Penthouse* wanted the chairman of the Senate Intelligence Committee to write a letter of praise.

I was about half inclined to recommend that Church honor the request. Years before the campaign of 1976—during which Gerald Ford and other silly old twits came unglued over Jimmy Carter's admission in a *Playboy* interview that he lusted in his heart after other women—Frank Church had appeared in *Playboy*. Church wrote a straight foreign policy essay for the magazine. He lusted only after peace in Indochina.

Unfortunately, the article appeared in the very first edition in which *Playboy* threw caution and its undies to the wind and began showing pubic hair in public. Worse, Church's article began on a facing page to one of the raw, new nude shots.

Apparently I was about the only one who gave much notice. Even though Idaho is a rather upright state with a pronounced Mormon influence, there was hardly any mail. Maybe that was because anyone who didn't approve was in no position to admit where he had seen the offending article.

I figured, if the *Playboy* essay had passed unnoticed in an earlier, more sweaty time, then surely *Penthouse* would be no problem in this day and age. Moreover, the youngish *Penthouse* readership was a prime possibility for forming part of the constituency for the committee's campaign to rouse the country against the CIA's democratically abnormal methods. But I stalled the man from *Penthouse* until I had a chance to double-check my hunches.

Verda Barnes, Church's chief of staff at the time, voted no. She had once seen the magazine on an airplane. "It's pretty rough," she said, "a lot worse than *Playboy*."

I was inclined to dismiss her judgment as a trifle square until the man from *Penthouse* returned later in the week with an advance copy of the latest edition. Flipping casually past the yawning organs, he pointed proudly to the latest article on the CIA. He wanted me to take the magazine home and see for myself what a responsible publication *Penthouse* is. He wanted me to see how much it deserved to be praised by the chairman of the Intelligence Committee. I was having a little trouble concentrating on what he was saying. I've always found it difficult to think about the CIA so soon after having seen full-color pictures of sex organs. That may be unpatriotic, but I'm funny that way.

I took the magazine and, trying to look dignified, told him I would read it and get back to him. Obviously, I couldn't sit in the middle of a U.S. Senate office building reading *Penthouse*. A taxpayer might drop in and misunderstand. I would have to wait until I got home to study the magazine.

I went home early.

First I flipped through the pictures. I might as well clear that hurdle first because, if I didn't, it would only nag at me while I was reading the CIA article. The pictures were what are usually called "full frontal nudity." But that was an understatement. They were exceedingly frontal.

Next I read the article on the CIA. In truth, it was first rate, neither preachy nor shallow, but straight, sober reporting.

And then, because of Church's unfortunate placement years earlier among the pubic hair of *Playboy*, I examined the general content of the magazine—to judge the context in which his requested praise of *Penthouse* would be found.

Verda Barnes was right. *Penthouse* was not a subtle magazine.

And it was more the words than the pictures that made me wary of recommending that Church become associated—as we Victorian press secretaries would put it—with "that sort of thing." One salacious article in particular seemed to stand out, along with most of its readers, I assume. Toward the back of the magazine was kind of a kinky Dear Abby—a standing feature, I was told. Xaviera Hollander, author of *The Happy Hooker* and similar books, gave advice to the lewdlorn. Some of it was pretty far over the line. For instance, one joker wanted to know if he and his girlfriend might not be a trifle weird because they enjoyed peeing on each other.

Why of course not, Xaviera comforted. As long as you respect each other and don't do anything degrading or in bad taste, peeing on each other can be exhilarating.

Or something close to that.

I was struck that night with a thought that crossed my mind dozens of times as I labored for the taxpayers in Washington: What a strange way to make a living.

There I sat in my apartment, working overtime (who says bureaucrats are lazy?) reading *Penthouse* magazine for the good of the republic.

And somewhere else in Washington that night, a CIA press secretary was doing the same thing.

* * *

The Senate Intelligence Committee was my first brush with the Washington way of scheming within a bureaucracy. The more experienced members of the committee staff soon noticed that, though I had the chairman's ear, I didn't maneuver against them. They concluded that I was either toothless or didn't choose to bite. I was a virgin and they had their way with me.

My only previous experience with internal politics was one term as president of an elementary school PTA. God knows that got vicious at times, but I usually came out on top. After all, I was the president.

I rarely came out on top of the Intelligence Committee staff. I suppose I should have warned them that I was a former PTA president. That would have put the fear of God in them. But I assumed at the time that knowing the committee chairman personally would be enough.

It wasn't.

My needs were simple. All I wanted was an even break for the press. The press created the Senate Intelligence Committee. It was a series of investigative reports, initially in *The New York Times* and subsequently elsewhere, that convinced the Senate that its committees charged with oversight of the CIA, the FBI, and other intelligence organizations had been fast asleep for years. So the Senate created, in January 1975—over the objections of its slumbering watchdogs and assorted other apologists—a committee with a title in keeping with the windy Washington tradition of naming committees and agencies: "The Senate Select Committee to Study Governmental Operations With Respect to Intelligence Activities."

It took longer to say the name than it takes the CIA to topple a government.

The committee, in its year of existence, documented, among other transgressions, that:

> —The CIA plotted assassination attempts against a half dozen foreign leaders, developed deadly toxins and James Bondish poison dart guns, caused the foreign mail of American

citizens to be opened, intercepted the foreign phone calls and cables of American citizens, and generally tried to manipulate the world while invading the privacy of the people it was paid to protect.

—The FBI had similarly violated the civil rights of its patrons. And former FBI Director J. Edgar Hoover had waged a personal vendetta against Dr. Martin Luther King, Jr. Hoover saw to it that the FBI bugged King's hotel rooms, eavesdropped on his telephone calls, tried to frighten him out of accepting the Nobel Peace Prize and, in an especially small act, tried to prevent King from being granted an honorary degree from a university that had honored Hoover earlier.

I didn't know the committee had learned any of that at the time. I had decided against seeking security clearance, not because I had given aid and comfort to the commies, but because I was determined to give aid and comfort to the press. I would be their advocate within the committee. If I knew nothing but the nonclassified details of the committee's work, then everything I knew of the committee's work would be legitimate public information and should be shared with the press. That would be in keeping with a free society, as I understood it. Thus, by urging openness on all that should be open, I would be serving the republic, the committee, and the committee chairman, who had manifested an abiding affection for democracy.

If I had been granted security clearance and been routinely filled in on all the dark secrets as they unraveled inside the committee, I probably would have become as paranoid about the press as most of the committee staff. I probably would have joined them in the practice of keeping from the public a great deal more than was necessary—just to prove how important we all were.

I noticed while I was in Washington that keeping secrets has something to do with the pecking order. The more important you are, the more secrets you know. And vice versa. Consequently, if you don't actually know many secrets, you must treat as secret some information that should not be a secret, thereby establishing your claim to clout.

With members of the committee staff snickering at me behind my back because I alone didn't know any secrets, it was sometimes tempting to uphold my honor:

REPORTER: How old is Senator Church?
PRESS SECRETARY: I'm sorry, but that information is classified.
REPORTER: My God, I didn't realize you were that important!

The committee and the staff were unusually goosey because the investigation had begun amid accusations by the American right that, to paraphrase, "the Church committee would leak like a sieve, leaving America naked and vulnerable to her enemies." The committee was determined not to do that, and it certainly didn't. But in its caution, the committee, like its critics, overlooked the point that most of the CIA's adventures were already known to practically everyone except the American people. For instance, Fidel Castro noticed right away when the CIA began trying to kill him. Castro has always been quick about things like that. It was only the people whose government had decided to snuff Castro who were kept in the dark.

Church thought the CIA was out of control and could be brought into line with the country's customary principles only if the public believed what the committee had learned and demanded change. To that end, Church wanted a unanimous final report—a report signed by all 11 members of the committee, especially including the committee's token cold warrior, Barry Goldwater. So Church tended to bend over backward toward the Goldwater wing of the committee in deciding what could be made public.

Most of the reporters seemed to understand that at first. But they had their other needs. After the first three or four dozen members of what was to become a staff of 120 had been hired, reporters came to me wanting their names and backgrounds.

"My God, you can't give them that!" an agitated committee honcho protested, a nervous little knot of her fellow bureaucrats gathering around to back her.

"Is it classified?" I asked, knowing it wasn't.

"No, it's not classified, but if the press knows the names of the staff, they'll call them at home and try to pump leaks out of them."

"I don't doubt they will," I said. "But if it's a matter of public record, all you can do is make it inconvenient for the reporters to get the names. All you can do is make them mad. They'll get the names anyway. You'll have to guard against leaks by hiring people you can trust to keep their traps shut."

She shifted gears on me: "The chairman insists we guard against leaks. And I know you want me to carry out the *chairman's* wishes."

We were now playing "The Chairman Says." In Washington, underlings invoke the name of the appropriate high official in argument whenever there is doubt that they might be outranked by the person with whom they are arguing. One does *not* say, "I don't think we ought to do that." One says, "The chairman wouldn't want us to do that."

So she had me there, but only for the moment. I went to the chairman. "We can't keep the staff list from the press," he said, astonished at the suggestion. "It a matter of public record. You tell them I want those names out."

And so, having tattled, I went toddling back to the committee, rehearsing my lines for my inning at bat in the game of "The Chairman Says." I figured I'd open with something mature like, "The chairman says you better give me those names, and right now!"

It was great training for the White House, but I felt silly. There was something familiar about all this, something reminiscent of simpler days on an Idaho farm:

> "Bobby stole my slingshot."
> "You tell Bobby I said to give you back your slingshot."
> "Bobby, you little rat, Daddy says you better give me back my slingshot, and right now!"

I marched into the committee's quarters, an eerie and intimidating world in which to try to assert superiority. Uniformed officers guarded the doors 24 hours a day. Authorized visitors like me had to sign in each time we entered. Inside were row upon row of cubicles where the sifters of secrets worked probing individual facets of the intelligence establishment. They learned what other sifters were doing in other cubicles only if they had "a need to know," secrecy within secrecy. Around the room were high-security filing cabinets with combination locks on each drawer. Here and there were waste baskets with hinged lids marked "classified," their contents doomed to the fabled Washington shredders.

Into that atmosphere I marched on my mission, wearing a green "visitor" badge, betraying to everyone my lack of security clearance and advertising to those I would confront that I was the only one in the room who didn't know any secrets.

"I'll need those staff names," I snapped. "The chairman wants them given to the press right away."

And they were sore afraid. Naturally, if that's really what the chairman wanted, they would get right on it. Obviously, they had underestimated the virgin from Idaho. He wasn't such a pushover after all.

Except that over the next six weeks they beat me senseless with the bureaucrat's ultimate weapon—inertia. Almost daily I shuffled into the committee quarters to see if the list of names was ready yet for the reporters.

Some days my tormentor, apologizing profusely, had simply forgotten all about it. Some days the list was just about ready, but a few more people had been hired at the last minute. There hadn't been time to add their names to the list.

"Just give me what you have," I whimpered. "You can give me the other names later."

"No, we can't do that," she said sweetly. "The *chairman* wants the press to have *all* the names, right up to the minute. I think you understand we have to do what the *chairman* says."

I understood all right. I might get some action if I tattled to the chairman, but what little dignity I had left wouldn't allow me to do that. I kept nagging. It was weeks before we finally did what the *chairman* wanted.

*   *   *

In the fall of 1975, after months of closed-door hearings, the committee finally opened its sessions to the public and the cameras. It was time to bring in the bad guys and shake the truth out of them with the nation watching. The open hearings fulfilled the usual purpose—to parade in public what had already been learned through private interrogation. Most of the witnesses had been caught red-handed at some violation of American principle or law. The public hearings were intended to document graphically what had been going on by forcing the bad guys to sweat under the klieg lights while singing out their sins. It's a great moment for those who relish going in for the kill. I never had much stomach for it. I don't think Church did either. There were days when I sat at the press table, with other people slavering all around me, feeling traitorously sorry for the bad guys, the overzealous guys, the guys who had let their patriotism run off with their brains. Most of the witnesses knew damn well the committee had the goods on them. So the smart move was to admit everything, to get it over with as fast as possible. The witness who lies, or becomes evasive, or gets hostile, or—like Nixon aide John Ehrlichman before the Senate Watergate Committee—becomes a bit of a smartass, provokes senators and brings out their mean streak. The witness who strays from the straight and narrow is begging to have the truth pummeled out of him. They'll get him for that.

But a Senate investigation of government wrongdoing is no picnic, even for the cooperative witness who respectfully spills his guts. At the very least, even he must spend some time on national television acknowledging—before his mother, his children, and his God—what a son of a bitch he has been.

Most of the witnesses before the Senate Intelligence Committee were well advised. They recited their sins, genuflected a lot, and got the hell off the stand as fast as possible.

But there was one type of witness who was so truthful that the committee could only stare in amazement—the witness who almost boasted of what he had been doing for the government and who truly couldn't understand why anyone would object. After all, in a harsher time, the spooks had been considered heroes in some circles for their manipulation of other governments, and for occasionally snuffing someone on the other side who really had it coming.

Typical of those witnesses was a Dr. Strangelove involved in producing lethal toxins developed to kill people discreetly. He was somewhat oblivious to the moral questions involved but intrigued with the scientific challenge of his work. He could hardly contain his enthusiasm—or his pride—even before a committee that had summoned him as a symptom of an agency with a diseased attitude. His nature was best revealed one day during the preliminary chit chat just before the hearing began. A senator asked him about his hobbies.

"I like to kill fish," he answered, startling the chairman, who did the same thing but called it "fishing."

*   *   *

I sat in on nearly every interview and press conference that Church granted. So I usually had in my head, up to the minute, just about everything he was at liberty to say in public about the progress of the investigation. But there came a day when I was stumped for an answer to a reporter's question.

"Who is this guy who's replacing you as the committee's press secretary?"

"I beg your pardon?"

"You know, the guy who starts next Monday."

I didn't know. No one had told me I was being replaced.

I did know that I would probably be phased out sooner or later for the simple reason that the growing workload on the committee would eventually require a full-time press secretary. And it wasn't fair to the other senators that the committee press secretary actually worked for the chairman alone. The other members couldn't tell me what to do, even by a ten-to-one vote, if that one vote was the chairman's. And then there was also the matter of those menacing rumbles about my work from Senator Goldwater.

Occasionally a reporter would misunderstand that it was neither professional nor healthy for me to get my name in the paper. Senators hire press secretaries to get the names of senators in the paper. But sometimes, instead of reporting the thinking of the committee chairman, as I had explained that thinking, the reporters would, to my horror, quote me by name. And sometimes they would quote me, while citing "a committee source."

It didn't happen often so I never got much flak from Church. But word came to me that Goldwater was having a snit. He was essentially in disagreement with making public any of what the committee uncovered. In fact, he wasn't too crazy about the entire investigation.

"Since the Select Committee came into being . . ." he wrote in his portion of the report on the CIA's foreign assassination attempts, "it has been my belief that the investigation should be held in executive session with one final and complete report to the Senate and ultimately to the American people. The difficulty of distinguishing between those matters that are part of the public record from those that must remain classified are difficult to keep in mind. Accordingly, members of the Select Committee and its staff are now faced with an increased possibility of inadvertent disclosure of information that could be damaging to America's foreign policy."

One day, a somewhat embarrassed member of the committee staff came to me and asked if I was the "source" quoted in a clipping he handed me. Goldwater, who had also raised hell about stories quoting me by name, had demanded that the staff identify the source quoted in several stories. He had issued the demand in a letter to his committee colleagues. The thrust of the letter was that, just as he had warned, the committee was leaking like an old boat. Staff members were dispatched, brandishing a stack of clippings, to locate the leak. Apparently I was their first stop. No one looks as leaky as a press secretary.

Yes, I confessed, emulating a contrite Watergate conspirator and wondering what my lecture fees would be, the source quoted in several of the clippings was me.

I had spilled information of two kinds. One had to do with what had once been fresh news—details I had heard Church give to reporters, details I had later repeated to another reporter who mistakenly thought it was such hot stuff that he protected me by attributing it to "a committee source." The other type of information had to do with procedural details (also based on Church's public pronouncements) such as his estimate that the committee might wrap up its work by the end of the year, or the revelation that the committee would not be meeting again until the following Tuesday.

I doubt that Goldwater was actually all that upset about the stories. I think he was waving my "leaks" at Church and at anyone else on the committee who was inclined toward openness as a way of keeping that faction on the defensive and fulfilling his wish to tell the public next to nothing. The old rascal was probably just maneuvering.

Of course, it's always possible that Goldwater actually saw me as a threat to the committee—and thereby to national security. He had no way of knowing I was a former PTA president. And I may have looked like the type who would leak our nation's secrets. If so, his suspicion was ironic. Nobody would ever tell me anything. They wouldn't even tell me the nonclassified information. They wouldn't tell me who all those people were working in all those committee cubicles, let alone what the CIA had been up to all those years.

But thanks to Goldwater, I held my head high for a few days around those snobs on the committee staff. They hadn't even regarded me as a threat to their mission to keep staff names from the press. But Barry Goldwater—former candidate for president of the United States—considered me a threat to the free world. Barry Goldwater had enough respect for me to try to get my butt fired.

He succeeded, too. The reporter who called was right. The committee had a new press secretary. Someone had forgotten to mention it to me. Another secret I didn't know.

*   *   *

The intelligence investigation had a purpose in common with the Watergate investigation before it. Neither was conducted simply to bring the individual abusers of power to justice. Both investigations attempted to shake some sense into the country, to generate a backlash against practices that seemed to be escalating toward democratic perdition.

By that yardstick, the orchestration of the backlash against Watergate was a howling success. The nation no longer worships its presidents; it watches them.

The attempt to stimulate equal vigilance to the habits of the CIA had more of a mixed result. On the positive side, the public climate today is, if not entirely hostile to the CIA's KGB tendencies, no longer quite so hospitable either. And out of the Church Committee investigations came a new permanent oversight committee which was—for a time at least—more inclined to perform its function than the old committee, which didn't even meet for one entire year.

Church told of a conversation during his early years in the Senate with one of the members of the committee then charged with keeping an eye on the CIA. The old senator boasted to Church that, almost as a measure of his patriotism, he didn't know what was going on inside the CIA, "and what's more, I don't want to know."

Perhaps the most significant victory in the Church Committee's efforts to alert the public to that self-indulgent agency was the apparent success in reaching one American in particular. In the closing months of his campaign for the presidency, Jimmy Carter began denouncing CIA excesses. It was apparently more than a coincidence and more than another campaign promise.

In the epilogue to its report on assassination plots, the Church Committee declared: "The United States must not adopt the tactics of the enemy. . . . Crisis makes it tempting to ignore the wise restraints that make men free. But each time we do so, each time the means we use are wrong, our inner strength, the strength which makes us free, is lessened."

Carter echoed that thought in his inaugural address: "We will not behave in foreign places so as to violate our rules and standards here at home, for we know that the trust which our nation earns is essential to its strength."

The Church Committee also had its large failures. Paradoxically, the effectiveness of the Watergate investigations is one reason the intelligence probe was less effective. To succeed to the fullest, the Church Committee had to shock the country to its senses.

How could you shock anyone after Watergate? The country was virtually shockproof—and its spirit so low after so much bad news that it was in no mood to listen to any more. To make matters worse, the intelligence investigation dragged on well beyond the public's painfully maimed attention span. The CIA apologists were able to lie low and buy time until they were handed a moment that allowed them to mount a backlash of their own.

That moment was the murder, on December 24, 1975, of Richard Welch, the CIA station chief in Greece. Welch was killed by Greek terrorists, but the canard soon sounded across America that Welch had been killed by the carelessness of the Church Committee and by the recklessness of a similar investigation in the House. The CIA apologists let the story bloom, and then helped it along a little, though they knew better.

In the first place, Welch was living in a home well known in Greece as the official residence of the CIA station chief. He was far from a deep-cover man.

Moreover, while many Greeks knew who he was and what he was doing there, the Church Committee didn't. Welch's name never came before the committee, and for good reason. The committee had specifically asked that it not be given the names of individual agents still active in the field, lest those names inadvertently leak and cost someone his life. The committee was interested solely in the policies being carried out by agents around the world, not in the names of the individuals carrying out those orders. The committee wanted the blueprints, but deliberately declined the names of the carpenters.

Of course, the CIA apologists knew that. But the general public didn't. When Welch was killed, hundreds of scathing "Murderer!" letters flooded Church's office from people across America who honestly and instantly assumed that the terrorists had learned Welch's identity through the Church Committee investigations.

Official Washington nurtured that notion:

> —White House Press Secretary Ron Nesson noted darkly that the president had warned Congress to be careful with its investigations.
> —President Ford ordered a show-funeral at Arlington National Cemetery, invited the cameras, and positioned himself next to Welch's widow at the grave.
> —Conservative members of the House took to the floor to blame the congressional investigations for Welch's death.
> —Church's colleague from Idaho—conservative Republican Senator James McClure, normally a fair person—toured the home state, telling his constituents and Church's that Welch's murder was an example of what can happen if a congressional investigation is not prudent with the lives its work affects. He didn't mention Church by name. He didn't have to.
> —For good measure, small newspapers and broadcasters around the country—without reporters of their own in Washington to set them straight—picked up the theme and weighed in with angry editorials. Several of them mailed their words to Church to make sure he knew what a piece of garbage they thought he was.

The campaign was transparently that—a campaign. The reporters covering the committee scoffed at the obvious orchestration. But with about three exceptions, none of their newspapers or networks reported it. My fellow bureaucrats sneered that the press had run out of guts, that it was too terrified, in that climate, to say what it thought.

Perhaps. It did get a little rough there for a few days. But solid newspapers rather relish the role of speaking the unspeakable when the politicians dare not. There are several solid newspapers covering Washington. But most of them were considerably less outraged than Frank Church's press secretary over what was happening. The press was getting terribly bored with the CIA investigation. After the glory that was Watergate, the CIA story had seemed pale by comparison. And it had slogged on—mostly behind closed doors—for months. Editors were beginning to yawn. The presidential election year was dawning, with the New Hampshire primary just around the corner. Washington is essentially a one-story town. The next story was moving into position.

One day I cried on the shoulder of syndicated columnist Mary McGrory (with *The Washington Star* at the time), one of the exceptions to the general silence of the press. I asked her why so few of her brethren were reporting the eagerness and the guile with which Ford and associates had pounced on the opportunity to spare the CIA further embarrassment.

She wondered why the chairman was not speaking up for his own investigation. Many in the press would stand behind him, she said, if he would lead the charge. It was his committee. If he wouldn't go to bat for it, why should anyone else?

Church tended to pout a bit when things didn't go his way. Maybe most of us do. But he took only a few stabs at sticking up for his committee—usually in response to provocative questions from reporters. That left no one to answer—neither the press which spawned the investigation nor the chairman who led it. Nobody was anxious to take on a president who had wrapped himself in the widow of a man killed in his country's service. So the cause of creating a public demand for CIA reform dwindled down toward an indefinite conclusion. Some initial concern had been generated. But in the end, no lasting outrage was mounted against an American agency that was mimicking the moral standards of the Russians.

*   *   *

Dear Xaviera,

Is it normal for a proud republic to pee on its principles?

Kinky Country

Dear Kinky,

Certainly. As long as it's in good taste and you don't do anything those filthy Russians wouldn't do, peeing on your principles can be exhilarating.

Love,
Xaviera

Chapter Four
Honk If You Love Silence

Washington is truly a city where everyone toots his own horn—incessantly.

Bus drivers honk. Taxi drivers honk. Commuters honk. The president's Secret Service driver honks on his behalf.

The horns of Washington are used not simply to clear the way or as a friendly warning to careless pedestrians. There is nothing friendly about it. All that honking is an expression of rage against the conditions Washington commuters endure getting to and from work.

Washington is a national transportation composite. It can't decide whether to be New York or Los Angeles. It is New York in the hordes who pour daily from the suburbs into a few square miles. It is Los Angeles in the way most of them choose to get there—by private automobile. Washington has the worst of both worlds. A Los Angeles flood of cars doesn't fit in a Manhattan-sized city.

In 1976, Washington opened the first tiny segment of a new subway system which, for some years thereafter, was built at a congressional pace. It would be years before most commuters would have more than the chronic choice between a bus or an automobile. However, now that that day has arrived, Washington has one of the cleanest and most user-friendly subways in the land.

But before the arrival of the subway, most Washington workers chose the automobile—and many still do—because, as aggravating as that can be in the daily squeeze, it is still about twice as fast as a bus. A bus stops every two blocks. On a good day, a car doesn't. So Washington, like Los Angeles and many other cities, spends much of its life in an automobile.

I tried buses at first, although it is a foreign form of travel to someone from one of the many little LA's of the West where the car is king. I never felt so much alone as when riding in a Washington bus filled with people.

There are two unwritten rules followed by people riding Washington buses—no talking and no touching. You can crowd 80 people, sitting and standing, into a D.C. bus, give them nothing to do for 40 minutes but get where they're going, and they won't say a word to each other. People board the bus, recognize friends, give them a secret little wave, and even stand beside them for blocks without speaking.

And you might as well grab someone by the rear end as let your elbow or hip so much as brush the person seated next to you. My first day on the bus, we lurched around a corner and my shoulder made firm, lascivious contact with the shoulder of the woman seated next to me. She reacted like she had been molested.

Similarly, one must never sit next to someone on a bus if there is a seat anywhere else on the bus with no neighboring seat occupied. If you can avoid sitting with someone, but sit with him or her anyway, that person will sometimes become alarmed. He will suspect you have settled down next to him because you get your jollies snuggling up against strangers. He will suspect you sat with him, not because it was the nearest seat, but because you really wanted to sit with him.

The law against touching is followed to the extreme. I have what might be called your slightly-below-average, skinny-little-male fanny, taking up most of the space of one person. But I have had, as seatmates on the bus, enormous women with your much-larger-than-average fanny. They occupied a seat and a half, leaving half a seat for me, with no touching allowed. I soon learned that the only way to avoid being glared at like a pervert was to perch one cheek on the remaining edge of the seat, leaving the other cheek dangling in the aisle. I was uncomfortable but I wasn't the only half-assed press secretary in Washington.

Conversely, there are also situations in which it is possible to offend by declining to sit next to a fellow passenger. A form of rejection takes place on a bus. For instance, if there is one empty seat left, and that is next to a slobbering drunk, that seat will, of course, remain unoccupied. Sometimes there will be two dozen people straphanging while that drunk sits there alone with that vacant seat proclaiming him a pariah. One drunk got so upset with me over being rejected that he broke the no-talking law.

"Come on, buddy, get the load off your feet."

"Thanks, but I've been sitting all day."

"Aw, come on, have a seat."

"No, I mean it. I really enjoy standing for 12 miles."

The hardest part for the beginning bus rider is sitting in one of those seats facing another seat across the bus. You find yourself staring into the eyes of a stranger at 7:30 in the morning. I learned that makes people fidgety, especially if you smile a lot. You mustn't do that.

At first I tried lifting my eyes and gazing at the little advertising signboards above the seat across from me. But how long can you look at some trendy jerk in a beer ad without getting carsick?

The solution, I eventually learned, is to put on a big-city poker face and throw your eyes out of focus, as if daydreaming. That way you can be aimed right at the person across from you and not really stare at him. You may look a trifle catatonic, but so does everyone else on a bus.

Some months after leaving Washington, I took a bus to the state Capitol one morning in Boise, Idaho. People I had never met nodded and smiled as I walked down the aisle. I took a seat toward the rear—all by myself—the way any decent person would. But at subsequent stops, the people occupied the first open seats next to the other passengers, gradually filling the bus from the front to the rear. And they were talking to each other! And their shoulders were touching!

I had never known there were so many perverts in Boise, Idaho.

Shortly before I left Washington, a change came over bus riding. Some social-working do-gooder had started a friendly driver contest. The pictures of the winning drivers began appearing in advertising signboards above the seats. I remember thinking what a gushy idea it was—until the damn thing began to work. I traveled several routes on which the drivers knocked themselves out to be civil to the passengers. And the passengers began in a shy way at first, to reciprocate. The atmosphere on the buses of Washington, D.C., began to lighten.

"How are you today?" a driver chirped the first morning I encountered the new program.

My first thought was that I had stumbled onto a tour bus from Utah.

"I'm fine, thank you," I finally said, recalling the old ritual.

The other passengers had the same reaction. First, a doubletake, then—only a little rusty—a pleasantry of their own. They came down the aisle with a surprised little smile on their faces.

It was the same at the end of the day.

"Have a good night," the driver said as each passenger exited.

"You do the same," they snapped right back, really starting to get the hang of it.

I was aboard a bus one day that stopped at Union Station to change operators. The departing driver stood at the head of the aisle and cleared his throat to get our attention. I was sure there was something wrong, that the bus had broken down.

"Ladies and gentlemen," he said. "I want to thank you very much for riding with me this evening."

We were stunned for a moment. But then we all called back a thank you of our own. As we pulled away with the new driver, the passengers talked with each other about the incredible event—and soon about other things as well.

The unwritten law against talking on buses had been broken.

A few nights later, on another bus with a happy-talk driver, a hobbled old white man with curvature of the spine boarded on 16th Street, early in the run, where there are rarely any empty seats. With his gnarled spine, he was hanging rather awkwardly from the overhead rail. A middle-aged black woman stood up and tried to give him her seat. He was too proud to accept, but as she sat back down in front of him, he gave her a pat on the shoulder.

The unwritten law against touching had been obliterated.

*   *   *

In addition to the bus and the private automobile, there is, of course, the taxi. In one sense, Washington may have been the best cab town in America during my time there. The cabs were almost as numerous per capita as in New York, and they were much less expensive. You could ride several miles through downtown D.C. for a buck and a half.

But I would rather ride with a New York cabby. New York cab drivers are talkers.

If a Washington driver talked at all, it was often in English so broken he couldn't be understood. That is true many places in America, including New York. But it was more pronounced in Washington at the time with so many foreign students attending college and picking up extra money driving independent cabs. I wearied of trying to explain to Iranians what a press secretary does for a living. It's hard enough to explain to Americans.

To an Idaho ear, there is some doubt whether native New York cab drivers speak English either. But whatever it is they speak, it's worth straining for the meaning. They aren't just talkers; they are entertainers. One New York cabby almost had me convinced that the weather had changed because astronauts going to the moon had punched a hole in outer space letting in all that cold air. He also assured me that the astronauts had found life on the moon. In fact, they had encountered monsters so horrible that fear had blotted the experience from their minds. That's why the astronauts, great patriots who would never knowingly lie to the American people, thought they were telling the truth when they said they found no life on the moon.

"But if they were the only ones who saw the monsters, and they can't remember what they saw, then nobody would know they ran into monsters?"

"I know," he said, mysteriously, "I know."

I can't imagine a similar conversation in Washington—some eccentric cabby insisting there is life in the Pentagon.

You may have to mortgage your mother to ride in a New York cab, but at least they give you a good show.

*   *   *

After six months of living on Capitol Hill, I fled to the suburbs—Silver Spring, Maryland. I rode the buses at first. But after a few weeks of 80-minute rides, with two transfers out in the rain, I bought a car and joined the pack.

That's what Don Watkins, Church's assistant press secretary, named the waves of cars during commuting hours—the pack. Because of the traffic lights, the cars came in waves. The street would clear for a few seconds, a light would change, and then a pack of maybe 200 cars, three lanes wide, bumper to bumper and traveling about 40 miles an hour, would come thundering down the street.

That wave would pass and there would be a few seconds of eerie silence again. And then the next wave. If you're crossing the street, it's easy to believe that a pack of menacing machines, like a herd of buffalo in the West, is stampeding toward you.

But the pack is more suicidal than homicidal. I used to stand at the bus stop as the cars stormed by and wonder what madness would ever possess anyone to get into a car and join that daily dash for downtown Washington. One false move in that tailgating pack and everyone would be wiped out. After I bought a car and joined the pack, arriving at work in half the time, I used to feel sorry for the poor slobs we blew past at the bus stops.

Even by car, the suburbs seemed a long way out. But not to most people who work in Washington. Washington has been brainwashed by real estate ads. The ads all say the same thing: "Only about 30 minutes from downtown Washington."

The people who buy the houses believe the ads. Ask any suburbanite in Washington how far he lives from work and the answer will be "only about 30 minutes." They don't finish their sentences. What they really mean is "only about 30 minutes—if I drive it early Sunday morning after the tourist season in a month beginning with an R." They lie to themselves because no one can admit driving 45 minutes to an hour—and sometimes considerably more—twice a day, through that kind of traffic, and still keep his sanity.

Anyone who has ever visited his nation's capital by car knows that it is a typical American city: The street signs are useless. They are so small that you can't read them until you are already in the intersection and it is too late to make the turn. The natives find their way around because they have memorized the streets. The tourists and the newcomers get lost a lot. That's unfortunate because Washington requires better street signs than most cities. Thoroughfares like the fabled Pennsylvania Avenue sort of get lost winding around the White House and the Capitol. Indeed, Pennsylvania Avenue becomes symbolically devious whenever it comes near an executive or a legislative building. Some streets blend into other streets for a time, compromising for a few blocks on a common name, and then double-crossing each other and moving off in opposite directions. And worst of all are what Washington calls "traffic circles," named in honor of the direction the government is heading most of the time. At repeated points throughout the city, six or eight streets converge on a common circular drive like the spokes of a wheel. You are expected to drive around the hub to the point where you find the matching spoke—halfway around the hub—of the street you were traveling when it ran into the circle.

It might work, if the traffic were slower and the signs larger. But it all moves too fast and you lose your bearings. It is like trying to spot your mommy from a merry-go-round. I usually made six or eight revolutions of the circle before spotting my street and exiting, frequently discovering it wasn't the right street after all. Conservative Republicans are less impulsive when driving the circles; they stay on them until they are certain they are getting off on the right street. That's why there are so many dizzy conservatives in Washington.

Liberal Democrats, by contrast, often don't know where they are going, but at least they are making progress and they aren't going around in circles.

I finally memorized my way through the traffic circles of Washington, but not before I began fantasizing that I saw the same driver every time I was in Dupont Circle—a gaunt Flying Dutchman of the Washington street system, a ward heeler from Kansas City who came to Washington in 1951 to look up Harry Truman, got caught in the circle, and was doomed to drive its endless curve for eternity.

I became something of a Flying Dutchman myself on the streets and highways of Washington's Virginia suburbs. Whenever I headed for a location in Virginia, I filled the tank beforehand because I always got lost. I was lost one night—at 60 miles an hour—for three hours. It is disconcerting to travel at that speed on a freeway and not have the slightest idea where you are or in what direction you are heading. You keep thinking that, at that rate, if you don't learn where you are soon enough, you will wind up in Nebraska. But what saved me was that, like anyone who is lost, I seemed to be going around in large freeway circles rather than heading straight for Nebraska. Every 15 or 20 minutes I would recognize some landmark like the Washington Monument, glowing in the night, tantalizing me from across the Potomac. But every time I spotted a familiar sight there seemed to be no way to get off the freeway to head for it.

Eventually, there would be an exit ramp which seemed to be heading in the general direction. I would turn on it, but it would turn out to be, not truly an exit, but a ramp leading to still another freeway. Away I would go in some new direction as the familiar landmark faded from sight.

The night I was lost for three hours I finally strayed onto what I recognized as the George Washington Parkway, heading for Dulles International Airport. I didn't want to go to Dulles International Airport. But at least I knew where I was. I knew that within a mile or two I would come upon an exit I had used before. From that exit I knew my way back to Washington, to which I was determined to retreat. The Virginia dinner party, which had been my original destination, was undoubtedly drawing to a close anyway.

I couldn't remember the name of the exit, but I was pretty sure I would recognize the terrain. At the last minute, I did. I cramped the wheel and sailed off the exit ramp past a large red sign reading, "WRONG WAY!"

Around a curve, three abreast, horns blaring, roared the pack, coming straight into my teeth.

I spotted a little grassy strip next to the guard rail. It looked about three feet wide. My little Japanese car was about four feet wide. But if I could get a couple of wheels on that grass, there might be room for the pack to squeeze by.

Through some miracle, I got all four wheels up on the grass without touching the guard rail. The strip of grass was wider than it looked. Or my little Japanese car sucked in its sides as hard as I did.

The pack never slowed. It stormed by, horns bellowing all the way. I controlled myself. I swore a little. And I almost wet my pants. But I never honked.

As the months wore on, I became rather proud of myself. Other drivers honked at me daily, but I always turned the other cheek. I refused to respond in kind. That's the trouble with Washington, I thought. One person loses his temper and honks. That infuriates the victim, and he in turn begins honking at other cars, who pass it on to still more cars.

I figured somebody had to show those animals how to resist anger and remain civil. But sooner or later in a large city the right combination of pressures will develop, and then even the most sanctimonious driver will crack. I finally did.

It was one of those days. The phone constantly screamed for attention. A typewriter gave out halfway through an urgent press release. David Martin, our Associated Press reporter (now with CBS) was in one of his snotty moods. Church was having a cranky day. Out of some sense of loyalty, I also became cranky, bickering with the rest of the staff.

To make matters worse, I had to meet an Idaho constituent downtown at the Mayflower Hotel right after work. As I headed for the parking lot, it began to pour. Conservative Republicans dominated traffic and it inched along. The headlights of other cars bounced off the wet pavement into my eyes, giving an extra dimension to my burgeoning headache. And as usual, the city steamed with humidity.

I had no hope of finding parking on the street that time of night, so I headed directly for the parking garages in the vicinity of the Mayflower.

They were full.

I kept driving around the Mayflower waiting for something to open up. The rain finally ended, but I was already half an hour late for the meeting and there was no telling how long it would be before I could find a parking place. I was beginning to wonder what else could go wrong when an enormous gob of bird crap scored a direct hit on the windshield.

I couldn't believe it at first. It must be a joke. But there was no doubt about it. It was bird crap all right. And such an incredible amount! What kind of bird could possibly deposit that much?

I suppose it was just a pigeon using high altitude for maximum spread. But I was so crazy by then that the only big bird I could think of was an eagle.

Suddenly I knew. It was the ultimate indignity—crapped on by an eagle in our nation's capital during the Bicentennial!

I had barely recovered from that humiliation when I rounded the corner of the Mayflower, plowed through a generous puddle, and doused a distinguished old gentleman who was furling his umbrella.

He had quick reflexes for an old guy. He bashed his umbrella over the top of my little Japanese car before I could travel three more feet.

That did it! A rage swept through me such as I have never known. It was something about the imagined injustice of the situation. How dare he punish me without waiting to see whether I would stop to apologize and offer to pay the cleaning bill for his suit?

I haven't struck anyone since my last kid fight with my younger brother when I was 15. But I was suddenly capable of more than merely punching someone. I was capable that night of snapping that old man and his umbrella in two. And I might have jumped out and done so, but the traffic wouldn't let me. The traffic kept moving. I circled the block and came back down the street where I had last seen my aged attacker and his unjust umbrella. By then I had decided to let him live. I was determined to roll down the window and shout something mature like, "Clean your own suit, you rotten old bastard!" But he wasn't there.

It was three days before I could admit I had been in the wrong and that the old guy who bashed my car was probably in the right— the son of a bitch.

And so Washington finally got to me. It finally beat me down to the level of every raving driver in D.C. But I managed to retain one last shred of dignity: I might have been ready to leap out in the street and pummel an old man. But I didn't honk.

However, one day I finally did.

A scruffy mongrel dog strayed into the street ahead of me. He probably would have got out of the way in time anyway. But it was my chance. And it wouldn't compromise my pledge to myself. I would be tooting in kindly warning rather than in anger. I pressed the horn gently for the first time.

It was embarrassing. My little Japanese car had a high-pitched, nasal little horn with unmistakably effeminate overtones. If I had ever used that horn in a fit of macho bravado to swear back at another car, the pack would have laughed me off the road.

*   *   *

I was exiting one day from "the tunnel"—the underground freeway beneath Capitol Hill. My passenger was the senator's son, the Rev. Forrest Church. Confused as usual as to what lane I should be in, I touched the brakes to buy time for the right decision. In the process, I caught a tailgater by surprise. He nearly plowed into us. And he was furious. He began leaning on his horn, really leaning on it.

He finally stopped scolding and whipped around us. He was a black man, and he was mad enough to snap an old man's umbrella. He cruised alongside for a moment, literally shaking his fist at me and screaming something vile before going on his way, pounding the horn a couple more times for punctuation.

"I think you just got told off with an automobile horn," Forrest said.

I explained to the young minister my no-honk policy and the Christian reason behind it.

"Well, then," said Forrest, "at least he can't call you a honky."

I wonder if the Lord will forgive a minister for a pun that lousy.

Chapter Five
Let's See How Long Castro Can Stay in Power Without His Whiskers

Only once during the months of Washington pressure did I truly think I had lost it. And that was just for an instant. I came around a corner and plainly saw Abraham Lincoln sitting in the outer office. He was smiling at me through that gaunt, melancholy face and those warm, civilized eyes.

I had been deep in thought, drifting around out of synch inside my own head and feeling rather disoriented, as usual. The first thing my mind focused on was Abraham Lincoln. For a moment, I thought I had passed through a time warp.

I finally realized it must be an actor or a mental case and snapped back to reality, sticking out my hand and saying, "How are you today, Mr. President?" If it was a mental case, it would be prudent to humor him. If it was an actor, he would enjoy my playing along with the pose.

It was neither. Abe Lincoln, whose real name I never did learn, was a Capitol Hill fixture. He was a nice old gentleman who died not long after I left Washington. He bore an uncanny resemblance to Lincoln. He completed the image with the classic Lincoln beard, the stovepipe hat, the whole costume. He was shorter than Lincoln and quite a bit older than the sixteenth president lived to be. But his hollow old cheeks merely added to the illusion of that celebrated face as we know it best from the Civil War pictures, when it was sunken and exhausted.

The pretend Lincoln used to hang around the Hill touting such highly generalized causes as "the good of our youth." I saw him many times thereafter. But the first time was a shocker.

Others had to catch their breath when first meeting Abe Lincoln in the twentieth century. John Squires, a constituent from

Pocatello, Idaho, met the pretend president during an unforgettable lunch in the Senate cafeteria. Actually, there were two Senate cafeterias—back to back with a common kitchen in between. They were identical in size, in seating, and in the plastic flower decor. Telling them apart took practice.

John was finishing his lunch with his wife and with Don Watkins of the Church staff when he discovered he had run out of cigars. Watkins directed him to the tobacco shop in the long hallway that connects the two cafeterias. When John left the tobacco shop, he turned the wrong way and entered the opposite cafeteria, not knowing there was an opposite cafeteria. He strolled absentmindedly around a pillar to his table and discovered his wife was missing. In her place sat Abraham Lincoln, crushing crackers into his Senate bean soup.

"Hello," said the apparition, extending a frail hand coated with cracker crumbs, "I'm Abraham Lincoln."

John wondered for a moment what kind of funny weeds are used to make the cigars sold in the Senate.

Other people are attracted to the Senate who are not as pleasant to talk with as Mr. Lincoln. Indeed, a good many of them are downright dotty. Washington is a magnet to the mentally ill. And they don't all work for the taxpayers. You can get the impression, serving in a Senate office—and especially during something as melodramatic as an investigation of the CIA—that half the country needs treatment. Unbalanced people flock to Washington from throughout the nation—people seeking notoriety, people with ugly grudges, and especially paranoiacs weary of being hounded and persecuted by "them."

Sometimes the paranoiacs come to the capital believing pathetically that all they need do is tell their senator about the devils chasing them through their minds and the government will put a stop to it.

Sometimes they come on the mission of alerting their government to the trickery of the communists hiding among us everywhere. Sometimes they are desperate to make their senators believe that FBI or CIA agents are treacherously reading the minds of the people.

The Intelligence Committee investigation attracted the tormented in droves. The gritty secretaries on Church's personal staff and on the committee were extraordinary in their patience and in their kindness—and occasionally in their courage. Several of the more manic visitors came unhinged, escalating suddenly from tears to threats.

When I arrived in Washington, most of the CIA and FBI calls were shifted to me because I was the only member of the chairman's personal staff working directly with that committee. I had also had experience dealing with the mentally dispossessed. Not all of the mental cases in America are congregated in Washington. Newspapers also attract their share. As an editorial writer, criticizing the government and afflicting the establishment, troubled subscribers sometimes regarded me as an ally against their demons. They have contacted me by the dozens over the years. They often called at odd hours, after the eight-to-five social workers had gone home. I have talked a couple of people out of suicide, but most aren't that desperate. They're lonely. They just want to hear another voice.

Some of the callers are baffling. I'm still trying to fathom the woman who demanded I write an editorial blistering Jimmy Carter for thinking he could grow cabbages in a rock pile. And I had to drive one young woman to the hospital after she freaked out in my office. I sat with her in the waiting room for an hour while she alternately cried softly and yelled, "I am not a slut!" causing others in the waiting room to misunderstand and glare at me in utter contempt.

But for all those earlier years in the newspaper business, I've never seen anything to equal the parade of paranoiacs who passed through Frank Church's office during the intelligence investigation.

A woman stopped by one day to leave word for the chairman that the CIA, knowing she had the goods on them, had caught her on the hospital operating table and forced the doctors to perform a hysterectomy as a warning to keep her mouth shut. But they couldn't intimidate her. She insisted she would tell all on national television. She owed it to her country. And what more could they do to her anyway, she asked.

A man called from Virginia to say he had been ill for months because the CIA had been beaming X-rays through his home. Columnist Jack Anderson, the celebrated master of the government exposé, had attracted similar people for years. He told me the X-ray complaint has long been common. Anderson said Brit Hume, who worked with him during my time there and is now with ABC television, once offered one of the poor souls the solace of a make-believe remedy to cope with the make-believe X-rays. He asked one of the X-ray people if he had ever heard about "grounding." He explained that, if a person grounds himself, the X-rays are ineffective. Hume pulled a coat hanger off the rack, twisted it apart, straightened it, and hung it from the back of the man's trousers, with the end trailing on the floor. "The man left the office happy as a clam," Anderson said.

During the height of the intelligence investigation, a call came from a woman in Denver. She wanted me to inform Church that both the CIA and the FBI had been bugging her telephone for years. "And tell Senator Church that I'm not afraid to testify against them."

I tried to give her some hope, suggesting that she see her attorney.

"Never again," she objected. "I tried that once. My attorney called the CIA and the FBI. The lawyers all work for them, you know. The CIA and FBI agents broke into my home and put me in a straight jacket and took me into this little room at a hospital where they tore off all my clothes and squirted me with cold water."

I tried another gambit. "Is your phone still bugged?"

"Of course."

"Are they listening now?"

"They're *always* listening."

"Gentlemen," I said, trying to sound official, "this is Wilbert D. Hall, press secretary to Senator Frank Church, chairman of the Senate Intelligence Committee. If you don't get the bug off this patriotic lady's telephone, I'm going to report you to the senator and there will be hell to pay."

The basic information from such calls was always referred, on a just-in-case basis, to the Intelligence Committee staff. I was reasonably sure the tipsters were imagining things, but it wasn't my job to sort the calls, only to forward them. And I was nagged by the thought that one individual out of a thousand might call with a legitimate complaint that sounded as zany as the rest. How could that information get through if some yo-yo on Church's staff, without benefit of psychiatric training, routinely pronounced people mentally ill and filed their complaints in the waste basket?

I wonder, for instance, what my reaction might have been if someone had called from Miami, saying, "Listen, I can't stay on the phone long because they might be bugging me. But tell your senator I have solid evidence that the CIA had a plan to paint Fidel Castro's shoes with a special shoe polish that would make his beard fall out."

Naturally, I would have jumped to the conclusion that it was still another mental case. But I would have forwarded the tip to the committee, just in case.

And a good thing, too. The committee learned that the CIA did indeed have a plan to place a chemical in Castro's shoe polish that would have made his beard fall out, costing him his trademark and, according to the nuts who dreamed it up, giving him image problems. You would think the CIA, of all people, would have remembered false beards.

I passed one complaint on to the committee that I didn't take seriously enough for my own good. In December 1975, a deceptively calm, middle-aged woman brought me what she insisted was documentation that the communists had installed "piezoelectric crystals" in her tooth caps. Moreover, the crystals had been secretly installed, with the aid of disloyal dentists, in the teeth of countless other Americans. She explained that piezoelectric crystals "turn people into radios, which permits monitoring of their speech and body functions, including brain waves."

I stood there nodding, wondering what in hell piezoelectric crystals are. The dictionary later informed me that they are crystals that produce charges of electricity when pressure is applied. It occurred to me that radios powered by pressure-activated piezoelectric crystals would function best in the mouths of people who gnash their teeth a lot, which would include most Americans who live in fear of communists.

(I had several expensive capped teeth myself at the time, but the only broadcast I had ever received on them was the faint sound of my dentist giggling at his ski lodge where he goes to count my money.)

I dutifully forwarded the woman's "documentation" to the Intelligence Committee and forgot about it. Five months later, I was served with the papers. The woman with the piezoelectric tooth caps had filed a complaint against me in the D.C. small claims court, asking a judgment of $750.

"I'm sick and tired," she wrote in the statement of claim, "of being ignored, brushed aside, neglected, by public servants who are paid high salaries from the taxpayers' money, but who fail to perform the duties of their public offices in behalf of these taxpayers. On Dec. 14, 1975, I handed to Wilbert Hall, press secretary to Senator Church, chairman of the Intelligence Committee, a case file covering my efforts to secure help and expose a Communist surveillance technique—highly secret and intensely guarded—of which I, among many Americans, have been a victim since 1957. . . . I respectfully request that this court determine the reasons for the lack of action on Wilbert Hall's part."

She filed similar complaints against President Gerald Ford, the Pentagon, and Senator Ted Kennedy. I might have been flattered by the company I would be keeping in small claims court, but I was too angry. We were in the middle of a frantic presidential campaign. And now I would have to squander half a day in small claims court, or cough up $750—and all on a complaint so frivolous I couldn't believe the court clerk would have done me the injustice of processing it.

I ranted so much around campaign headquarters about the D.C. courts leaving lawful citizens at the mercy of piezoelectric dingbats that Jerry Murphy, the Church campaign attorney, volunteered to serve for free as my lawyer. But he made the mistake of thinking the lawsuit was funny.

"No!" I insisted. "That's the point. Why should anyone have to lift a finger just because some crackpot got her piezos out of whack and filed a groundless complaint? The system must be taught to protect people from things like that. I'm not going to move a muscle. Let them stash me in jail. It'll make a hell of a story, and we'll expose the incompetence of the D.C. court system. You want press coverage in this campaign? I'll get you press coverage!"

Jerry wasn't laughing so much by then. He didn't think it would be prudent to get myself thrown in jail. If I wouldn't show up for the hearing, he'd be happy to appear in my place.

"No!" I fumed. "Why should this incompetent court inconvenience you either with its slipshod screening of nut complaints?

But you want somebody to go to court? I'll go to court. I'll put on a clown suit and go down there and show my respect for the D.C. court system."

Jerry wasn't laughing at all by then. He thought that would be a very bad idea. He insisted on appearing for me—in his regulation lawyer suit. No clown suits, please.

And he did represent me. Because of my tantrum, Jerry Murphy took half a day from his own work load. The case against me was dismissed, of course. But I was told that both Jerry and the judge, realizing the woman was ill, patiently heard her out and then explained that, though she might feel wronged, I had broken no law. The court was powerless to act. In other words, they gave her a little moral victory in their respect for her frustrations and in their full, official attention to her complaint. With slight inconvenience to everyone—except the defendant sulking back in campaign head-quarters—the court had shown some humanity and let a woman, who lived with greater pressures than I, feel she had been heard by her government.

Maybe the D.C. courts aren't so incompetent after all.

*   *   *

The only times I ever met that gentle man, Senator Philip Hart of Michigan, was in the Senate corridors where walked prima donnas and where also walked Philip Hart, dying of cancer, nodding hello to everyone, and treating members of the Senate staff like human beings. After he died, the press rediscovered him and sang his posthumous praises. But the Senate staff knew him as a saint long before that. So I flatter myself to believe that my mind was running in the same track with Phil Hart's mind that year, for we were both nagged by a similar thought.

I had been concerned since the fall of Richard Nixon over the consequences of watching some of the wildest charges by the pro-testers of that period proven true. Not every wacky charge against the government is accurate, not by a long shot. But I worried it would become more difficult to dispute even the most preposterous assertions now that so many bizarre charges had been confirmed. For instance, a self-righteous student at the University of Idaho insisted early in 1972 that Nixon's Committee to Re-elect the

President had a plan to capture protest leaders at the Republican National Convention in Miami and hold them prisoner on a boat offshore until the convention ended.

I chastised the young man for babbling such absurd delusions, noting that he risked discrediting the anti-war and anti-Nixon efforts. There were sufficient sane grievances to dwell on, I lectured, without turning people off with baloney like that.

In deference to my more mature judgment, he fell respectfully silent. And then that fink Nixon left me with egg on my face. It was revealed that there had, indeed, been some Liddyish discussion in the inner sanctums of that campaign about a plan quite similar to the one the student had heard of through some protest grapevine.

Philip Hart confessed a similar embarrassment during the hearings of the Senate Intelligence Committee. Just out of the hospital and with his life ebbing, Hart was temporarily back in place at that sprawling hardwood table in the historic Senate Caucus Room where the truth about Richard Nixon had also been uncovered three years earlier. Hart and his colleagues on the committee had been hearing testimony about the FBI's systematic violation of the elemental rights of war protesters and civil rights leaders.

"I've been told for years," said a sobered Hart that day, "by, among others, members of my own family, that this is what the bureau had been doing all the time. As a result of my superior wisdom and high office, I assured them that they were on pot. It just wasn't true. They [the FBI] just wouldn't do it. What you have disclosed is a series of illegal actions intended to deny certain citizens their First Amendment rights—just like my children said."

I know the feeling, senator. And I wonder about those other "children" of that period. As the committee confirmed each adventure by the FBI and the CIA, it routinely vindicated the young cynics of several years before.

Would that their vindication will teach their parents to question their government more often in the future—without teaching the young cynics to question their government too often.

I also wonder about all those sick people who marched their personal hells into Frank Church's office and pleaded for protection from "them"—for their government's protection against their government. The undisciplined excesses of the FBI and of the CIA during those years knocked a crack in nearly everyone's faith. But the meanest sin of those two agencies was to give some credence to every paranoiac's delusions.

How do you convince a sick woman that the CIA wasn't responsible for her hysterectomy when she has just heard on television that the agency conceived a plan to make Castro's beard fall out?

Chapter Six
Who Rules the Senate—the Senators or Their Aides?

I had just boarded a Senate Office Building elevator, heading for the basement, when the call buzzer sounded three times from the floor above.

"I'm sorry, sir," said the operator, telling me what I already knew. "That's a senator. I'll have to go up and get him."

Senators have priority use of elevators, to speed them to the floor for votes. To exercise that priority, they push the call button three times. The command had sounded. Up we went.

Waiting as the door opened was a seasoned senator in his sixties, although he appeared more ancient. At his elbow was an aide in his early twenties. The aide led the shuffling old man with the spaced-out look aboard the elevator. As we descended to the basement, I realized that this zombie, once one of the crack minds of the Senate, was so drunk he was almost paralyzed. He was not merely a seasoned senator. He had been marinated as well.

We arrived at the basement and the young aide, thoroughly embarrassed, took the old boy gently by the arm and steered him from the elevator toward the little subway train that speeds senators the two blocks to the Capitol. As the aide guided his charge to the train, he counseled him patiently, in the manner of someone dealing with an addled grandfather.

"Now, you remember how to vote, Senator?"

"Right," the boiled senator slurred, "this one's a yes."

"That's right, senator, a *yes*," the aide emphasized, leaning on the word, driving it home one more time.

The senator shuffled a few feet toward the subway platform, then stopped.

"Shoe. Shoe," he repeated, indicating his right foot. The lace was missing from his right shoe.

"Don't worry, senator," the aide soothed, steering him toward the subway. "We'll get you a shoelace as soon as you cast that *yes* vote."

"Right," said the senator. "This one's a yes."

It was 11:30 in the morning.

The senator's senior aides had decided how he should vote— or, if they were a loyal staff, how the senator himself would want to vote if he had his wits about him. The senior aides had not even bothered to accompany the old man to the Senate floor themselves. Leading him to the floor and making certain he voted as they thought he should had become such a routine task in that office that they had assigned a little make-sure-you-vote-yes machine.

The senior aides didn't have time for such trivial chores. They were too busy being senator.

That inebriated senator was, of course, an extreme example. But he was no exception. More and more, senators—even the most sober senators—have become puppets of their aides. It is not a conspiracy. It is Parkinson's Law.

The senators are caught in the vicious circle of their own bu- reaucracy. The more staff they have, the more legislation that staff originates. And the more legislation there is, the less the grasp of the senators on the details—and the more they need additional staff to keep abreast. So the senators—usually at the suggestion of aides—vote themselves more staff. That additional staff, in turn, originates even more legislation, making it even more impossible for a senator to know the details of each bill. And so on.

There is by now so much staff originating so much legislation that there are few senators remaining who aren't heavily depen- dent on the advice of aides each time they head toward the floor to cast a vote—with a snootful or without.

In the best offices, it is, of course, the established practice for aides to write brief memos honestly spelling out both sides of an issue and leaving the final decision to the senator. And with such senators, woe be to the aide caught loading the case in one direc- tion or the other to fit his personal agenda. But it is possible, and sometimes happens, that an aide steers his senator toward the aide's idea of how best to run the republic.

Worse in its way is the tendency of staff in most offices to point a senator toward a safe vote in harmony with the senator's political popularity at home—on which the continued employment of the aides also depends. Because of that, there is less and less opportunity for a senator to change his mind, to break with past patterns, and to cast an audacious vote. Instead, there is a tendency to program senators to vote the passing emotional urges of the home-state electorate.

Given the growing workload, no senator can consistently do all his own thinking. But one reason I thought Frank Church might be equipped for the presidency, with its even more massive volume of detail on an even wider range of issues, was that he was one of the few remaining senators who still commanded the details—and thereby his own staff—most of the time. Frank Church had a photographic memory.

I drafted a 300-word statement one day—as always, along the lines Church dictated. When I handed it to him, he entered an almost-trance-like state, oblivious to everything around him, mumbling the words aloud. I think he read through it twice. And then he turned to other business.

Several hours later, a reporter asked him a question on the subject of the statement. Church, in a conversational tone, repeated the statement—verbatim. I just sat there, mouth open, trying to remember what I had eaten for lunch that day.

But there is a price for such powers of concentration. A head that holds such sober detail has no room for less weighty matters. Frank Church's staff used to spend some portion of each day looking for his eyeglasses, for his car keys, frequently for his briefcase, and even for his car. Church could never remember which parking lot he had used when he arrived at work that morning. Members of the staff routinely went out in search of the senator's car. But, of course, that's preferable to sending them with him to the Senate floor to help him find his way to the right vote on a bill.

I think it was while searching parking lots for Frank Church's car that I first decided I wanted to do more with my life and tried to quit. As much as I worry about where the staff-orchestrated Senate will lead us as a nation, I would frankly have taken the same perverse pleasure in manipulating a senator as some other aides did. I expected Senate work would involve helping the senator find his way through the murky issues of our time rather than helping him find his automobile. But Frank Church was a proud loner who kept his own counsel. He never once asked what I thought we should do to keep the pushy Russians in their place. He never solicited my insight on inflation. He was deaf to my remedy for the excesses of the international oil cartel, though I knew several Arabs personally. And he never sought my formula for bringing peace to the world in this century.

Mostly he wanted to know if I had seen his briefcase, and, if I had, would I mind fetching it for him. So I invited him to lunch one day after about five months of briefcase fetching. We took a table in the Senate Dining Room, beneath the stained glass portrait of George Washington astride a white horse. Washington was scanning the Delaware as usual. Most people speculate that he is looking for an easy river crossing. I'm convinced he is looking for the aide he sent forth to fetch his briefcase.

I told Church I was uncomfortable as a butler and would be returning to the *Lewiston Tribune* in Idaho. To make the point that I had felt underutilized, I finally forced some advice on him. I counseled the ranking member of the Foreign Relations Committee to refuse any offer of Secretary of State should the Democrats reclaim the White House and want him for the job.

"Any president worth his salt will be his own Secretary of State. You would be no more than an errand boy. You would be miserable as an errand boy."

And so I served notice. But I hadn't counted on the tenacity of the senator's only powerful and truly influential aide—his wife. Bethine Church remained convinced that I had been responsible for the biggest wave of publicity the senator had received in his career—the stories spontaneously generated by press interest in the Intelligence Committee investigation. She began lobbying me, calling several times a day. She suggested I might enjoy Washington more if I received the higher salary to which I was surely entitled. She hinted that the senator was intrigued with some of my recent advice (probably "I think you left your briefcase in the cloakroom, Senator") and would be depending on me for more advice in the future ("Where did I leave it this time, Bill?").

Most of all, she went for my stomach. The best restaurant in Washington was the Church home. Bethine practices an addictive style of cooking that is the best of two worlds—Idaho farm kitchen and French cuisine, meat and potatoes with a French accent. I was living alone in an apartment and she knew I doted on her cooking. She mentioned more frequent invitations to dinner.

The senator, by contrast, seemed to accept my leaving and to respect my reasons for it. But he was also being lobbied. He warned me one day that Bethine had made up her mind and that there might be nothing either one of us could do about it. It might be, he said—in the mood of a man not only resigned to his fate but intrigued by the inevitable—that neither one of us had the strength to withstand the heat.

He was right, of course. Eventually I had to agree with Bethine that I was vital to the future of Frank Church, which, at the time, seemed to mean that I was vital to a confused world that required a new American president with me at his side to whisper in his ear—and, of course, to fetch his briefcase.

*   *   *

The Senate is widely trumpeted as one of the great debating societies of the world. It could be, but it isn't any longer. In recent years, the Senate debates, if it debates at all, mostly on television.

Church, a champion debater in college and a former courtroom lawyer, had relished his early years in the Senate during the 1950s. In those times, he had joined with gusto in the exposition of the issues of the day during extended floor debates.

But that practice petered out. He complained about the change one day over lunch with me and with John Simonds, then a Washington correspondent with the Gannett chain and later an editor of the Honolulu *Star-Bulletin*. Most of the time, Church said, there were about six senators on the floor—and about the same number of reporters in the gallery. The committee load had mushroomed, dragging senators off the floor. The commercial jet liner came along and made it possible for senators to go back to the home state for a weekend. So they were expected to do so—frequently. As a consequence of those and other distractions, the traditional Senate debates had mostly come to a close. All that remained was a disjointed, electronic form of debating. As a new issue swept the capital, the networks would grab a couple of senators on either side of the question and give them each 15 seconds on the evening news. That had become modern Senate debating.

Senate speeches came to be delivered more and more often away from the Senate—before gatherings covered by the television cameras and without other senators present to rise and glibly poke holes in a colleague's reasoning. The era arrived when a senator was more likely to have his views heard by the country if he addressed a labor convention in Chicago or a peace rally in Boston or the American Legion's annual binge of jingoism in Seattle than if he spoke in Senate chambers. Church told Simonds and me that senators were rarely on the floor any longer because they were off chasing cameras.

Cameras were still banned from the Senate that day Simonds and I had lunch with the senator. So Simonds suggested wryly that perhaps the remedy would be for one of the networks to construct a mock-up of the Senate chamber and invite members to appear there nightly in televised debates.

Church laughed and said it would surely work. And I thought he was right.

But it didn't. Some years thereafter the Senate finally agreed to permit television cameras in the chamber. But except for rare debates of crucial consequence and the occasional Senate scandal on that center stage, the senators are still largely absent from the chamber. They still prefer to make their points in television interviews rather than gather in that historic place and try to live up to the once-proud designation "the greatest deliberative body on earth."

Today most of them do their part to live up to the new and less proud designation, "the greatest television prima donnas on earth."

*   *   *

Technology has had another detrimental effect on the modern Senate: Long-distance phone calls were once reserved for exceptional matters. Today, the long-distance call is so commonplace that each senator has his ration of nationwide toll-free lines. Senators once corresponded—in writing—with colleagues, governors, and all the other movers and shakers. Today, they use the telephone. Today, we all use the telephone rather than write. But that loss of a printed record is all the more unfortunate among the 100 members of the U.S. Senate, with its congregation of party leaders, future cabinet officers, and possible presidents. If historians aren't crying in their martinis about that, they should be.

Indeed, it was such concerns that moved Richard Nixon to secretly bug the Oval Office, to record his every momentous utterance. But, of course, doing that—without bothering to mention it to his unwary visitors—was going a bit far in a free society.

I am without a solution. I have only a curse—for the telephone, that technological toilet down which so much American history is now being flushed.

*   *   *

Frank Church began opposing increases in Senate staff in the later years of his time in office. He could see the day when even his retentive mind would no longer be able to keep on top of all those issues and all those aides. As the Senate staff grows, not even the ablest minds will be able to escape becoming puppets of their own underlings.

And how that staff has grown. Until 1909, 92 senators and their few aides were housed in quarters within the Capitol building itself. Today, 100 senators have three huge office buildings in Washington, with more aides and additional offices scattered all over their home states.

Some small part of that growth is attributable to more Americans placing more demands on their respective senators. If the growth were all devoted to serving constituents, it might be easier to defend. But the increase in staff members directly serving the folks back home is the least of the expansion. The bulk of the growth is in specialists—especially on committees. The rationale is that Congress needs more help producing its own separate assessments of the issues, independent of the overpopulated executive branch— as if Congress could ever hope to equal the executive branch in the number of personnel.

And no matter how sound the rationale may seem, the fact is that the growth in staff is robbing the senators of a more crucial form of independence—the freedom to actually *be* senators, the ability to make decisions independent of how they are programmed by their unelected aides.

The day is at hand for some senators—and approaching for the rest—when they will be little more than the dashing front men and women for a Senate constituted, not of 100 duly elected legislators, but of 100 bureaucratic oligarchies:

> "Senator, we, your board of advisers for the Senior Senate Seat of Idaho, have determined how you will vote on today's bills."
>
> "But I wanted to decide for myself how to vote on some of those bills."
>
> "Senator, surely you're not suggesting that you know as much about any of this legislation as we do?"
>
> "Oh, no. I would never be that presumptuous. I know you people have studied these matters much more thoroughly than I ever seem to have time for. I just thought . . ."
>
> "Senator, every one of these votes has been screened by the computer for constituent-arousal potential. All are quite safe. Any deviation and we might all be out of work after the next election."
>
> "Forgive an old man his occasional delusions. I'm sure you people know best."
>
> "Good for you, Senator. . . . Steve, comb the senator's hair. . . . And mix him a weak Scotch and soda."

Chapter Seven
The Senator Had a Secret

I haven't underestimated the American appetite for every private detail on every public person since one morning over breakfast when I read the latest rectal temperature of the President of the United States.

Dwight Eisenhower had been seriously ill. The whole country was uneasy until the press presented us with the ultimate proof he was on the mend—a perfectly normal rectal temperature. What a comfort that was.

As a consequence of that experience, I knew when I left for Washington that, sooner or later, under the best of circumstances or under the worst, the public would learn that presidential candidate Frank Church was missing a testicle.

There was no point in quibbling whether the public had any right to such details, or whether the press should censor such information—as it did the dreadful state of Franklin Roosevelt's wartime health a generation before. The fact is, whether anyone might wish otherwise, the public today insists on and will be given every last detail about the health of every presidential candidate of any consequence. The only question about Frank Church's missing testicle was how that loss would be made known to the public.

Would it be supplied forthrightly by him, long before the campaign began, thereby making the point that his loss was hardly shameful and demonstrating also that his health was so secure that he would talk easily and openly about once having had cancer? Or would it be discovered furtively in the middle of a presidential campaign and reported over his furious objections, thereby indicating he might have something about his health to hide, and indicating also that losing a testicle is something disgraceful?

I knew what the answer to the question should be. I knew that the information had to be brought out early, casually, and with nothing held back if this man was serious about running for president. He must, as one wag in the press was later to advise me, stop short only of emulating Lyndon Johnson and showing the scar from his operation.

But you never know how a presidential candidate is going to react to the need to let people know he is missing one. Some presidential candidates with one testicle are probably a little stuffy about that sort of thing.

It was not a point I brought up in my discussions with Church before taking the job. But I was tempted. That kind of candor represents something of a test case—both whether the candidate and his family are ready for the unrestrained probing they will undergo during a campaign, and whether they know the first rule of handling a sticky truth: Volunteer the information.

If Church himself began talking freely about cancer and his missing part in occasional interviews—long before the press got wind of it—he could convert a potential liability into an asset. The reporters would regard the man who nonchalantly talked about such a detail as a guy with his head on straight.

Church faced the same situation as Betty Ford and her missing breast. There wasn't a prayer of keeping the illness of a First Lady quiet anyway. Had she tried, had she so much as flinched at talking about it, all the nitwits would have felt vindicated in doubting whether she was any longer a normal person. But Betty Ford had her head on so completely straight that the only course she ever considered was how to discuss her loss in ways that would be most likely to give social courage to other women in the same situation. Because she reacted that way, because she met the issue squarely and apparently without social qualms, breast surgery today has lost much of its stigma. And Betty Ford has become, not less a woman, but more.

But it's easy for me to talk. I have yet to lose either a testicle or a breast. So I could understand, given that tittering herd of perpetual sophomores among the general public, if a presidential candidate or a First Lady did not so quickly grasp or relish the finer PR moves required in dealing with a testicle or a breast operation.

For one thing, some medical procedures provoke more mirth than others. Dwight Eisenhower and his aides probably had no qualms about discussing the president's heart attack. But it's possible they resented—especially in that less candid age—the reports on Ike's rectal temperature. Is nothing sacred?

Not any more it isn't. So imagine the possible reaction in this swaggering macho country at any hint of a sexual handicap. A missing testicle invites gags potentially damaging to a candidate running for an office requiring toughness in a country that equates manliness with toughness by charging that weak people have "no balls." There was bound to be a certain amount of giggling, and for a time there was. One story involved not only Church but also presidential candidate Morris Udall, the representative from Arizona. Udall, a former basketball star, was missing an eye:

"What has one eye, one ball, plays basketball, and wants to run the country?"

"A Church-Udall ticket."

The only antidote to that sort of thing was to bring out the details early and let them get the giggling out of their system. I hoped that we could convert the whole business into an old joke that everyone would be tired of by the time it mattered.

But would Frank Church share that attitude?

I thought he might. In the first place, Church had never hidden the fact he had been stricken with cancer as a young man. He had lent his name in previous years to the National Cancer Society as a cured cancer victim. Moreover, it was no secret in some circles in Idaho what kind of cancer had hit young Frank Church half a lifetime before, or what he had lost in the process. Most Idaho politicians knew about it. The details had never been reported to the general public only because the health of senators, unlike that of presidential candidates, is not a matter so plainly in the public interest. A senator doesn't have his finger on the nuclear button. It doesn't matter so much when facing the need for a quick response to some hot war if a senator keels over and dies.

Some national reporters knew about Church's lost organ and had never reported it for the same reason. But early in 1975, as a few reporters began zeroing in on the possibility that Church might run for president, I began getting The Question:

"What kind of cancer was it?"

I answered that I would have to check.

It was largely a stall, of course. I was virtually certain what kind of cancer it was. But I wasn't sure Church was ready to deal with the question. The moment had arrived. We had better give them a quick answer or lose the initiative. But I was uneasy about bringing up the subject with the senator. You never know how a guy is going to react to a question like that. So I did what anyone else did in the Church office when wary of upsetting the senator: I called Bethine Church and asked her advice.

"Tell them it was cancer of the groin," she said.

"I don't think they'll buy that."

"Well, then," she said, hesitating for only a moment, "tell them it was testicular."

That they would buy. It was the truth—the whole truth and more truth than they might expect a guy running for president to part with so casually. It would answer the question. And it would make him look good in the candor department.

So I was able to call back quickly to the reporters and, treating it like any other routine question, tell them it was "testicular." I also volunteered the added details Bethine had supplied: The left one removed, along with the lymph glands on the left side of the groin. And I offered also, as Bethine had suggested, the good news: "Fortunately, the human body is gloriously redundant," I told the reporters. "You can get by very well with one lung or one kidney or one eye—or one testicle. You only need one, you know."

Like youngsters not wanting to appear any less well informed on sex than their peers, the reporters quickly assured me that, of course, they knew that. Some actually did. They volunteered the point on redundancy before I could get it out—almost in atonement for having asked such a nosy question and wanting to guide me toward the added information that might help blunt the giggling of the macho crowd.

After several days of answering The Question and finding that the unembarrassed candor from the Frank Church office was being well received by the reporters, I was elated. The Churches were indeed realistic and rational enough as politicians to know they had no choice but to part gracefully with the details. We—the Churches and I—had passed our presidential PR test with flying colors. We had crossed our biggest hurdle.

A few days later, a magazine writer presented me with a slightly larger hurdle: "But can he get it on?" she asked delicately.

I had thought she was up to something a couple of hours earlier when she interviewed Church in his Capitol office. She sat on the carpet at his feet, instead of in a chair. And her blouse was half unbuttoned, exposing most of her talented lungs. I not only noticed but I found it difficult to concentrate on Church's answers to her questions.

But Church, like any senator, had no trouble concentrating on his own words. Indeed, he was enthralled. She asked foreign policy questions, and Frank Church was a foreign policy junkie. When he got on that subject he was as oblivious to anything else as a bowler discussing the day he rolled a 300 game.

But she wasn't interested in bowling.

"You know," she said later over a drink. "I don't get much reaction from him . . . no man-woman reaction, if you know what I mean. I'm not suggesting I'm irresistible, but I usually get some reaction. And some of these old bastards in the Senate aren't safe to interview alone in a private office."

"Oh, hell," I said, "haven't you ever been that way—so full of your own brilliance that you can't concentrate on anything else? I'm the same way once I start talking politics—and I'll bet you are too."

She admitted she was.

"But if it's any consolation," I told her, "I wasn't talking during your boob test so you got a reaction from me. My hands were shaking during the whole interview."

She denied she had deliberately exposed her cleavage, but accepted the compliment with a laugh.

"But now be serious," she said. "Off the record, can he get it on?"

"On the record," I answered, "there are only two people who know the answer to that question. I ain't one of them, I ain't going to ask, and you shouldn't either."

She let it drop.

Of course, the question came up again from time to time. I gave all the reporters the same none-of-your-business answer, which most of them more or less agreed with on reflection. It was by no means certain at that point that Church would be running for president. As long as they had him down as a doubtful starter, they would permit some privacy. But if he did run, several reporters gave me to understand, the question would come up again—certainly not from them, mind you; they were too tasteful. But there were certain to be some reporters around who lacked their refined standards on how much the slavering public absolutely has to know.

At the time, I really doubted it would come to that. After all, there must be some limit even to the coverage of a presidential candidate. I put the impertinent question about my candidate's sexual competence out of my mind.

Meanwhile, the more graceful crusade to give the country the full details, good and early, of Frank Church's bout with cancer proceeded with the complete, civilized cooperation of the Churches and utterly without visible qualms. As the presidential candidacy appeared more probable, Church fielded the cancer questions as blithely as a man discussing a boyhood bout of prickly heat. He made it easy on the reporters, sparing them any embarrassment over asking the question his looming candidacy now required them to ask.

Discreetly, story by story, the information went out that the senator from Idaho was minus one of his testicles. No one blew it out of proportion. Invariably, it was just another detail slipped gently into the lower paragraphs of each story. His manner made the difference.

Church also agreed during that period to do a first-person article on his struggle against cancer for *Good Housekeeping* magazine. He dropped the article on my desk one day and asked me to look at it before he mailed it.

It was a moving story—a love story. Frank Church hadn't simply been stricken with cancer; he had been given a death sentence, which his strong-willed young wife commuted to life in tandem.

As a law student, with a wife and baby son, Church had developed pains in the small of his back. The doctors diagnosed it at first as "student backache"—too many hours at a desk poring over books. Not to worry.

But the pains grew worse, more tests were run, and the doctors came to a dreadful verdict—utterly untreatable cancer. They gave him six months, more or less.

Thereafter, without any real hope, but because one must at least try wild shots in the dark, the doctors cut away everything that appeared cancerous. And then, in those early days of rudimentary remedies, they showered his entire torso with a desperate, deliberate overkill of x-rays. Actually, they considered the x-rays futile, except perhaps to buy a few more months, but they felt they had to go through the motions.

The treatments amounted to an attempt to sicken every cell in his body, in the hope that the normal cells could be taken merely to the edge of extinction while mortally wounding cancerous cells. In Bethine's words, "They burned him up." His six-foot frame shrank to 90 pounds. Worse in its way, the x-ray treatments left him so thoroughly nauseous, so miserable from constant dry retching, that his reaction was not so much fear of death as a feeling of maddening frustration. He recalled thinking, "If I'm going to die anyway, why are they doing this to me?"

Bethine never gave up. Except for the x-ray treatments, she took charge of the patient. And then that Idaho farm girl proceeded to put up one hell of a fight to save her young husband.

An initial crisis came with dehydration and the alarming loss of weight. She experimented, trying to find some liquid he could hold down. Nothing worked until she tried root beer.

She flooded him with root beer.

Next she worked on solids. She discovered that he could sometimes handle lamb chops.

She virtually force fed him lamb chops. He began gaining weight.

Meanwhile, one tenacious doctor decided to take a second look at the cancer cells. Sweet Mother of Jesus! It was a slightly different strain than they had diagnosed. And it was treatable!

The doctors and the young wife heaped remedies on the future senator. And they saved him.

But there was more to his story as he wrote it in that magazine article. It came through, between the lines, rather unintentionally but vividly, how much he loved that woman. The experience didn't simply bring them together; it combined them. I have never seen such a complete merger of two individuals. They were virtually a single personality, a single mind, the kind of union in which partners finish each other's sentences. They always had similar interests, ideals, and ambitions from the days of their high school romance. But that illness and its outcome obviously sealed the bond.

I returned the draft of the article to Church and told him what a touching story it was. But he was uncomfortable with it, not because it mentioned the loss of a testicle, but because he had never written anything quite so personal. He didn't approve of the genre of articles written by senators on their own heroics: "It sounds like one of those stories some of my colleagues write—'How I found God and became wonderful.'"

But he had already promised the article. And I promised never to speak to him again if he didn't send it to *Good Housekeeping*. And so he did.

The article, with its "before" picture of an emaciated young Frank Church, plus a color picture of the mature Frank Church, robustly healthy, produced a warm wave of letters and phone calls. For once, there was no true hate mail, although one woman wrote to ask why he was so terribly grateful to his wife and to his doctors, but had neglected to mention his God.

"Tell her I thank God every day I'm alive," he said.

Some messages were more difficult to deal with. A senior citizen called and asked me to thank the senator. The old man's wife, in her seventies, had been hospitalized two times previously, with a cancerous breast removed each time. And now she had returned to the hospital a third time. He was confined to a wheelchair at home and didn't have the money for a taxi, so he hadn't seen her in a week. The doctors had told him by telephone that she was filled with cancer, that she was terminal. But he no longer believed them. Frank Church's article had persuaded him otherwise. His wife was going to make it, just as the senator had.

I didn't know what in the world to say. I just listened and thanked him for calling.

At the other end of the scale were those who called to say they had lost a member of the family to cancer, but wanted to thank the senator for talking openly about his illness. It might help end the notion among some people, they said, that cancer is untreatable. It might get them to the doctor in time.

The most touching messages came from men who said they had lost a testicle to cancer and had hidden the fact until then. They would hide it no more. If a presidential candidate could talk about it so openly, who were they to act like sexual lepers?

Chalk one up, not only for Betty Ford, but for Frank Church as well.

*   *   *

As the campaign drew near, the question persisted of whether Church was sexually functional. Peripheral questions cropped up about Chase Church, the family's younger, adopted son. Was there some reason they had adopted a child after the illness instead of following the usual practice?

The question seemed outrageous at the time. Perhaps many will still be appalled to know that the press goes that far in covering presidential candidates. And the political system certainly could survive without such indelicate detail. But the consequences of reporting on Eisenhower's rectal temperature, Betty Ford's mastectomy, Frank Church's missing testicle (and eventually Vice President Hubert Humphrey's missing bladder, with that little waste pouch he and other Americans found themselves wearing), caused me to consider another point of view. I can't help but notice that people are less uptight today about such illnesses than they used to be. And that includes me. The irrational stigma once attached to such maladies is disappearing along with the social taboos against discussing them openly. That must be a blessing to men and women afflicted with the same indelicate diseases as those more celebrated citizens. I'm far from certain that every reporter who asked the sticky question always did so with the best of motives, but the social results seem to have been for the best.

Perhaps it would also be good for the morale and for the treatment of several million sexually dysfunctional Americans to know that a president or a presidential candidate has had to cope with the same condition. Indeed, it is almost certain that several of the old boys who have occupied the White House have been impotent in more ways than one—just as some of them have known excess in the opposite direction. So such questions, though really none of the public's business—unless the president is having at the wife of the ambassador from some unfriendly power—could serve a social purpose. But I certainly didn't think so at the time. I thought the reporters were pretty damned cheeky.

It was Mary Perot Nichols, then of the *Village Voice,* who tilted me toward believing that, fair or not, the question could not be avoided. The same rules applied as to questions having to do with missing a testicle. If we didn't at least answer the question, the public guessing—and giggling—would begin. The best course would be to volunteer the information, the same as with the cancer operation. Mary casually added that she was the kind of reporter who could most tastefully handle the story.

Once again I called Bethine. I told her the question and that I had been receiving it for months. It wouldn't go away.

Bethine was steamed at first, not at me, but at the lack of limits on public curiosity. Nevertheless, she heard me out on the arguments in favor of still more candor, almost audibly shrugged, and then agreed to accept a call from Mary.

The story in the *Voice* had a slightly hypocritical theme—the gall of some other reporters in how far they would go in asking questions. Good Lord, they now had the bad taste to actually ask Frank Church whether he could function sexually. Are there no limits to what those animals in the press will ask?

But as long as those vulgarians had brought up such a sleazy subject, Mary wrote, the answer, for the record, is yes, Frank Church can function very well, thank you. His wife said so. In addition, Mary had double-checked with a New York doctor who said of course he could. In addition to the redundancy of the human body, it is even possible to be sexually functional with both testicles removed. The doctor said impotence is mental, not physical.

I should have known that. As a farm boy, I remember a very active gelding.

The clincher was a quote from Bethine. She said that despite his being quite conventional in his capacity for sex, there was one thing about Frank Church's sex life that a town like Washington would regard as highly abnormal: "He's monogamous."

And that was that. I never again heard the prying questions about lost organs or doubtful potency, even deep into the presidential campaign.

Of course, Bethine was not the only member of the Church family to whom I had put the final uncouth question while Mary Nichols prepared her article. Two people knew the answer.

"Senator," I began, feeling cheap, "I have to ask a nosy question I've been getting for months. I've ignored it until now because I thought it would go away. It won't. I don't know any easy way to put this, but . . . can you get it on in bed? It's the cancer thing."

He blinked a couple of times and said nothing. I quickly explained the reasons why I thought the question could no longer be avoided.

And then, without the slightest hostility and trying to put me at ease, he said, "Well, if they really have to get into that, then the answer, happily, is yes. I'd have been in a padded cell long before this if it hadn't been for the pleasures of sex."

I thanked him profusely for being so understanding—indeed for not pitching me straight out the window. I started to remove my boorish person from his civilized presence.

"Now wait a minute, Bill," he said. "If it's gone that far, you'll be getting questions on this, too: Those radiation treatments were massive, over my entire body. I'm sterile. We thought at first it was a tragedy because it meant we couldn't have any more children. But of course, it's turned out to be a great blessing. If it hadn't been for that, we would never have found and adopted Chase. And I think you know how much we love him."

Neither Frank nor Bethine Church ever showed the slightest resentment over my part in the general impertinence of asking anyone such questions for publication. The only time I ever heard of it again from either of them was one day some weeks later when we were compiling his financial records for distribution to the press.

"I'm sorry to keep pestering you with these money questions," I said, interrupting him at his desk.

"No problem," he said, smiling. "I'm just grateful you've finally got your mind off my sex life."

And then he roared at his own joke. So did I.

I don't think most politicians could have handled those same questions with the grace and humor that Frank Church displayed. I don't think most politicians would have been man enough.

Chapter Eight
Dinner with that Charming Henry Kissinger

I had just finished changing into my tuxedo when *Playboy* magazine called. It's gratifying what the right clothes can do for a man.

The *Los Angeles Times* had invited me to the annual dinner of the White House Correspondents Association. Strictly black tie. A tuxedo was not my customary weekend wear. Indeed, I spent most of my early weekends in Washington in blue jeans and tennis shoes, just kicking around Capitol Hill by myself. I kept track of the flower beds around the Capitol, stocked up at the Pennsylvania Avenue wine shops, and frequently drifted into that giant greenhouse, the National Botanic Garden, where I had located a little indoor forest and could pretend I was in Idaho.

The first weekend in May, 1975 was to be different. I was due that Saturday night, along with President Jerry Ford and half of Congress, at the International Ballroom of the Washington Hilton. Jerry and I had both been reminded to wear a tuxedo.

I understand Jerry already owned one. I rented a tux in a shop on Capitol Hill under the motherly eye of Myrna Sasser, Church's veteran chief in charge of constituent problems. She pushed me past the more colorful plumage, so popular at teenage weddings, and toward a basic black job. I tried it on and stepped out of the dressing room for an examination. Myrna nodded her approval. There would be no embarrassing Frank Church in something so somber.

The clerk then inquired if I would like a plain white shirt or something more audacious. I looked at Myrna, a slight pleading look in my eyes, the taste of a teenage bridegroom welling up in me.

"Live a little," she said, doubting I could go too far wrong.

The clerk produced a charcoal gray, a lime green, and a pale lavender with dark lavender trim. All had frilly fronts, the kind that could get you stomped in an Idaho beer bar. But what the hell? When in Rome . . .

I took the lavender.

Myrna rolled her eyes.

I picked up the tux on the Friday before the dinner and brought it to the Church office for modeling and pictures. The pictures were to send to the relatives. The modeling was to give Church's secretaries a look at a real stud in black and lavender. They had been envious in a friendly sort of way that I would be attending one of the social events of the season. But they wanted to give me a chance to lord it over them. And they wanted an opportunity to coo over me, just because they were affable people and wanted to butter my ego.

So, in response to numerous requests, I went into the office bathroom and stuffed my standard white body into the ruffled lavender shirt and the basic black tuxedo. The requisite cooing had barely begun when one of the secretaries informed me I had a call from *Playboy.*

We all laughed.

But the secretary insisted. I really did have a call from *Playboy.*

And I did. A woman with a soft bunny voice was calling from Chicago, asking that I pass the word on to Church that they were running an article on the CIA and would be sending him an advance copy.

I have never been more suitably dressed for a telephone call.

*   *   *

The White House Correspondents Dinner is, as the Indians of Idaho would say, no pile of chopped liver. The evening begins with cocktail parties, hosted by newspapers and magazines. Famous faces are everywhere, both from the government and the media. Everyone stands around in evening clothes, looking elegant as the devil and wearing the smug smiles of those from a powerful inner circle. The newspapers, networks, and periodicals all invite guests from the government. Not just senators and representatives, but also members of the Cabinet, members of the Supreme Court, heads of federal bureaus, and the principal aides to all those people, including four of us from Frank Church's staff. I had received invitations from three different publications and chauvinistically accepted the one from the *Los Angeles Times,* because it is a western newspaper

and because my host for the evening would be *Times* D.C. correspondent John Averill, a former Idahoan and a genial drinking
companion.

The International Ballroom was about the size of a velvet foot-
ball field. On one side stood the platform where the orchestra and
the entertainers (Danny and Marlo Thomas) would do their thing.
On the other side—running from about the 35-yard line to the 35-
yard line—was the ostentatiously elevated head table where sat 40
demigods, including the Fords, most of the Cabinet, and the officers of the White House Correspondents Association. Down on
the velvet playing field were the Christians and the lions, the government officials and the reporters, ten to a table.

The gathering was so large—about 2,000 people—that the
Correspondents Association provided a thick booklet for a program,
cross-referenced with the names and table numbers of everyone
present. From the center of each table rose a little standard bearing the table number. The booklet served not only as a means of
finding your seat and your dinner companions, but also as a table-
hopper's guide to others in the congregation. It answered such
questions as who that distinguished but slightly loaded gentleman
is at Table 27. And it made it easier for everyone to find Dan Rather
and Senator Kennedy. No one was neglected. Jerry Ford and I were
both in the guide, our table numbers listed after our names for the
convenience of those who failed to recognize either one of us:

> Ford, Gerald R., President of the United States......Head table.
> Hall, Wilbert, Office of Senator Frank Church......Table 132.

Following the after-dinner program, which consisted of little
more than gridiron jokes by the press at the expense of the president, and vice versa, Jerry and Betty went home. The rest of us
rushed upstairs for more cocktails and a little more mingling with
the mighty.

John Averill of the *L.A. Times* was like an uncle taking a kid to
the zoo, having more fun himself because of my wide eyes beside
him. And what a zoo. He showed me a flighty senator from South
Dakota, a graceful female Cabinet secretary, a nervous covey of
California congressmen, and a strutting network correspondent.
And he walked me straight into the *Time* magazine enclosure where
a huge crowd had cornered a preening Secretary of State with a

deep voice and a soft German accent. I boldly shook hands with the creature despite its belligerent reputation.

I think everyone in Washington who has ever met Henry Kissinger described him with the same word—charming. People who worship Kissinger rave about how charming he is. People who detested his policies and sometimes the man himself would recite his offenses against reason and humankind, and then add, "But the son of a bitch is charming socially."

And he is. Indeed, Kissinger goes a step beyond charming. He is disarming in the full my-defenses-are-down use of the word. He transcends common political charisma and instills in those around him some inferior urge to stay on his good side for fear he will never again let you bask in the glow of his droll and articulate presence. Henry Kissinger, the warrior-statesman, could be lovable at a party.

It is easy to see how senators, prime ministers, and potentates, determined to resist his entreaties to do things his way, found their resolve melting as soon as Kissinger started purring and rubbing up against their egos. This man, with what I assume is a deserved reputation for brutal command of his staff and for rather heartless manipulation of lesser nations, could be a seductive pussycat in a social setting.

I had no chance at more than the exchange of a couple of pleasantries because there was such a mob of senators and network stars—most of whom professed to disapprove of his policies—pressing around us to touch Richard Nixon's (and Gerald Ford's) Secretary of State, the last great guru of the cold war era. It was the measure of Kissinger's sorcery that most people that night, given a choice between rubbing elbows with Henry or with the President of the United States, made a beeline for the Secretary of State.

Somewhere over the next couple of hours, hopping from hospitality suite to hospitality suite, I lost my guide, John Averill. And so, much the worse for wear, I flagged a cab and headed home.

The taxi driver was new, a college student fresh from Kentucky and quite starstruck. He knew what was going on at the Hilton that night and had been cruising the place all evening, picking up the distinguished guests, taking them safely home from the biggest binge of the Washington social season. He was visibly disappointed when he learned all he had bagged was a lousy press secretary to a senator. But he pumped me for details of the evening—who was there, what we had been served (breast of capon cordon bleu), that sort of thing. He didn't even mention Jerry Ford. But after the preliminaries were over he asked the prime question: "Did you meet Henry Kissinger?"

"Yes," I said, leaning back in the seat nonchalantly, crossing my legs, "Henry and I exchanged a few words."

"What's he like?" the driver asked in hushed tones.

"Charming," I said. "He's charming."

*   *   *

Like everyone not born with a silver credit card in his mouth, my models of how to conduct oneself in a quality restaurant come from the movies. There are two basic styles. One is Orson Wells, the arrogant aristocrat who tastes an unremarkable wine, turns purple, expectorates in his glass, and thunders, "You dare serve me this filth!" as the staff scurries to the cellar to find something worthy.

The second style is Tom Hanks, unpretentious, egalitarian, and easy to please. He is welcomed to the restaurant by the entire staff, all of whom are genuinely delighted to see nice Mr. Hanks. They give him the best table, the best wine, and something special from the chef because it is such unqualified joy to have him on the premises.

My model in Washington restaurants was Tom Hanks. I was cordial and undemanding like the former busboy I am. And I found one restaurant in particular—Agostino's on Connecticut Avenue—where they reciprocated my Hanksian manner. Agostino's was a medium-priced Italian place with a wine-cellar motif, strolling musicians, and an especially creamy fettuccine—one of those cholesterol creations they should serve with a cardiologist.

Most of all, Agostino's offered a smiling *maitre d'* who said, "Good evening, Mr. Hall. Your usual table?" And it had Agostino himself, the owner-manager, who would send an after-dinner cognac by the table with his compliments and then sit briefly with me and my guests to learn what fascinating thing Mr. Hall had to say that evening.

I was a sucker for that place. Each time I dined there, I was given to understand that I was an unqualified joy to have on the premises.

But my more frequent hangout in Washington was a modest restaurant on Capitol Hill known as Mike Palm's. It was near Church headquarters and members of the campaign staff ate there often. The clientele was mixed—very mixed. Tourists would stray in from the nearby Capitol. And I came to realize that some of the couples who frequented Mike Palm's were gay, apparently Capitol Hill workers stopping by for a drink or dinner, just as the Church people did. It wasn't every restaurant where you dined simultaneously with Republican implement dealers from Des Moines and with gay bureaucrats from the U.S. Senate.

I stopped by Mike Palm's one evening with Debbie Herbst, assistant press secretary to the Church campaign. We were seated at a small table, sandwiched between couples on either side. On one side were two middle-aged men in business suits. On the other side were a man and a woman in their fifties wearing tourist clothes. It soon became apparent from the conversations we couldn't avoid overhearing that the couple on the left were a Rotarian and his wife in town from the Southwest for whatever it is that Rotarians do when they are in Washington.

The two men on the right were also married, or at least they had been shacking up for years. Both couples were having trouble making a selection:

"How about the filet of sole?" said one partner on one side of us.

"You know I don't like filet of sole."

"Since when?"

And then from the other side:

"Why do you always have the French dressing? Try the Roquefort."

"You know I can't stand Roquefort."

"You used to eat it all the time."

And from the other side:

"I ought to know whether I like filet of sole or not."

"You ought to, but you don't."

And from the other:

"I'm the best judge of whether I like Roquefort."

"I'd think you'd get tired of French dressing."

And the other:

"Filet of sole is tasteless. I'd rather eat a block of wood."

"Suit yourself. But you know you like it."

"I give up! You want me to eat the goddam sole, I'll eat the goddam sole."

And:

"I don't know where you get these crazy ideas. I've always detested Roquefort."

"Eat what you please. I don't care. But you love Roquefort."

"OK! I'll take the damned Roquefort. Anything for a little peace."

And so on for 45 nagging minutes. Debbie and I kept our heads down, not daring to look each other in the eye for fear of dissolving into disgraceful giggles. Finally, both couples left. Debbie looked up with a straight face.

"Try the filet of dog," she said.

"You know I don't like filet of dog," I snapped.

Then we both cracked up.

I apologize if people who favor that life style are offended by our mirth. But you have to understand: Neither Debbie nor I have spent that much time around Rotarians.

*   *   *

In February of 1976, Frank Church was invited to address the World Conference on Soviet Jewry in Brussels, with a stop in London for a visit with the Prime Minister. The senator kindly ordered me to advance his trip. I flew overnight to London, which is to say I was awake all night. I find it difficult to drop off to sleep when I'm at 35,000 feet and there is an ocean down there in the darkness. I arrived at mid-morning on a Saturday and hustled to the American embassy for a couple of hours to make arrangements for the Church visit, planning to catch an afternoon nap and then spend a night on the town. But as I left the embassy, I couldn't wait. My English-Irish ancestry beckoned. I had been in London for two hours and all I had seen was the American embassy, a tacky ostentatious monolith topped by a huge gold eagle, shouting its vulgar American presence like a Texas tourist. If there was ever a building that typifies our foreign policy during most of the period of post-World War II, it is that rude, overbearing American building in gentle London.

Across the street is London's revenge—a little park in Grosvenor Square, built around a statue of Franklin Roosevelt.

There is Roosevelt, cape flowing, in a heroic pose. And there are the London pigeons, cooing in British accents, crapping all over an American president, and with one of their number strolling around in an impertinent little circle on top of his heroic head.

If the English didn't like the way Roosevelt was always trying to run the war, why didn't they just say so?

From the embassy, I took off on foot across London. Before long, I had entered my first pub, a wonderful homey place where the drinks were uncommonly inexpensive and no tipping was permitted. Tired as I was, I stood at the bar, the way the comic-strip lowlife Andy Capp does, sipping a pint of stout, and drinking in the accents and conversations of those about me. I felt that self-centered glow of Americans who return to what they imagine they came from. These were my people and I was content at first to be among my new-found cousins.

But then I noticed something: there wasn't an attractive face in the room. Indeed, I had never seen such a collection of clock-stopping faces in my life. Thereafter, I saw the same thing all over London—protruding, pointed chins, pasty complexions, squinty eyes, tight little mouths, and frizzy, brownish-red hair so thin the pink scalp shows through on the women as well as on the men—hair like mine!

I had come to London to find the fount of our laws, our language, and our gritty spirit. I had found as well the source of my pinched face, my freckles, my bald spot, and my needle nose. I have never looked into such a discouraging mirror. We may have given the world noble institutions, but, my God, we are such an ugly race. No wonder Hitler never crossed the channel.

I had intended to go to the theater that night, but I never made it. I lay down to take a nap and slept past curtain time. And a good thing, too. After discovering such gnarled roots in that little pub, I needed all the beauty sleep I could get.

I met the Churches at the airport the next morning at 7:00. They had flown overnight from Oregon where they had been making appearances in that crucial primary state in preparation for the presidential campaign they would begin officially in about a month. Church would sometimes pretend to sleep on airplanes, but he really didn't fly much better than I did. He arrived exhausted, went directly to the hotel, and slept for the next 12 hours while the European press tried to get at him through me. Church was chairman of the Senate Subcommittee on Multinational Corporations. That subcommittee had just blown the whistle on the bribery of foreign leaders by Lockheed and other American corporations. The European press was after him for hints on whether their governments would be the next to come under the committee's eye.

I could have fielded the calls from my room, but that would have been too much. I was seeing precious little of London as it was. So I established myself near a phone in the lobby where I could at least watch all my ugly cousins stroll by. It was a Sunday morning and, fortified with a heavy stack of London newspapers, I settled down for the next 12 hours, reading, taking calls from reporters all over Western Europe—and drinking tea.

In my experience, most dishes and drinks for which given cities or countries are celebrated are interesting, but not all they're cracked up to be. Not so the tea of London. The English really do know a teapot from a kumquat when it comes to brewing tea.

"A cup of tea, please," I said to the Jeeves-like gentleman presiding over the serving station in the center of the lobby. He returned shortly with:

A steam-heated cup and saucer.

A thick crockery teapot with the tea leaves—not a tea bag, you ninny, but the leaves—already steeping.

A small crockery pitcher of scalding water to dilute the tea if it became too strong.

A pitcher of hot milk.

A dish of lemon wedges.

A bowl of sugar.

A dish of biscuits.

A fork for the lemon, a spoon, and, of course, a cloth napkin.

Each time I ordered a "cup" of tea that day, the waiter, balancing a large tray, scooped up everything and returned a few moments later with another load, gently arranging everything in its place. I missed the changing of the guard at Buckingham Palace a few blocks away, but I doubt it could have held a candle to the maneuvers that resulted from the command, "A cup of tea, please."

* * *

The extreme highs and lows of a presidential campaign came into sharp focus after that trip to Europe. One night I dined with the Churches and a dozen international high rollers at the French restaurant atop the Brussels Hilton—turbot with white sauce, a different wine with each course, and a huge chocolate souffle, followed by Dom Perignon champagne.

Two nights later I dined at the Capitol Hill Roy Rogers—a hamburger with Roy's special barbecue sauce, French fries, and a vanilla milkshake.

I was once partial to Roy and Dale Evans. I did my time in the Saturday matinees of that era. And there was a period when I admired Roy, even if he was merely a drugstore cowboy, a frilly shirted, sissy tenor who would get laughed off a real western ranch. What tore it with me was when his horse Trigger died and Roy, rather than giving his horse a decent burial, had his loyal friend stuffed and put on display. It was enough to make me wonder what he would do if Dale died. It occurred to me that it would probably be the first time she'd been mounted in years.

I was eating at the Capitol Hill Roy Rogers one day when a man I would see many times thereafter entered. In his mid-sixties, he wore what had once been an expensive pin-striped suit, a white dress shirt, no tie, no socks, and a pair of expensive shoes. He hadn't shaved for a couple of days, but he was clean, with his hair neatly trimmed. I guessed that he had been used up by Washington, reached the age of legal senility, and had been banished to stroll the streets of Capitol Hill, his career finished and without enough purpose left in life to bother shaving.

I saw something very much like him the night after attending the White House Correspondents Dinner—in my mirror. I was hung over, unshaven, and listless. Crumpled on a chair were my tuxedo and my lavender shirt. A cuff link was broken. I think I stepped on my wrist on the way home.

I decided to get some fresh air. Donning my jeans and tennis shoes, I left the apartment for a stroll around the Capitol grounds. I had not gone far when I encountered the old bureaucrat from Roy Rogers, out for his own healing constitutional. He was strolling casually behind young women, watching their fannies jiggle. As we passed, he recognized me and nodded, the warm greeting of one fading fraternity brother for another.

It was depressing, of course. I knew Washington was a town where you could be on top one day and at the bottom the next. But I didn't expect it to be quite so literally true. The night before I had been standing at the Hilton in my tuxedo exchanging small talk with Henry Kissinger. The next morning I was stumbling unshaven around Capitol Hill with the other dirty old men, admiring fannies.

How quickly the mighty crumble in that town.

I wonder what ever happened to that charming man Henry Kissinger.

Chapter Nine
Running for President with the Senator and the Secret Service

Politically, we are nearly all stereotyped. Most Americans have at least one characteristic that is supposed to preclude their trustworthy performance in a life-and-death job like the presidency. Millions of our fellow citizens, for their own peculiar reasons, would not vote for a president who is female or from one of the forbidden ethnic groups.

But stereotyping does not end there. Millions of male WASPs are similarly excluded from common consideration for the presidency. Indeed, some of them are likely to be refused long after women, Latinos, Jews, and blacks have entered the White House. What are the odds, for instance, against electing a candidate in the next quarter century with a disfigured face? Or the most sound mind in the nation if its owner has cerebral palsy and tends to drool a bit during speeches? Or a dwarf? Or someone named Sylvester Hitler? Or, in this television age, someone as ugly as Abraham Lincoln?

And of course, to a lesser extent, the electorate has always felt a trifle superior to a candidate from given states or regions. Would you really be comfortable, for instance, with a president who grew up in Jackson, Mississippi? We all know what kind of attitudes are constructed in that environment. Besides, people from Mississippi talk funny.

How about a president from Boise, Idaho? Sleepy, square, culturally deprived, frugally educated, socially stifled, little Boise, Idaho?

You must be kidding. Some of my best friends eat potatoes, and all that. But Boise, Idaho? Let's not get giddy about picking our presidents.

It was in Boise, Idaho, in the fall of 1974, that Governor Cecil Andrus (could you respect a president named Cecil?) cautioned me against underestimating Jimmy Carter of Georgia as a contender for the presidency. Carter could go all the way, Andrus insisted.

Neither Andrus nor I had any indication at that point that Frank Church from Boise, Idaho, would enter the race, so we were still shopping. There were several promising prospects. But Jimmy Carter? From Georgia? I thought Andrus was out of his mind. The country simply didn't elect someone from the South to the presidency, not from Arkansas, not from Mississippi, certainly not from Georgia.

And we all knew then that governors—not to speak of governors like Carter no longer in office—are routinely passed over for the presidency in favor of senators. Senators are national government and international affairs. Governors, in the second half of the century, have become peanuts and potatoes. Indeed, at the time of my conversation with Andrus, governors were still the untouchables of national politics. They couldn't be elected to the White House, even if by some miracle they were the exception and had somehow schooled themselves in national and international subjects. I wrote off the Andrus attachment to Carter as the empty hope of a member of the national political underclass that one of his kind could make the grade and erase the stigma on an entire, generally inferior class of politician.

Two years later, Jimmy Carter (who would make Cecil Andrus his Secretary of Interior) wept as he stood before the people of Plains, Georgia, to claim his victory over Gerald Ford. They were tears of triumph, but not just for himself. They were also the tears of fraternity with his fellow townsmen. They had dared to assert that their kind was good enough to go to the White House, and had been sustained in that conviction by their countrymen. Jimmy Carter's election was a political emancipation proclamation for people from places like Plains, Georgia, and Boise, Idaho, and even Hope, Arkansas. Their children could, too, grow up to be president.

There is something special in the air when the native son of such a place reaches for the prize that has fallen so unremarkably in the past to the sons of the large urban centers of the North and West, with their much more massive payoffs in electoral votes. That was why Jimmy Carter and his townspeople wept especially proud tears that day. The first president from Georgia stirred deeper emotions than the latest president from New York or California.

And so it is with a presidential contender from Idaho. But the moving moment of Frank Church's campaign came at the beginning, not at the shriveled end. And it was in a place no larger than Plains or Hope and with no more promise of a president. Idaho City is the shrunken remnant of a once-bustling gold rush. It was also the home of the first Church in Idaho, the senator's grandfather, Frank Forrester Church, appointed chief assayer for the Idaho Territory by President Grover Cleveland. From the platform built on the porch of the wooden frontier courthouse we looked out that day on a town of 200 souls, temporarily swollen by a crowd of 5,000 Idahoans who had come to see one of their kind announce for president. There were tears in many of those eyes that day as their candidate seemed to be saying that, by God, a person from a state with a measly four electoral votes could, too, become president.

And of course, a person from Idaho or from the South can indeed become president. But not Frank Church that particular year. He was beginning his bid precariously late. It was March 18. It was the spring of the presidential primary season with delegates by the dozens already decided.

"It's never too late, nor are the odds ever too great—to try," said Frank Church with a flourish of bravado at the close of his announcement speech. And of course, the crowd roared its agreement.

But it was terribly late, and the odds were god-awful great, even to try.

You get so caught up in the blather of your own propaganda during a campaign that it's difficult, even now, to sort out the press agentry from what we actually thought his chances were. Suffice it to say that, even at a date so late and with odds so great, we could construct in our minds what seemed like a vaguely plausible scenario for catapulting Frank Church from the meager start of his campaign to the front ranks of the contenders within a matter of weeks—if everything broke just right.

Carter was already rolling by the time Church entered. Carter was so far ahead that much of the media had all but conceded his nomination. The Georgian was knee-deep in delegates when Frank Church first waded in and started to get his toes wet.

Myrna Sasser, Church's veteran aide, had introduced me weeks before to some affable Washington know-it-all named Mark Shields. I had never heard of him, but Myrna told me he was as astute as anyone in Washington. She said I should listen to him.

I listened but I did not hear. He said Frank Church was an able senator and a fine man but that we were too late. He said the new rules of the Democratic delegate process ruled out a late start because the primaries were no longer winner-take-all in each state. He pointed out that an early candidate winning second or third or fourth place in all the states would defeat a late candidate winning first place in a dozen states.

I didn't want to hear it. And maybe it's just as well for me, if not for Frank Church and America, that I ignored Mark Shields. If I had listened carefully, I would have known he was right and would have headed back to Idaho, never to see a national presidential campaign.

But I'm not surprised that Shields went on to become a premier political analyst for PBS.

I wasn't willing to listen because I was high on the excitement of a presidential campaign. And we had a glib but flawed answer for people like Mark Shields. As we so often reminded reporters, Carter was playing a delegate game. We would beat him with a momentum game—slowing his and starting Church's. Carter was committed to stretch himself thin over all the primary elections in the land but one. (All candidates had heeded the demand of Senator Robert Byrd to stay out of Byrd's West Virginia.) Church would choose his shots, defeating Carter wherever they met head-on. Church would focus on six or eight primaries and, because he was a better campaigner and not stretched nearly so thin, would win every one. There would be a cumulative effect on both the Church and the Carter campaigns—the effect of an unbroken string of victory headlines for Church, and the effect of doubt-spreading, Carter-stopping headlines for the front-runner. About the time the country would begin wondering about Jimmy Carter and begin to think that this Frank Church must really be something, we would go in for the big, loud finish in California—a Church victory over Carter in the largest state in the union. In California Barry Goldwater upset and destroyed Nelson Rockefeller in 1964. In California Frank Church would clobber and perhaps fatally weaken Jimmy Carter in 1976.

The arithmetic worked out that no one, not even Carter, could come out of the primary with a first-ballot convention majority. We would try to send a message to that convention that Carter had faltered in the stretch, that maybe he would do the same in the general election.

Our line to the press was that Church was unavoidably detained by his work with the Senate Intelligence Committee, so he could not enter all the primaries. Nonetheless, we told the reporters, he would enter "a representative cross-section of the nation's primaries." That meant Rhode Island in the East, Nebraska in the Midwest, none in the South, and a half dozen elections on Frank Church's home ground in the West. Not really much of a cross-section, but it was the best we could do entering so late. By declining to bite off more than he could chew, and by proving to be the more dramatic campaigner, Church would win all the primaries he entered. So we would be in a position to say to the convention, "Whenever and wherever the Democratic voters of America were asked, 'Who do you prefer for president, Frank Church or Jimmy Carter?' they answered—without exception—'Frank Church!'"

And we would ask the convention delegates what they thought it was about Jimmy Carter that, despite an overwhelming head start, far more money, and much heavier media exposure, he still couldn't manage to defeat a last-minute candidate like Frank Church? We would ask them if they still thought it safe to let Carter carry the Democratic standard into the fall wars.

In short, the initial goal of the Church campaign—what he called "the late, late strategy"—would be to knock a big, fat crack in Carter's credibility. Our strategy was to send the convention into a second ballot where anti-Carter, non-Carter, and doubting-Carter delegates would look for a place to coalesce. And of course, Frank Church, as the soaring new personality who had stopped Carter in his tracks at every turn, would become a prime prospect for the nomination.

The strategy worked up to a point. But of course, it also faltered at other points. One hitch was financing. A new campaign finance law, with its limitation of $1,000 per contributor, made the mechanics of scooping up money fast enough for the next primary too cumbersome for all but a front-runner like Carter. Front-runner groupies were throwing money at Carter; the Church campaign was chronically undernourished.

So Mark Shields was correct. The rules had changed. No more winner-take-all primaries. Each candidate in a given state primary won a number of convention votes in direct proportion to his percentage of the vote. That factor kept Carter from locking up a majority of the convention delegates in all his early wins. But it also meant that, even in losing to Frank Church, Carter still added to a total already large enough to panic the pros toward his bandwagon. Carter's strategy of entering all the primaries but Byrd's West Virginia was paying off. He could finish second or third in all six primaries on a given day and still add more delegates to his overall total than candidates like Church who finished first in one or two of those same primaries without entering the rest.

But the biggest fly in Frank Church's ointment was a character named Jerry Brown. "My mistake was not patenting the late, late strategy," Church said when it was all over.

California Governor Brown had also been laying back, waiting for the field to thin. Brown was a dramatic, charismatic campaigner who could easily upstage the less colorful Carter. And of course, Brown would surely cost Church California (and another state Church had been counting on—the California media suburb of Nevada). Some of the top Democratic politicians in California had quietly pledged their support to Church—if Brown didn't run. California Assembly Speaker Leo McCarthy, for example, had agreed to be Church's state chairman, providing the home-state boy didn't announce.

The home-state boy announced. McCarthy became Brown's state chairman.

It was already apparent that Brown was going to louse up our act by the time Church was ready to declare his candidacy. Church, a political realist, was virtually certain he was wasting his time.

But he announced anyway. Campaigns, once geared up, aren't geared down; they are only beaten down. There was too much go-get-'em-tiger money in the tank, and too many grand expectations in Idaho and elsewhere to deny the crowd the old college try.

In truth, Church talked more often those days about the vice presidency. It isn't a simple matter of secretly running for vice president in the pose of a presidential candidate. Church was of two minds. There were moments of dreaming about everything breaking right and first place on the ticket falling in his lap. But there were more moments of realism. As early as Church's trip to London and Brussels in February 1976, he was still among those who thought Carter was an early fluke who would stumble in the stretch. Church was still talking privately over dinner with Bethine and me in London about the inevitability of stop-Carter forces gathering around Hubert Humphrey and pushing him, without Church's blessing, into the nomination. Church preferred Carter. He thought Humphrey, whatever his former greatness, had become something of a posturing, chronically ambitious hack.

"But if I win the western primaries," Church said one evening in a London restaurant, "Hubert will have no choice but to choose me as his vice president."

Before the spring was over, the observation had been modified: "If I win the western primaries, Carter may have to choose me as his running mate."

* * *

We had it easy compared with most of the other campaigns—ten weeks of frenetic campaigning and it was all over. But even that was enough to make a person wonder about the candidates and their helpers who pursued the presidency for as long as two years— an almost inconceivable grind. Walter Mondale had terminated his campaign for the presidency late in 1974, saying it would be insane to spend the next two years living in Holiday Inns, wondering what day it was, what state he was in, and, eventually, what his name was. It was no accident that interest in the Mondale candidacy, not forthcoming while he was still a candidate, soared a bit when he left the race for the reasons he gave. It was as if the press and the party leaders concluded that anyone level enough to realize running for president is insane would be suited to the presidency.

Conversely, anyone willing to do what is now required to win the job is demonstrably too crazy to be president.

But ordeal or not, there were moments in the early insanity of our own brief campaign when we stepped high. A presidential campaign, with all the modern trappings, can be very tall clover indeed, even for those with only slightly arrested emotional development.

As Church finished his declaration of candidacy at Idaho City, the Secret Service rather dramatically drifted out of the crowd and slipped in around us. Suddenly we were in another world. For the next two and a half months (and again briefly while Carter considered Church for the vice presidency at the New York convention), the Secret Service accompanied our candidate 24 hours a day. Wherever he was—at home, in a hotel, in his office, on the Senate floor, or even in the bathroom—the Secret Service was just outside the door. They formed a little ring around him pushing him through a crowd. They were at his side as he strolled down a street. They raced him down the corridor while he rushed to make a vote on the Senate floor. And of course, as he addressed an audience, they were scattered throughout the room, with a couple of their number behind him on the stage, their eyes sweeping the crowd.

Church may have required protection more than most presidential contenders that year. He had led two inflammatory investigations. There was his probe of the CIA and the FBI, with vile mail, including some death threats, pouring into the office. And there were his revelations about the bribery of foreign governments by American multinational corporations, which had prompted one Japanese extremist to call a press conference in Tokyo to announce he would kill Frank Church. For good measure, the multinational inquiry had revealed that Arab states had a blacklist of American businesses who sold goods to Israel. It occurred to me at the time that there were a few cranky Arab terrorists running around the world.

I and others on the staff tried to persuade Church to let us see what we could do to bring the Secret Service aboard a few weeks early. But he would have none of it. It was partly the usual fatalistic streak in a candidate. But I think it was also the realization that, if lightning did strike and he made it to the White House, those few weeks would be the last in his life without the Secret Service hovering in the background.

Nonetheless, once the agents fell in behind him, he adjusted instantly. He acted like there had always been bodyguards strolling around his backyard at night. Indeed, he and all the rest of us came to enjoy the company of the agents. They were an intelligent, witty, and gregarious group. The Churches and the agents—who seemed wary at first of the man who had stuck it to their brother intelligence agencies—grew genuinely fond of each other. Bethine mothered them as mercilessly as anyone else. And though they were studiously apolitical in public, more than one agent wore a Church button beneath his lapel.

Early in the campaign, when we still traveled by commercial airliner, it was the usual practice to put the Churches in the very front seats, with an agent across the aisle and a row of agents and staff in the seats behind them on either side of the aisle—a buffer against menacing cranks. I sometimes sat with the agents in the row behind the Churches, chatting with the armed men on either side of me and with my feet on the strange, long, flat suitcase containing, I discovered later, a sniper rifle.

We learned, as did all candidates that year, that the Secret Service could inadvertently make it possible for a beginning candidate to lease his own plane sooner than would otherwise have been the case. We could charge each agent first-class rates, as well as any reporters along for the ride. In combination with what we would have spent anyway on the Churches and staff for commercial flights, it made charters possible that much earlier. And of course, with charters, you are no longer at the mercy of airline schedules. It becomes possible to take maximum advantage of the candidate's waking hours.

The Secret Service also solved ground transportation problems for the candidate and his wife. The government supplied the automobile wherever the Churches went, for the simple reason that the agents needed a car fully equipped with communications gear, which candidates don't ordinarily have. All we had to do was present the Secret Service with Church's schedule and there would always be a car available to take him wherever he was going whenever it was time to go. The staff car was the only ground transportation expense to the campaign.

Secret Service protection produced another inadvertent advantage to all presidential campaigns: It gave the nobody candidates a little more credibility than their chances warranted. If a candidate strolls into a room with his wife and one aide, that is one thing. But when he sweeps into the room, ringed by a dozen imposing government body guards, that is dramatic. Somebody important has entered—a candidate for President of the United States!

But there were limits to what the agents could do. They were not authorized to protect Bethine, though I doubt as big, strong friends they would have stood by if someone had made a move at her.

And they were not authorized to carry a candidate's luggage. One afternoon a few days into the campaign, Church took a rest break at the home of a relative in Los Angeles. When it came time to leave, the hulking agents stood by as the scrawny press secretary fetched a half dozen heavy suitcases from a second-story bedroom. Ernie Olsson, the head of our detail, explained why: "If we have a dozen agents on a candidate, and one of them is carrying luggage, that means either that we needed only 11 agents to protect him and the twelfth is a waste of the taxpayers' money, or that we have one less man watching the candidate than is needed, and we are therefore placing him in danger."

I couldn't argue with that explanation. But I was wishing that afternoon that somebody would explain to me why Bethine had to stuff so damn many heavy things in the suitcases.

*   *   *

After Church's announcement at Idaho City, we climbed into a Secret Service motorcade and, with the crowd still waving, swept away down the mountain highway to Boise Airport. It was small potatoes at first, but I was suddenly very much aware that I was inside a presidential campaign. The Churches, their son Forrest, two agents, and I boarded a Lear jet and headed for Portland, Oregon. I was flying high that day. There I was in an executive jet, drinking the coffee passed back to me by a Secret Service agent, alternately discussing strategy with a presidential candidate and dictating letters to my personal secretary. (I forgot to turn on the record button.) On our right wing was another jet load of Secret Service agents, keeping us in sight and, it almost seemed, watching out for any Russian fighter planes intent on stopping the probable president who would give those commie bastards such a hard time when he took office.

Portland Airport, in the largest city of that crucial primary state, produced our first big airport crowd. As Church, in a cocoon of agents, walked through the airport lobby, I led the way, carrying two briefcases decorated with Church bumper stickers, letting the crowd know who was coming. The television cameras took it all in, the crowd applauded, and a senior citizen band serenaded one of its favorite senators, the chairman of the Senate Committee on Aging.

Suddenly an agent grabbed the wrist of a man rapidly approaching Church with his hand on what looked like a holster. I froze. Agents descended on the man.

It was a tool holster, holding a pair of pliers. With apologies and then a quick handshake from the candidate, the agents released the startled man.

(After a time, almost everyone, except the Secret Service, became as fatalistic as the senator, rarely thinking about the human time bombs in the shadows of modern American politics. But it always made me a little itchy as we passed with the senator through those hotel kitchens and back corridors that were the common access to banquet platforms. They all reminded me of the one where Bobby Kennedy was murdered. Bethine confessed similar thoughts.)

Church gave a quick airport speech and press conference at Portland and we flew on to Los Angeles for a fund-raising party with show business notables. It was early evening of the first day. We were already in our third state.

The Hollywood party produced the first problem for the press secretary. Most of the stars present were already committed to other candidates. But they had come to have a look at the latest contender anyway. With the new $1,000 contribution limit, and with so many of the guests only rubbernecking, we wouldn't raise enough money that night to pay the rent on the Lear jet. All we could hope to get out of the evening was television time, and an ABC crew was present. But our host didn't want the notables bothered by tacky television cameras, and I couldn't talk him out of it. Church had to intervene, persuading him to admit the cameras that might give the candidate some national exposure. Our host wanted a private party. Our candidate wanted to get elected president.

With the objections finally swept aside, the cameras captured Church with the stars present—Dennis Weaver, Ed Asner, Steve Lawrence and Eydie Gorme, and Milton Berle, among others. I took it as encouraging when, after Church's speech, both Uncle Miltie and the bartender snatched campaign buttons from my lapel.

I don't know whether Milton Berle was with us all the way or just being friendly in the excitement of the moment, but it is a strange union that takes place between political and show business stars in an election year. There is often a kind of mutual marveling among political and entertainment personalities. The same senator or governor who is awed at meeting a star doesn't always realize that the star is equally awed. The politicians and the stars need each other. Theirs is a symbiotic relationship. The stars draw crowds and television cameras to the politicians. The politicians fulfill some yearning for substance in the stars.

There was always a small dither in Church's Senate office when a movie or television notable dropped by. Some were more popular than others. Two of the coldest fish who ever entered that office were Jane Fonda and her then-husband Tom Hayden. Maybe they were just having a hard decade and were normally affable as all get out. But on that particular day, they gave the secretaries frostbite. However, most of the stars ingratiated themselves. And some caused quite a stir.

Paul Newman was in town on one occasion in those years before he began accepting more mature character parts. He created excitement all day long without even entering the office. Church was due that night at a party with Newman. The secretaries joked that they were going to crash the affair.

"Senator," I said that afternoon, "it's cruel not to find a way to take the secretaries to the Paul Newman party."

"What is there about him, anyway?" Church asked. "He's a very engaging man, but what is it that women see in him? He's just a little, short, middle-aged man."

"I don't know either, Senator, but they always mention something about his blue eyes."

"Yes, isn't that strange," Church said.

Newman was a ripple compared with the day Robert Redford was due in the office to discuss with Church their mutual attachment to conservation causes. The secretaries and female aides in our office were mature young women of considerably-above-average intelligence. But they went bananas. One 30-year-old woman marched up to my desk and informed me she was trading desks with me for the day because I had a view of the waiting room where Redford would enter and she didn't.

"Move!" she said menacingly.

I moved.

Redford was overdue. Little work was done while the women in our office peered around corners and gasped each time the door opened. In a vicious excess, I slipped out the side door and popped in the front door, quickly, in the grand manner of a star.

They tensed as I entered—and then lashed me with indelicate language when they realized they had been duped. I was warned not to do that again.

"How would you like it if you were expecting Robert Redford and nothing but you walked in?" one of them scolded.

It wasn't just our office that was disoriented that day. Up and down the long corridor in that wing of the Senate Office Building coveys of secretaries stood vigil in the hallway, waiting for HIM! They were waiting again later as he left.

I should include something about what Redford was like, but I never met the guy. Pushed out of my desk and stuck in the back room, I didn't get a look at whatever it was that walked in that day. But if they find a way to bottle it, you could finance a campaign with the proceeds.

*   *   *

My first night of the campaign, I entered another new world— tucked away in my bed with Secret Service agents stationed outside my door. The candidate and his wife were usually stashed in a secure room at the end of the hotel hallway, with the personal staff in adjoining rooms, serving as an added buffer against the baddies. A key was in the lock on the candidate's door at all times, for quick entry in case of emergency. For good measure, there was always, wherever the candidate slept, an ominous black telephone on the stand beside his bed. It was an alarm. No dialing necessary. If a person so much as lifted the receiver, the agents charged into the bedroom without knocking. A couple of times the phone was accidentally knocked off its cradle. Bethine Church teased the red-faced agents standing over the bed, asking them if they wondered how it might have happened.

For reasons I never learned, there was also a key in the staff door—the room occupied by Administrative Assistant Mike Wetherell, and occasionally also by me. I assume that key was for quick access to aides in case more help was needed in a real crunch.

But there are certain things you don't think about until later. I didn't ask. And the agents never volunteered the reason.

Before bed, we often kept the doors open to the Churches' room and to our room, wandering back and forth. Bethine would come into our quarters to watch a different network on our television set, or we would go into the Church room to use the extra telephones. With the door open to my room, I could glance up from my work and watch the agents stationed in the hallway throughout the night. The agents alternated in modest shifts of less than an hour each. But it was still impressive that, no matter how late I glanced out at the agent I never saw one with his eyes glazed with boredom. Those eyes were invariably on full alert, covering the hallway.

*   *   *

Church went into the May 11 Nebraska primary the hard way—without a prayer. He was almost blanked out of the national media. Carter had been on all three network newscasts every night for weeks, Church only rarely. Our workers kept running into Nebraskans who said they would vote for Church, "if I thought he had a chance." The networks kept telling them that he didn't. And the day before the Nebraska primary, both *Time* and *Newsweek* had Carter on the cover. With few exceptions, the national press didn't send reporters to Nebraska; to them, it was clear who was going to win. Indeed, most of them scoffed at the thought that Church might defeat Carter in Nebraska.

Carter also scoffed. Except for one perfunctory visit, he looked ahead to other primaries.

By contrast, the Church organization put all it had left into Nebraska and then some. Church mortgaged his home to buy television and radio time. And we almost emptied national headquarters. Most of our D.C. workers were pulled off their desks and sent into Nebraska. If we didn't win there, they wouldn't be needed after May 11 anyway. We provided each of them with $10 per day, leaving it up to them to find room and board for that figure. One contingent, by crowding together and sleeping on the floor of a single upstairs room, found housing for $1 per day each. But it was sometimes a little noisy at night. Those nice young ladies in the downstairs apartments turned out to be hookers. A bawdy house and Church camp all in the same building.

Meanwhile, Church spent most of the last week and a half dazzling the Nebraska electorate with his old-school, stem-winding, political-stump oratory. He filled those voters with his own outrage at the malfunctions in American foreign and domestic policy. The number two man on the Senate Foreign Relations Committee told them that most of America's troubles—including domestic headaches—stemmed from a faulty foreign policy. "There is nothing foreign about foreign policy," he said. Foreign policy is a dominant force in domestic affairs, affecting everything from the price of gasoline to the price of wheat to the price of a pointless war in distant Indochina, he told them.

But his biggest applause line was aimed at Midwest fury over administration embargoes on the export of grain and at general isolationist unease over American armaments sales to belligerents on both sides of confrontations around the world. He questioned the cost and the morality of such a policy. And then, eyes flashing with anger, "I say America should be the breadbasket of the world and not the global cannon factory." It always brought down the house, and Carter appropriated the line for his fall campaign against Jerry Ford.

Church's own strange blend of liberalism and populist isolationism struck a Nebraska nerve. And Carter struck out. Church won the May 11 primary by only a handful of votes, but it caught almost everyone by surprise. Nebraska was a small thunderclap. Nebraska blurred Church's can't-win disadvantage. David had toppled Goliath. It made good copy in the national media for several days. A few more reporters began trailing the Church campaign. They thought Nebraska was probably a fluke, but maybe this guy had something that they should keep an eye on.

Later that year, Jimmy Carter's son, Jack, told me during a campaign visit to Idaho, "We underestimated Frank Church in Nebraska, and it gave us fits the rest of the way."

And so it did. The Carter runaway slowed. There was a little crack in his credibility.

The crack widened the following Tuesday, May 18, when Jerry Brown clobbered Carter in Maryland and Mo Udall came within an inch of winning in Michigan where Carter had once been far ahead. It was beginning to sink in with the press that Carter might not do so well when not running against the large field, now gone, which had fragmented the non-Carter vote in the early innings. But of course, even in losing, Carter continued to add to his bulging total.

On May 25, two weeks after Nebraska and one week after Carter's loss to Brown in Maryland, Carter suffered another setback in the momentum game. But he minimized the damage with a clever PR move.

There were six primaries that day. Carter lacked serious opposition in three of them—Tennessee, Kentucky and Arkansas—so they were no test of voter appeal. Brown was unbeatable in a fourth primary—Nevada—with its daily bombardment by the California media. Church was unbeatable in a fifth primary—his home state of Idaho. The only significant test that day was in Oregon. Church, Carter, and Brown slugged it out for most of the week preceding the vote.

Church won rather massively. But Carter created a distraction. Realizing late in the game that he might lose Oregon, he was in New York the night the returns came in. Rather than appearing on television from Oregon to concede another defeat, he appeared at a New York news conference to announce another triumph—three victories that day out of six primaries, more than anyone else. Most of the eastern press bought it.

Nonetheless, it didn't hurt Church's growing credibility to win the big one. Carter was so far ahead on delegates that hardly anyone thought Church would win the nomination. But Oregon convinced some reporters that it was at least theoretically possible. The late, late strategy, hopeless or not, remained on schedule.

However, by then we were approaching what was supposed to be our big finish in Jerry Brown's California. And our campaign was beginning to get spread a little thin. The week before California, Church was entered simultaneously in Montana and Rhode Island. To make matters worse, we got too big for our britches and decided to go not only for California, but also for Ohio on that same final day of the primary season. That was asking for it.

On June 1, the voters of South Dakota, Montana, and Rhode Island were to vote for their presidential preferences. We were leaving South Dakota to Mo Udall for a one-on-one shot against Carter. (Udall stayed out of Nebraska and Oregon. And we agreed to stay out of New Jersey and South Dakota, which we couldn't have handled anyway, for all the good it did Udall.) Church hoped for and needed a double in Montana and Rhode Island—demonstrating western and eastern appeal on the same day and continuing his string. At that point, it shouldn't have been too difficult. Neighboring Montana, so much like Idaho, had turned heavily toward Church almost from his first campaign visit. Little time was required in that state. But Church also had an opening in Rhode Island. No two people were more insistent that Frank Church run for president than Rhode Island Senator Claiborne Pell and Rhode Island Congressman Edward Beard. Together, they constituted half that small state's congressional delegation. Both men pulled out all stops campaigning for Church. Moreover, Church was such a skyrocket on the stump that he could carry almost any small state with the dramatics of his style. That's how he won Nebraska. But he didn't get his full quota of appearances in Rhode Island. We took him away from that state for events in impossible Ohio. To make matters worse, Jerry Brown grafted himself to an "uncommitted" slate in Rhode Island and spent several days there campaigning in his own splashy style.

Udall lost South Dakota. Church defeated Carter in Montana by more than two to one. But in Rhode Island, the people voting for Jerry Brown and the people voting unwittingly for Brown when they sincerely voted for what they thought was an uncommitted slate, gave Brown what was heralded as a victory. The Brown/uncommitted slate attracted 19,035 votes in an astonishingly low turnout. Carter had 18,237, and Church 16,423. Our candidate simply hadn't made himself known to enough voters.

And so, instead of a double victory on top of the Nebraska and Oregon wins, Church lost his first head-on meeting with Carter, breaking the string. And suddenly, only a week away, our little one-horse, pathetically funded campaign faced two killing races on the same day in the huge-population states of California and Ohio. Church was smothered in both states.

It would have happened anyway, but the margin was magnified by a strep throat that laid Church low for one day in California, and by the collapse of the Teton Dam in Idaho. The latter cost

Church a day in Ohio when he flew home to be with his stricken people, some of whom lost more than a mere election. But even without those twin misfortunes, a week was far too little time to give a late-blooming candidate sufficient exposure before two such massive electorates.

Some thought we should have conceded Brown his home state and gone full tilt into Ohio. But hindsight has tempted me to believe we should have taken a far crazier gamble: I think we should have skipped Ohio and gone straight into Jerry Brown's teeth in California. Any seasoned politician would have told you that was insane. But we had nothing to lose at that point. And there was, I learned, an outside chance of another miracle.

I spent the final two weeks of the primary season marauding for publicity in California and I made two discoveries there that cast doubt on the supposition that Jerry Brown was utterly unbeatable.

A poll, brandished all year by the national press as proof of Brown's supposedly incredible strength, was a gross oversimplification. The standard interpretation of the poll was that it showed Brown with a popularity in California of 85 percent!

Brown was popular all right. More than 50 percent of his constituents had answered flatly that he was doing a "good" job. But the 85 percent popularity figure also included those who thought Brown was doing only a "fair" job. In politics, fair isn't exactly passionate approval. Or in any other realm:

> "How was the movie?"
> "Fair."
> "How is the pot roast, dear?"
> "Fair."
> "What kind of governor is Jerry Brown?"
> "Fair."

Moreover, the 85 percent figure dated back to before Brown, the celebrated anti-politician, had revealed a rather common streak of raw political ambition by announcing for President of the United States halfway through his first term at the tender age of 38. That turned off some voters. And that was my second discovery. I kept running into Californians who told me what a fine young governor they thought Brown was. But they didn't think he was ready for the presidency. They thought he was getting ahead of himself, trying for the White House before mastering the job he had. Many of his own supporters were against his running for president. That was exploitable.

Forgive an old general for rehashing these battles, but Church should have gone into California with his standard personality blitz, speaking directly to the point that the governor was not only Brown, but a bit green as well. Church could have damned the young governor with the faint praise of what a promising young governor he was, but saying bluntly how cheeky it was of him to strike out so soon for the White House. Brown would have plenty of time to run for president. What was his all-fired hurry?

As a matter of fact, Church had tried such lines in several California appearances earlier in the year. He had noted that some candidates appeared a trifle eager to start at the top, whereas he had prepared himself for the presidency with two decades of seasoning in national and international affairs. "The White House is no place for on-the-job training," Church observed pointedly. The California audiences seemed receptive.

If Church had skipped Ohio, focused on California, and concentrated on Brown's weakness, I am convinced he would have finished at least second in that state, ahead of Carter, rather than the miserable third he eventually ran. That probably wouldn't have been enough, though we could have made much of a second place finish. Carter did. Carter was able to say that, naturally, no one could expect to beat Brown in his home state, but the next best thing had been accomplished. We could have done the same thing.

And if the wildest longshot of all had paid off—if Church had defeated Brown in California—it would have stunned the nation. It could have denied Carter that stampede of delegates that took place the day after the June 8 primaries in Ohio and California. It might have kept the delegates hanging loose going into the convention.

Might. Maybe. Perhaps. If only. That's all in the iffy land of what might have been where all the losing politicians live. Church probably lost the nomination the day he announced—so deep into the presidential year that it was already much too late and the odds far too great to try.

My musings on Church's chances involve only his prospects for making it to the White House, not mine. I had decided against joining him there even if he had won. I had served notice—before the Nebraska primary—that, win or lose, I would leave the campaign after the final contests in California and Ohio. That was a natural breaking point if he was still in the race. The national campaign headquarters had become such a fractious and unpleasant place that I was more convinced than when I had last tried to quit the year before that the life of a political aide was not for me. My newspaper had called early in 1976, saying if I didn't intend to come to my senses and get myself back to Idaho, they would have no choice but to fill my job.

I told National Chairman Carl Burke as he left for the push in Nebraska that I would return to Idaho in mid-June. When Church won Nebraska the next week, I repeated my resignation, lest Burke think it had been based on my expectation that the candidate would be finished after Nebraska anyway.

I did rather expect Church to lose Nebraska. Worse, there were times when, for my sake, I almost hoped he would. That is when the thought occurred to me that nobody wins a presidential nomination; the people working on the losing campaigns sober up in time and give the election away.

It dawned on me that, when the campaign ended, so would my stay in Washington. The sooner Frank Church was blown out of the contest, the sooner I could return home.

Treason?

Perhaps. But the nonsense was mounting daily in national headquarters. Nasty infighting had begun. And in Idaho, it was spring; my peaceful garden beckoned.

Surely I was not alone among presidential campaign workers in thinking such seditious thoughts. Indeed, I suspect that any sane campaign worker, after months of going without sleep and fighting the infantile pecking-order wars within a national campaign staff, comes to the same rude realization that I did: If Church went all the way to the White House, there would be no end to the typical backstabbing of political intramurals for the next eight years. Any sane person coming to that conclusion begins finding ways, perhaps only subconsciously, to throw the campaign. Who wants eight years of that bull? So it may be the worst staff that wins—the staff that fails in every effort to throw the election.

By that standard, the ablest staff in the 1976 campaign was that skillful team that worked for Senator Birch Bayh. Those clever devils blew him right out of the first primary and then went happily home to Indiana.

The Church campaign was somewhere in the middle range. We managed a low enough level of general competence to make certain that Church didn't become a front-runner. But we were weak on control of the candidate. He kept breaking free from headquarters and—though I know he had his own reservations about eight years in the White House—gave into his instincts as a campaigner and dazzled his way to several dangerous victories. I kept thinking, first after Nebraska and then after Oregon, "If he doesn't knock that off, we're all going to end up doing time in the White House."

Most of the year, the poor Carter people couldn't do anything wrong. It was pathetic. Of course, they had their moments. Getting Carter to endorse the "ethnic purity" of neighborhoods, and topping that with a stand against "black intrusion" into white communities was a masterstroke. It almost cost Carter his crucial support among blacks. But the Carter people didn't keep an eye on their candidate. The next thing you know he was apologizing for the remarks, actually admitting a mistake, which of course endeared him to the electorate. That put him—and his aides—right back on the trail to the White House, the poor unfortunate boobs.

And the White House is precisely where Carter and his incompetent Georgians found themselves at the end of their campaign—not back home fishing, not sitting in the southern sun drinking beer and belching their cares away, but beating their butts off seven days a week in Washington's biggest stress factory.

They had it rough enough in that role without my rubbing it in after all these years. But candor compels me to note that, to the victor belong the toils.

And losing means never having to say good-bye to Idaho.

Chapter Ten
The Best of the Washington Press

In the history of journalism, there have been no four forces more likely to send a chill through a public figure than the merciless paparazzi of Rome, the teeming press battalions of Tokyo, the relentless waves of Washington reporters, or Rush Limbaugh on a really snotty day.

I have never had to deal with Limbaugh or with the paparazzi, and I regret that because I enjoy emotional people. But Washington reporters were my daily routine. And I encountered the Tokyo press corps on one occasion. Frank Church, as chairman of the Senate Subcommittee on Multinational Corporations, had revealed that Lockheed had slipped money under the table to high-level Japanese politicians. It created a Japanese Watergate. Frank Church became a principal figure in that Japanese melodrama.

When word of the scandal hit Japan, the leaders of the Japanese party in power and the leaders of the opposition parties announced separately that they were heading directly for Washington to confer with Senator Church. Worse, the word came to me that planeloads of Tokyo reporters were on the way. I felt like Pearl Harbor.

It is no mystery to a reporter why the Tokyo press corps has a reputation for aggressiveness. There are so many reporters in that city. Tokyo has a population of about 11 million people, and at last count, there were something like 12 million daily newspapers, each with hundreds of reporters. The competition is fierce. So are the reporters. Or at least that was what I had been told by knowledgeable Washington reporters kind enough to warn me.

For several days, Church's assistant press secretary Don Watkins and I, plus members of the subcommittee staff, were flooded with questions from the first waves of Tokyo reporters to arrive in Washington. They all wanted private interviews with

Church, which was impossible because there were so many of them. To my surprise, they took no for an answer. Exceedingly polite, they gave us no trouble at all when we told them Church lacked the time for so many interviews. However, Jerry Levinson, chief counsel to the subcommittee, answered a knock at his front door one night and found himself standing in floodlights, with microphones thrust in his face and shadowy figures calling out questions in Japanese accents.

The morning the Japanese political leaders were due to meet with Church, I stuck my head into the hallway and drew in my breath. Half of Tokyo was out there, armed with cameras. The sessions with Church were to be private, but the Japanese television reporters, and several from the United States, wanted a "silent filming opportunity." Silent filming is the method used to give the media pictures to illustrate a hearing or a meeting when that hearing or meeting isn't open to the press. You've seen it often when heads of state visit the White House. Before the president huddles privately with the foreign leader, the cameras are invited into the room for pictures of the two sitting together exchanging small talk. After a few minutes, the cameras are shooed from the room and the two heads of state go on with their discussion. The television news that night carries footage of the president and the foreign leader seated together, smiling and chatting, while a correspondent's voice tells you what happened:

> President Clinton met today at the White House with Prince Rainier of Monaco to discuss the sale of jet fighters to the tiny principality to protect its crap tables from Las Vegas goons.

The first time I handled a silent filming session I didn't know the ropes. William Colby, then head of the Central Intelligence Agency, was meeting privately with Church. I invited the camera crews in beforehand and they began filming. They continued filming for some time. Church and Colby were running out of small talk, beginning to look irritated and finally shooting dirty looks at me.

Daniel Schorr of CBS (now with National Public Radio) slipped up beside me. "You're supposed to call a halt," he counseled the green press secretary. "If you don't stop them, they'll film all morning."

"Thank you very much, gentlemen," I called out, using the standard time's-up signal.

"Just a few more seconds," a cameraman called back, continuing to grind away as Church and Colby began to fidget.

After calling out, "Thank you very much" a couple more times, the film crews finally condescended to leave and let Church and Colby get on with their business.

I remembered that incident as I peered into the hallway at all those Japanese reporters. I had heard horror stories about them swooping down in mobs and filming people to death. They were so hungry for the story of their tarnished government that I wondered how I would get them out of the room once they were admitted. Nonetheless, as Church and the ruling party leaders seated themselves, I opened the door and called out into the hall, "Gentlemen, you are welcome for two minutes of silent filming."

(I actually planned to give them about five minutes, but from what I had heard, I would be lucky to push them out in 10.)

The Japanese reporters and photographers, as well as a few of their American colleagues, rolled into Church's private office. They moved in waves around the dignitaries, trying for every angle.

I knew I was wasting my breath, but after precisely two minutes, I called out, "Thank you very much, gentlemen."

They all stopped instantly, turned crisply on their heels, and marched out of the office, sweeping a couple of reluctant American cameramen along with them. The last Japanese photographer to leave stopped for an instant, gave me a slight bow of his head, said "Thank you," and gently closed the door behind him.

I was stunned.

Half an hour later, when the opposition party leaders sat down with Church the same thing happened.

"Thank you very much, gentlemen," I barked with more authority, feeling the MacArthur welling up in me. Again, they promptly turned and marched from the room, sweeping several profane Americans along with them.

Washington reporters, like the Japanese that day, aren't ordinarily as difficult to deal with as their reputation would indicate—if you don't cross them. If you're somebody like Ron Ziegler, Richard Nixon's press secretary, peddling poppycock, they'll get you for that. But if you follow a few simple rules, such as being considerate of their needs and talking out of one side of your face at a time, you'll get along rather well—providing you're representing a politician they tend to trust.

But of course, that's a generalization. There are reporters and then there are reporters. There are reporters who concede a press secretary a certain amount of integrity, until such time as they are proven wrong. And there are terribly superior reporters who practice the cockroach theory of journalism—all politicians and press secretaries are cockroaches who must be stepped on at every opportunity.

A person might expect the most vile and unreasonable reporters would be in Washington where the competition is keenest and where they might be presumed to have climbed over colleagues to reach the top of the heap. Somewhat the reverse is true. It is often cream that rises to the top. There is a saying in the newspaper business that, among politicians, the bigger they are, the easier they are to deal with. That means you can stop a senator or a governor on the street for a few words, but you need an appointment to see a county clerk.

Most of the top reporters in Washington are equally easy to work with.

But beware the 23-year-old reporter covering the statehouse for a newspaper of 30,000 circulation. Like any puppy, he'll nip you with his sharp little teeth if you let him. He wonders whether he has sufficient respect. He has something to prove. And he's heard that press secretaries are professional liars, so he'll adopt a nasty tone just to show you he's not some hayseed who can be seduced by a whore like you. There is a direct correlation between a lack of seasoning and a lack of consideration.

Beyond a few beginners in the boondocks, about the only people I ever had much trouble with were young wire service reporters in Washington and some network radio people, mostly from New York. The veterans on the wire services were easy to work with. But the wires also brought in promising young reporters at the bottom of the Washington ladder. Some of the beginners tended to strut and posture and snarl a little to obscure how scared they were.

And some of the radio troops—particularly those serving weekend and late-night stints—appeared to be people within reach of the top who felt they needed just one more scalp to get there. They could be as pushy as a Bible salesman with a quota and sometimes a trifle unethical. I received a call one night about 2 a.m. in which an NBC reporter in New York began asking me questions about the Church Committee's investigation of the Central Intelligence Agency. I declined his invitation to be interviewed on tape. It was my job to bring attention to Frank Church, not to me. But I told him he could feel free to attribute the information to the senator because everything I could tell him would only be repeating what I had heard Church say on the subject. He agreed that would do nicely and proceeded to ask his questions. I noticed not far into the interview that each time I said something, the volume dropped slightly on the telephone—an indication he was recording my words.

"I feel I should warn you," I finally said in a husky, conspiratorial voice, "that this call is being recorded—not by you, I'm sure, because that would be unethical, and I know you would never do anything that tacky. It must be the CIA. Be very careful what you say, comrade."

"Oh, I thought I mentioned I would be taping you," he fibbed. We terminated the interview.

Another night, an NBC radio reporter called long after midnight wanting Church's home number for a quick quote. It was nothing urgent.

"I'm sorry," I said. "He's asleep now."

"That's OK," the reporter answered cheerfully, "I'll only wake him for a couple of minutes."

I thanked him for being so considerate but declined on behalf of the senator.

There was one other occasion, so traumatic I still get a sour stomach just thinking about it, when I did call Church and get him out of bed.

I had been shaken awake myself about 5 a.m. Standing over my bed in his underwear was Don Watkins, Church's assistant press secretary. (I was staying then with the Watkins family.) His face was lined with anguish. I knew instantly that something was dreadfully wrong.

Watkins had awakened in a nervous sweat two hours before, pretty sure he had neglected to mention to Church that the senator was scheduled that morning on ABC television's morning news show for a live network interview. Watkins had stewed alone in the

night, gradually digesting his own stomach, for as long as he felt
he dared before ending my sleep. When he gave me the dreadful
news, I jumped out of bed, also in my underwear (country boys
strangle in pajamas), and we rushed downstairs to the telephone.
We called Tommy Ward, Church's personal secretary and the
keeper of his schedule.

No, she hadn't told Church about the appearance. Naturally,
she assumed one of the press secretaries might have condescended
to let the senator know he was appearing that morning on network television. And she cautioned us, as if we didn't know,
that he wasn't going to be too crazy about the idea. Church liked
more warning on a 7 a.m. network appearance than two hours.
He was a little eccentric that way. Moreover, he was exhausted
from campaigning. This was to be his first chance in weeks to
sleep in.

I trembled as I made the call to Church. I often tremble when
calling senators from a chilly room in my underwear. His groggy
baritone came on the line and I inquired casually if he remembered
being due on network television in two hours.

There was a hateful silence on the other end.

"How could this happen?" he finally gurgled.

"Well, senator," I stammered, "I'm . . . I'm not quite sure,
but . . ."

I couldn't think of what to say next. And Church just left me
hanging there, groping for words.

In a supreme act of courage, Watkins grabbed the phone, saying it was all his fault and that he would consider it a personal favor
if Church would appear on network television that morning.

Church said he would consider it a personal favor if Watkins
and I would inform ABC that he wouldn't be appearing on their
wonderful network that morning and if we made it clear whose
fault it was. He also gave us to understand he would consider it the
greatest personal favor of all if we strangled each other. And then
he hung up.

"Jesus," Watkins said, "he's really mad."

For a moment we both just stood there in our underwear taking heartsick drags on sawdust cigarettes. Finally, Watkins, who
had made all the arrangements with an ABC producer, sighed a
melancholy sigh and picked up the telephone to call ABC.

I couldn't hear the other end of the conversation, but Watkins said stunning things like, "Well, I certainly don't blame you for being angry."

And then he said something that sent another chill through me: "All right. I owe you that. I'll call him back and try one more time."

He got lucky. Bethine answered. She said that, in all his years in the Senate, she had never seen her husband so angry over something an aide had done. But she felt sorry for us. She would calm down her furious husband and talk him into showing up for the interview.

Watkins, heaping the blessings of three religions on her dear head, hung up and quickly called ABC with assurances the senator would be there after all.

And then we collapsed into the nearest chairs.

After a few minutes of silence, I tried to comfort him: "It's all right, Don. He probably couldn't get back to sleep now anyway," I said, trying to make a little joke.

Watkins just glared at me.

In the year and a half I was with Church, I never saw him sharper in a television interview than he was that morning. It must have been the adrenaline.

*   *   *

During an early campaign swing through California, Church paid a courtesy call on one of his opponents, Governor Jerry Brown. Brown had been wowing environmentalists across the nation by breaking with the political tradition of constantly promising the people an ever-richer and more materialistic life. He called upon his California constituents to recognize that they must accept less of life in the future. He warned that we must all, in an era of vanishing resources, "lower our expectations." It had become almost the motto of his administration.

Church had quipped during several press conferences earlier that day that, "I have come to California to lower Jerry Brown's expectations." As we arrived for what would be a joint press conference, the Sacramento press corps was anxious to get Brown's reaction. Brown and Church huddled privately for a few minutes and then seated themselves on a comfortable couch in one corner of the governor's office. The reporters filed in.

"Governor," said the first questioner, "Senator Church said today that he has come to California to lower your expectations."

"What!" Brown said in mock outrage, his dark eyes dancing with Irish humor. "Did you say that, Frank? Why didn't you tell me you said that?"

"Yes, Jerry, that's what I said," Church answered good-naturedly, "and what I mean by that is that you are such an outstanding governor that the people of California must surely want to keep you on the job so you can get some experience before running for president some day."

Brown answered, still amused, that though he had been in office only a year and a half, he had been working 14-hour days, seven days a week, and that had given him more experience than most governors acquire in four years. He threw in the needle that senators, for instance, are experienced at administering only a few dozen staff members, whereas he had been running a state government much larger and more complex than all but a handful of the world's nations.

It was back and forth like that for several minutes. Church would take a verbal poke at Brown, and Brown's eyes would light up, seeming to say, "Nice shot, Frank."

Brown would then counter, and Church would twinkle, almost the proud professor enjoying a bright new mind holding its own against the veteran.

The reporters lapped it up and fed the combatants questions aimed at keeping them pitted against each other. Soon Church and Brown were virtually debating. It was good copy. But I looked at my watch and saw it was growing late. We couldn't let Church get any farther behind schedule. The press conference had to end.

In the Senate, by tradition, a press conference can be terminated by the senator, by a senior reporter, or by the press secretary. A press secretary can simply call out, "Thank you, ladies and gentlemen," or, more diplomatically, "We have time for one more question."

I thought we were running too late to be diplomatic.

"Thank you, ladies and gentlemen," I called out from the back of the room, and Brown and Church stood up to leave.

The office exploded in bellows: "Who said that?" screamed one livid reporter.

"Who's the son of a bitch who yelled, 'thank you'?" snarled another, racing around the room looking for someone to punch.

"Come on, goddam it, now who said that?" demanded the first reporter.

Church made his way toward the door with the dexterity of a combat veteran.

I had screwed up royally. It suddenly dawned on me, as a former statehouse reporter, that the state ground rules are generally different from the Senate. With governors and presidents, it is normally only the senior correspondent who can end a press conference, although he is usually told by the press secretary how much time the public official has to spare. It is a wise system, aimed at making certain a press secretary doesn't cut off the questioning just when the reporters have his client pinned. That's what they thought I had done. Worse, it was Brown's office and not my place to do anything.

I had to make good and not just sneak out, so I identified myself as the culprit. Most of the reporters were sane and merely annoyed. They just shook their heads and left. But four of their number couldn't let this insult to American journalism, this reflection on their manhood, go unpunished. They converged on me, all shouting at once and not wanting to hear any explanations.

"I'm sorry," I said, finally getting a word in, "but I'm accustomed to Washington . . ."

I was going to explain that, though it was no excuse, I had merely fallen into a Washington habit. But they thought I was starting to tell them that Washington ground rules are superior to Sacramento ground rules.

"This isn't Washington, you son of a bitch," interrupted one particularly furious reporter. "You can cram Washington. You're in Sacramento, and, by God, you'll play by our rules."

"That's right! Fuck Washington!" yelled another distinguished statehouse correspondent.

I tried again. I said, gently, that I should have known better because I had statehouse experience myself in Idaho. They exploded again, instantly assuming I was suggesting that Idaho also had a superior system to theirs.

"Fuck Idaho, too!" screamed the distinguished statehouse correspondent.

I was digging myself in deeper.

"Hall!" Church barked from the doorway in an uncharacteristically nasty command voice. "You're holding us up."

The reporters, startled, fell silent for a moment and I retreated to the skirts of my senator, getting out of the bear pit while the beasts were distracted. As soon as the door closed between me and them, the stern senator dissolved into laughter.

Thereafter, I never dealt with a local press corps without seeking out the senior reporter and learning the prevailing ground rules—before the press conference.

*   *   *

My most bizarre encounter with a provincial reporter was the fault of Bob Woodward and Carl Bernstein. Quite a few of the bizarre experiences politicians and press secretaries have had in recent years are the fault of Woodward and Bernstein. They not only helped bring down a corrupt government during Watergate, but they also created little media monsters all over America. A generation of young reporters arrived with dreams of following in their footsteps and becoming as tough as Woodward and Bernstein. The only problem is that the imitators sometimes get tough with people who are considerably less slippery and a good deal more honest than the principal slickers of the Nixon administration. Forgive me my vanity, but I have delusions of believing I belonged in that group of press secretaries who were more honorable than Nixon's hustlers.

Nonetheless, I was chatting on the telephone one afternoon with a young reporter from a small daily in Idaho. I had known him as an Idaho colleague and we were talking about my new job—how I liked Washington, that sort of thing. We got around to speculating whether Church would take the plunge and run for president. I said that, if I had to guess, and someone hadn't locked up the nomination by the time the senator had finished the intelligence investigation, I thought he would probably jump in. The reporter said that was his guess, too. And he asked me a couple more questions in that same vein.

Suddenly, among all that chit chat, he asked me what title I preferred to go by.

"You're not quoting me?" I asked. Church preferred that I get his name in the paper not mine—especially in Idaho.

"I certainly am," the reporter answered.

"I thought we were just chatting—for background."

"You didn't say anything about background," he snapped.

"I didn't know I had to. I thought it was obvious we were just shooting the breeze."

"You can't play that way," the grizzled, two-year veteran of the newspaper business instructed me, wondering if it was true that he resembled Bob Woodward. "You know I can't accept retroactive background."

I sighed and told him to let his conscience be his guide, which he did, giving me a lot of ink in Idaho the next day—and Church hardly any.

There was something about that term "retroactive background," that rang a bell. Suddenly I remembered: I had read the Woodward and Bernstein book, *All the President's Men,* only the month before. That night, I pulled it from the shelf, flipped a few pages and found the following passage:

> "You aren't quoting me?" Kissinger asked.
>
> Sure he was, Woodward said.
>
> "What!" Kissinger shouted. "I'm telling you what I said was for background."
>
> Woodward said they had made no such agreement.
>
> "I've tried to be honest and now you're going to penalize me," Kissinger said.
>
> No penalty intended, Woodward said, but he could not accept retroactive background.

I called the little devil back the next day and said, "I think I know where you got that business about retroactive background."

"Woodward and Bernstein," he said proudly.

"Now let me get this straight," I said. "Bill Hall, your former colleague from Idaho, is deserving of the same treatment as the members of the Nixon gang? As far as you're concerned, I'm just another Kissinger trying to cancel something I wish I hadn't said?"

He was kind enough to dispute that. And he said that, because he was now convinced I was sincerely ignorant of the big-time rules of Woodward, Bernstein, and guys like him, he would "let it go this time."

Damn Woodward and Bernstein anyway.

*   *   *

Surely there is no reporter in America with more contacts across the country than political writer David Broder of the *Washington Post*. I looked forward to meeting Broder when I moved to Washington, not just because he was so good at his job and a hero of mine, but also because I wanted to be able to hold my head up with Idaho politicians. Idaho is just one of 50 states, yet Broder has had contacts over the years from one end of Idaho to the other. During an election year, he would call them periodically to see what was going on, as he did similar sources in other states. Being called by Dave Broder became a status symbol in state politics.

He never called me. I was an editorial writer, specializing in politics, yet I never received a call from David Broder of the *Washington Post*. He routinely called party chairmen, legislators, behind-the-scenes operators, other reporters, probably even bartenders and barbers, if I know that man's unrelenting thoroughness.

But he never called me. I would be sitting in a cocktail lounge near the Statehouse in Boise with a pack of politicians and some subtle bastard would just happen to remark, "As I said to Broder on the phone today . . ."

"I don't agree with you," someone else would say. "I told Broder that . . ."

"What did you tell Broder?" someone would finally ask me.

"Oh, not much," I would say.

Broder could have wrecked my career if they had ever found out about his indifference to my observations. No politician would pay much attention to a political analyst who didn't get an occasional call from Dave Broder.

One political worker in Idaho became a bit of a pest about her Broder calls (and even an occasional letter, for God's sake). She was in the habit of repeating the calls verbatim to anyone who would listen. She got more calls from Broder than anyone else in Idaho and took to referring to him as "David."

"And so I said to David, 'Reagan will do well in Idaho,' and he said to me, in that cute, little-boy way of his, 'If you say Reagan's going to carry Idaho, he probably will.' And then I said . . ."

She's a dear heart, but Idaho politicians took to hiding in alleys when they saw her coming and the word was out that she had another cute-David story.

Broder has no idea that he does that to some people. He isn't a vicious person. Indeed, when I finally entered the ranks of those David Broder has talked with, he proved to be unusually considerate. He had heard through mutual friends that I was adjusting awkwardly to Washington and invited me to lunch shortly after my arrival. He even invited me to play with his Sunday morning tennis gang. I had to refuse because I have a tendency to hit myself in the right ankle while serving and could only have embarrassed myself. But I did talk with him frequently in Washington and had a drink with him on occasion along the campaign trail. So I can now sit around the table at Boise and drop stories about what Broder said to me one day over lunch while I was in the nation's capital.

(I wonder why he never calls me anymore.)

*   *   *

Columnist Jack Anderson practices an eccentric form of generosity. The first time I walked the celebrated muckraker to the Capitol for an interview with Church, he gave me one of his college lectures—arms waving, voice rising in outrage, and the purple prose of an accomplished scandal merchant pouring from his lips.

I thought he was a nut. I eventually realized that he feels some obligation to be on stage for people who meet him—like Bob Hope dropping one-liners at a golf tournament because it's expected of him. Jack doesn't want to disappoint anyone. They expect a muckraker; he gives them a muckraker.

Anderson and his co-columnist, Les Whitten, could strike terror in some press secretaries and politicians, but just as with many of Washington's celebrated press ogres, an honest office had nothing to fear from them.

Anderson and Whitten constantly kept tabs on everyone, including Church. A young Anderson-Whitten reporter would call our office and others on Capitol Hill almost every time there was a congressional recess. The legman wanted to know if Church was off on some free-loading, pointless foreign junket. After 18 years of finding Church ethically fit, and reinforcing that impression with periodic checks on his behavior, Anderson and Whitten never wrote anything more than mildly critical of the senator. Indeed, they frequently praised him in print. I was one press secretary in

Washington who could be told that Jack Anderson was calling without having a stroke.

As a small-town newspaperman, I was also partial to Anderson and Whitten because of a secret side they had that was typical of how big some big-time journalists can be. Across the country each year, there are usually several dozen obscure reporters who get hassled by legally frivolous, though sincerely apoplectic, lawsuits from local politicians. Occasionally they are ordered to jail on contempt of court citations from bush league judges who believe the First Amendment was all a horrible mistake. Anderson and Whitten were in the kindly habit of giving those small-time reporters moral support, both by telephone and in their national column.

As a consequence, there are a lot of small-time journalists around the country who think Jack Anderson and Les Whitten can walk on water. I am among them.

*   *   *

Perhaps the two most infuriating reporters in Washington during those years were two ogres still in fashion today—Rowland Evans and Robert Novak. And that's a compliment. It is their job to infuriate from the right just as it is the job of some liberal columnists to infuriate from the left. But Evans and Novak are better at their job than most.

Some reporters focus on hard-core corruption. Evans and Novak are after soft-core hypocrisy. Washington is their gold mine. They worked the classic good cop-bad cop routine and it may surprise some to learn that, during those years of the mid-1970s, Evans was the pompous heavy. Novak, the down-to-earth, straight reporter, tended to draw more out of politicians because he seemed to commiserate with them over what a son of a bitch Evans was.

It seems to me that they have switched rolls today. Evans has become the still-pompous but affable old twit and Novak has become the angry scourge of anything liberal.

But during the years of my dealing with them, Novak's questions were fair and straight down the middle. Evans threw screwballs. He spoke on the telephone in a supercilious tone meant to convey his conviction that the senator had surely been up to no good. He implied that he already had enough on the bounder to hang him and that he was merely calling, in the spirit of fair play, to give the victim a chance to offer some whining excuses. Of course, Evans was fishing for confirmation of some rumor. And he didn't make many friends that way, especially among those who had done nothing wrong and resented the pejorative style of questioning.

But to be candid about it, the prime reason behind the rather widespread hatred of Evans and Novak in Washington then and now has to do with the fact that they tend to specialize in puncturing liberal pomposity and hypocrisy. Washington, no matter what the party in power, is a liberal political community. Attacks on conservatives are regarded as justice triumphant. Attacks on equally seamy liberals are regarded as dirty pool. It is true that Evans and Novak tend to make mountains out of molehills on slow news days, but then so do the liberal critics of conservative targets.

Nonetheless, for all their cranky questioning and for all their inflation of minor foibles into pseudo-scandals, they do have their sources. They often get stories no one else is on to, partly because they are among the few working so hard on the side of the street where dwell the liberal sinners.

For instance, they came the closest of anyone to learning and reporting that Church was a lot more interested in a presidential campaign a good deal earlier than he publicly indicated. Several highly active volunteers around the country were putting together the bare bones of a presidential campaign long before Church became visible and admitted what was going on.

Evans called one day with a chilling question: Who, he wanted to know, was Tom Lantos.

Lantos was one of our deep-cover organizers in California. Lantos was trying to put together the beginning of an organization at a time Church was saying he didn't know whether he'd run for president or not.

Somehow Evans and Novak got wind of it. They had caught Frank Church in a hypocritical posture—pounding his chest over how faithful he was to his intelligence investigation, while actually making some preparations for a campaign he had already decided to enter. That is a rather common position for candidates who, for reasons of timing, aren't ready to announce their campaigns. But we had made rather much of Church's being so dedicated that he might give up his chance at the presidency rather than take any time away from the investigation of intelligence agencies. He wasn't spending a great deal of time on campaign preparations then, but it was more than we were letting on. Tom Lantos and several others across the nation were in rather high gear. So it was a bit unnerving when Evans dropped that name on me. But he wasn't sure of himself. I told him the man he asked about was a Frank Church fanatic who was adamant that the senator run for president, which was true. I said I didn't know much more about it than that, which wasn't true. I hadn't been told in so many words, but I knew.

That seemed to satisfy Evans and he let the matter drop. But he called again a couple of weeks later, asking for the telephone number of Tom Lantos. He would have been even more suspicious if I had refused so I gave him the number, demonstrating that we had nothing to fear. While I finished the conversation with Evans, a secretary called Lantos and told him to make himself scarce. It was the sneakiest thing I ever did as a press secretary.

So they never pinned it down. But Evans and Novak were, to my knowledge, the only reporters in Washington who got the scent so early. I was impressed. I still am.

*   *   *

The most fascinating interview I monitored was between Church and columnist George Will. Church and Will were both history buffs. Will may be the best read and most intellectual columnist in the city. And Church, a veteran member of the Foreign Relations Committee, had been a foreign affairs nut since he was a teenager. He knew the world, its history, and its latest political face as well as he knew his mom. George Will had come to have a look at the possible presidential candidate, to measure him for depth. For an hour they dueled. Their choice of weapons was historical trivia. It went something like this:

> WILL: As Henry VIII said of France—on, as I recall, February the 22nd . . .
> CHURCH: February, the 23rd. Remember? It was the day he threw a leg of lamb over his shoulder, splattering grease on the pale lavender gown of Katherine of Aragon.
> WILL: It was a leg of pork.
> CHURCH: You have me there, sir.

*   *   *

Syndicated Washington Post columnist Mary McGrory can flay the veneer from a phony with one slashing verb. But she is the epitome of the classic journalistic contradiction—teaching bullies the evils of bullying by bullying them in return. She is the champion of those who get kicked around, and the bane of those who do the kicking. She is a bleeder, standing up for war protesters, morally motivated draft resisters, welfare mothers, candid politicians, and other people the majority has little use for. She is an avenging angel, smiting the mighty and cutting them down to size.

Mary McGrory is Washington's Pulitzer Prize-winning queen of the well-slung phrase, but she could pass in person for an Irish peasant. Her syndicated column stands out in any newspaper with the brains to carry it, but Mary could get lost in a crowd. She is down to earth, refusing to be flamboyant and lacking the regal bearing of most major columnists.

Mary rarely writes from the ivory tower, but reports directly from the scene of any political crime. When she arrives for a congressional hearing or for a campaign speech, usually late and sometimes a trifle disheveled, she has the preoccupied look of someone's slightly dotty, gray-haired aunt. She is actually the Washington Slasher in disguise. Mary doesn't mince words. She minces her victims.

She has her favorites and, fortunately, Frank Church was one of them. She was with the old *Washington Star* then, and Church was among those she frequently praised in print, usually as a shining example for some stumbling public official she was tearing apart. But if one of her heroes also stumbles, she will roast him over the hottest fire of all because he, of all people, should know better. Frank Church sometimes felt that heat. Mary has no favorites when politicians stray from the correct, decent, and moral side of an issue.

She has a habit during congressional hearings of sitting at the press table and practicing her best lines in a stage whisper within earshot of a sinning senator or witness. It must be disconcerting to try to carry on with a hearing while that harmless-looking woman is giving you a preview of what she'll be doing to you in the next column.

Some of her victims get furious with her, but she is utterly fearless and quite irrepressible. Mary may write for newspapers, but she really works for all those underdogs that government bullies are kicking around. No editor orders her around. Her heart alone tells her what to do.

When I was in D.C., the *Washington Star* was still very much alive. Jack Germond (now with the *Baltimore Sun*) was the *Star*'s political editor and groused to me one night, "You know, technically, she works under me. But that's a laugh."

Jack couldn't get her under control. Nobody could.

I don't know why anybody would want to.

*   *   *

Sam Donaldson of ABC television is a trifle strange. He feels, in an exaggerated sense, that special obligation most reporters feel to bellow when he thinks a politician is trying to put one over on him and the public. He is Captain Wigout, defender of the First Amendment.

"Well, we've caught you lying to us again," he called to tell me one day.

"I've never lied to you, Sam, and what is this 'again' crap?"

"You said the committee wouldn't meet today. I called off my crew. And now I'm told the committee is meeting in secret. You've lied to us again."

"If the committee is meeting, it's news to me," I said. "Let me check and get back to you. I'm sure there's some explanation."

There was. The committee wasn't meeting.

But before I could call Sam, he called me. He said he had inquired some more and found it was all a wild rumor. He just wanted to let me know. He didn't call to apologize. To Sam, no apology was necessary—because it's good for press secretaries to be called a liar once in a while; it lets them know you're keeping an eye on them.

While standing around waiting for a Senate committee to come out of closed session—what the press calls a stakeout—Sam always felt compelled to entertain. He would dominate conversation with other reporters, making scathing jokes about whatever event they were covering. His voice would begin racing and take on an almost demented tone as he did little parodies of his own probable newscast that night: "In Washington today, the Senate Intelligence Committee discussed ways to foster open government during a four-hour closed hearing to which neither the public nor the press was admitted."

I encountered Sam in a Senate hallway one morning. It was before we had met and before he knew who I was or who I worked for. As we walked past each other he suddenly threw his hands in the air, looked straight at me, and said, about God knows what, "Madness. Madness. All is madness." I think he meant it as some kind of joke. Or maybe there really was an unusual amount of madness around that morning and he felt obliged to warn me.

That was before he was anywhere near as well known as he became in later years. And face to face he was so hyper I didn't take him seriously at first. I wondered why ABC would place someone so theatrical on a story as sober as the intelligence investigation. But he was only theatrical in person; when Sam Donaldson went on camera, a strange thing happened. He slowed down. He was controlled. And he consistently delivered solid, sometimes quite profound 60-second summations of what occurred during an entire day of hearings. He is a master, as television correspondents must be, of the succinct report.

Sam Donaldson was a little wiggy, but I should be so wiggy.

*   *   *

Legendary stories abound in Washington about the almost mystical ability of some politicians to remember thousands of names and faces. James Farley, the former postmaster general and Franklin Roosevelt campaign brain, is reputed to be the all-time champ. The veterans also tell astonishing stories about Hubert Humphrey and Richard Nixon, among others. But the ability to remember names is equally useful to reporters, so it should come as no surprise that some of those at the top of American journalism have good heads for names. David Broder of the Post is one. Jack Germond of the *Baltimore Sun* is another. Roger Mudd, then of CBS and now of public television, is downright eerie. I chatted with him for about five minutes one day while he waited to see Church. That was the first time he had ever laid eyes on me. And it was the last time he would see me until four weeks later. I was standing in front of a Capitol elevator. The door opened and out stepped Roger Mudd.

"Well, Bill Hall," he said, "how are you adjusting to Washington? Your family out here yet from Idaho?"

And I have such a common name. You might expect such a thing if your name is Mudd.

*   *   *

Charles Collingwood of CBS was a television news pioneer, a member of that distinguished fraternity that congregated around Edward R. Murrow. When I saw him, Collingwood still carried that golden beginning into the quality of his on-the-air work—and into his rather regal bearing as well. He was an accomplished dramatic news actor who gave great import in his grave manner to the subject of his interview, kind of the way George Will does today, only without being crabby.

Collingwood was especially skilled in handling a television technique that makes one camera do the work of three. When you watch a correspondent interviewing a politician on the evening news, you will usually see a few shots of the politician's face as he listens to questions from the correspondent, a few shots of the correspondent as he listens to some of the politician's answers, and quite a few shots of the politician talking. Only the last one is genuine. The other two are faked.

Network crews out in the field for an interview often use only one camera. The politician and the interviewer normally sit facing each other. The camera is aimed straight at the politician for the entire interview. After the interview is over, the politician is asked to remain in his seat, without talking, while the crew takes a few more seconds of his kisser in that pose. It is the listening pose. The correspondent usually chats with him—to give him something to react to. Sometimes the politician, for footage on an interview about the Soviet Union, is reacting to the correspondent's boasting about a recent fishing trip, or his observations on the weather that day.

Then the camera is moved to a position behind the politician, aiming over his shoulder at the face of the correspondent. That's how they get the shot of the correspondent listening.

The whole thing is edited together with sound over the top, creating the impression of three cameras. You could do great violence to a politician with that technique—splicing in a smiling shot of the politician while the correspondent is asking him about the starving children in an African nation. But I have never seen it abused. So the on-the-air impression of three cameras is a benevolent illusion, designed to avoid "jump cuts," where a person's face jumps around because of sections edited out. And the trick gives the audience some variety in the picture without costing the network an arm and a leg.

But it's a strange process to witness, made all the more unusual by an accomplished performer like Collingwood, and complicated the day I watched him by the fact that Church had to leave the room after his own listening pose had been filmed, leaving Collingwood to do his listening shots without anyone to listen to. He was left aimed only at a wall as the camera began recording his reactions.

At first, Collingwood simply stared intently at the wall, apparently fascinated with what it was saying.

"Now tilt your head, Charles," a crew member directed. Charles tilted his head a few degrees. His eyes narrowed. The wall had just said something rather puzzling.

"Now bring your chin slowly down and then back up rather quickly." Charles let his chin drift lower, and then snapped it back up again, his eyes growing wide. The wall had started to get a mite boring and he was beginning to lose interest when, suddenly the wall had made such a brilliant point that he looked up again in amazement.

"And now a quizzical look, Charles." The head tilted to one side again. The eyebrows went up. The distinguished brow furrowed. Could the wall possibly be correct about the astonishing observation it had just made?

"Great quizzical look, Charles," the crewman called out, and the filming ended.

Thereafter, I got to where I couldn't watch Charles Collingwood conducting an interview on television without chuckling. When friends asked me what I was laughing about, I just gave them a quizzical look.

* * *

I'm sometimes asked who I regard as the best reporter I met in Washington. There are several, of course, not the least of whom were unheralded reporters specializing in coverage for a single section of the country, such as John Simonds who reported for a few papers in the Gannett chain, and A. Robert Smith, a free-lancer covering for Northwest newspapers. It depends on the type of reporting. But for indefatigable digging on any story you pointed them toward, and for skillfully summing up what they had uncovered, I think especially of Daniel Schorr, then with CBS and now with National Public Radio, and of George Lardner of the *Washington Post.*

Schorr reminded me of an article I read years ago in a press photographers' magazine. Five newspaper photographers were presented with a hypothetical situation: "The clothes of a man standing across the table from you catch fire. On the table in front of you are a bucket of water and your camera. Which would you grab first?"

Four of the photographers said they would grab the bucket of water and skip the picture so the poor guy wouldn't have to suffer a moment longer than necessary. "I'd grab one quick shot," said the fifth photographer, "and then douse him with water. I can shoot really fast."

I wouldn't want that bastard around if my clothes caught fire, but I would want him working for my newspaper.

I wouldn't want Dan Schorr around if I were a politician who had been screwing the public. I wouldn't even want Dan Schorr around if I were innocent and he thought I had been screwing the public. If your integrity went up in flames, Dan would grab the camera. But I would feel fortunate to have Daniel Schorr working for my newspaper, even if CBS eventually found him too strong for network ulcers.

I suppose, now that he is a settled graybeard soberly commenting on everything under the sun for NPR, he is less aggressive. But he used to work right up to the ethical line. He would press as hard to get a story as the limit would allow and occasionally—seldom, but occasionally—would trip and fall over the ethical line. Moreover, he was no 8-to-5 reporter. He worked whenever the story was active—the morning news, all day at a hearing, late at night, on weekends. Whatever the story—Watergate or the Senate Intelligence Committee—it was his story and he would tap pipelines inside pipelines to get more of the story than anyone else.

In questioning, he was dignified, even respectful, and never strident nor devious. He would just bore in with hardballs right over the center of the plate. There was nothing accusatory in his questions, no hint of moral superiority that sometimes seems evident in the tone of a George Will or a Sam Donaldson. A politician or a press secretary with nothing to hide had nothing to fear from him. But if you had some seamy secret his questioning was likely to root it out because he had done his homework better than any other reporter covering the story. He had that master reporter's knack of finding two pieces of a puzzle and figuring out the whole picture.

Dan would keep driving on a story with a tenacity and daring that sometimes caused other reporters to shake their heads. On rare occasions, he would go too far. He once did a story in which he strongly implied that Alexander Butterfield (the Watergate witness who revealed Richard Nixon had been recording Oval Office conversations) had been a secret CIA operative spying for the agency inside the White House. Butterfield was no such thing. The story blew up in Dan's face. But he was heard to remark later that a reporter has to take a shot in the dark once in a while.

And of course, there was the case in which he got his hands on the report of the House Intelligence Committee, a report which the House had voted to suppress. Apparently unable to talk his network into more than a few excerpts, Dan unilaterally decided the whole thing should be made public and slipped his copy to the *Village Voice* in New York. The *Voice* reprinted the full report amid wails in Congress and the White House. Dan was suspended, with pay, by CBS.

He was later hauled before a House committee which demanded to know where he had obtained his copy. He refused to reveal his source. Though the committee could have cited him for contempt of Congress, and threatened to, it finally let the matter drop. With Dan no longer facing any formal charges of impropriety, CBS had the task of deciding whether to reinstate the high-rolling reporter with whom the network brass was so obviously uncomfortable. Dan took them off the hook. He resigned.

There is one principal difference between Daniel Schorr and that photographer who would grab the camera rather than the bucket of water. I would want the photographer on my news staff, but I don't think I would want to have dinner with the creep.

I'd be delighted to have dinner or lunch or espresso with Dan Schorr anytime. He made a couple of mistakes in practicing his profession over the years—the same as any doctor, lawyer, or journeyman carpenter. Nonetheless, he has done most of it right and he has practiced his profession to the fullest. After all, timidity is also a mistake when digging the truth out of the government of a republic. And that was one mistake he never made.

*   *   *

George Lardner of the *Washington Post* scared the hell out of me the first time I met him. In those early days, I expected something that doesn't exist—reporters who are at the top of their profession because they know strange and mystical ways of drawing out your most private thoughts and scattering them among the people. I expected great news surgeons who could dissect a politician and shake out all his secrets with one ingenious question.

There are some damn good reporters in Washington, but no supernaturally good reporters. They are gifted but mortal. The chief difference between reporters in Washington and those in the sticks is that most reporters in Washington are highly skilled, whereas many in the sticks are not. But a good reporter in the boonies could hold his own with the best in Washington. Indeed, most Washington reporters came from the boonies.

Nonetheless, I was braced in the beginning for the super reporters, those clever devils with their nasty bag of tricks. The first time I met George Lardner he seemed to match that image.

I see that he has grayed a bit in subsequent years, as have we all. But in the mid-1970s he wore a black, curly, Sigmund Freud beard and had the piercing eyes of a rabid weasel. He could take notes faster than any human reporter, racing a felt tip pen across the paper with a blood-curdling squeak-squeak-squeak similar to the violins that begin shrieking in the movie *Psycho* each time someone is about to be murdered. Lardner would write his abbreviated longhand notes without looking at the notepad for more than an instant now and then. His dark eyes would penetrate your soul. And he kept pushing you toward faster and faster answers, mumbling "Uh huh! Uh huh!" with the impatience of some pervert hearing the sordid details of your sex life and anxious for you to get to the climax. He would give you no time to think or to tidy up your answers. Worse, I learned at the outset that he is a semi-distant relative of Ring Lardner. And you know what that means:

Fiction!

Indeed, I was certain the first time I talked to George that he was one of those people Spiro Agnew, Nixon's vice president, used to warn us about, one of those reporters who would trick you out of as much as he could and then fill in the blanks with any distortion that would sell newspapers.

It was all my imagination. And Spiro's. I never met a reporter who more consistently mastered the daily struggle of accurately summing up a complex story in a few pithy paragraphs. George Lardner is a reporter's reporter, congenitally unable to write anything but the straight story as he understood it. I would sit through a four-hour hearing with him and then read in the *Post* the next day one of those accounts that cause you to say to yourself, "Of course! That's exactly what happened."

As for his demonic appearance during an interview, it's all that dark beard and his total concentration. I came to view him as a kind and civilized man. His soul is mellow and clean shaven.

But I was sorry some years later to hear that George Lardner had won a Pulitzer Prize. I was sorry because he won it by bravely writing about the murder of his daughter.

*   *   *

Hugh Sidey of *Time* magazine was one of the first of many reporters in Washington who tried to help me through my culture shock. Sidey and I had met some years before at a University of Idaho symposium. He invited me to lunch shortly after I arrived in Washington and brought along an engaging man who was probably one of the half dozen most popular reporters in Washington at the time, both among politicians and other reporters. Peter Lisagor of the *Chicago Daily News* was stretching himself too thin as it was without helping Hugh wet-nurse a recent arrival from the provinces. But Peter had Dutch-uncled dozens of newcomers over the years. He recognized that I was homesick and kept tabs on me after that. And he recognized that I was an especially difficult case the night we spoke at a cocktail party. In gesturing with my right hand, I knocked a glass of red wine out of my left hand and onto a white carpet that had been installed that morning. He checked with me frequently after that evening.

Peter Lisagor somehow remained a generalist in a town that had grown too complex for a reporter to be anything but a specialist.

He worked like three people. He was on the scene personally for most of the major stories in town. He was a regular on public television's "Washington Week In Review," and on a weekly television donnybrook among celebrated columnists, "Agronsky and Company." And he and his white shock of hair were something of a fixture on "Meet The Press" and other television interview panels. For good measure, he shadowed the president on foreign trips. In his spare time he dropped by the dinner parties of friends who, though he was exhausted, might be offended if he didn't put in an appearance.

Peter remained a favorite of other reporters despite being as critical of Washington news coverage as any Agnew who ever lived. He doubted that most of his colleagues were as professionally dubious of the latest leading lights of the government as they should be. He felt they were too easily dazzled by seductive government personalities like Secretary of State Henry Kissinger. Peter wasn't in the habit, for instance, of granting new presidents a honeymoon. He believed that somebody always gets screwed on a honeymoon.

I once heard him berating Hugh Sidey because *Time* had joined the then-fashionable honeymoon assessment of the new president, Gerald Ford. The magazine had devoted several stories to the popular thesis at the time that, agree with him or not, Gerald Ford was certainly a decent person and a nice guy to boot.

Peter was revolted. What the hell were reporters doing writing that kind of crap about a guy who would already be getting his boots licked every 15 minutes by his own staff?

"I almost threw up," Peter grumped, picking on *Time* only because it was the latest example of many. "Hugh," he scolded Sidey, "you're kissing his ass all over the magazine."

Peter said an odd thing to me one day. It was during my first, unsuccessful attempt at resigning and returning to Idaho. Peter had invited me to lunch to talk about it. Other friends tried to get me to stay. But Peter was intrigued with the thought I might actually leave. Indeed, if I went through with it, he wanted to do a column—"about somebody who has the guts to just pick up and walk away from all this bullshit." And then he added, "I've always wished that's what I had done."

To this day, I don't know if one of the most successful reporters ever to work in Washington actually wished he had left, or if he

, return to my element and was just trying to
fortable with the decision.

ome from a trip to China with Gerald Ford more
sual. He was having trouble breathing. He con-
ne call—the last time I talked to him before leaving
was "a little uneasy" about what doctors might find
ered the hospital that weekend for tests. "I hope it's
oddam fungus or something I picked up in China."
cancer. They put him through the treatment mill and he
ack.

months after I returned to my Idaho newspaper, I cov-
e Republican National Convention at Kansas City and
d in on Peter in the press tent. He looked fit and said he felt
me. Indeed, he seemed to be getting stronger every day. He
his fingers crossed, but he was beginning to believe he had it
pped.

He died four months later.

"With all the sonsabitches in this town, why Peter?" a young
reporter he had also Dutch-uncled through the early trauma of
Washington asked me the day the word spread through the city
that Peter Lisagor was terminally ill.

"Because he's already given this town 25 of the best goddam
years it's ever seen," I offered ineptly, rubbing the standard he's-
lived-a-rich-full-life salve on the eternal "why."

But actually I was wondering myself, why Peter?

Ten years later, I was strolling through Arlington National
Cemetery in a section that features more of the famous figures of
history than most of the plots in that place. And there was the grave
of Peter Lisagor. I always wonder what he would have thought had
he known it was Gerald Ford's decision to bury him there among
the nation's other honored dead.

Chapter Eleven
"Never Mind the CIA, Senator; Tell Us About the Spuds"

The 1976 presidential election was hardly a great year for Washington's political reporters. They were so busy gang-banging the front-runners that they missed a lot of the action elsewhere—and were constantly surprised.

I began to get the general drift of how the year might go for us when a New York producer called from NBC's "Today" show some months before we began celebrating the nation's bicentennial with a presidential election. The "Today" show would be celebrating with a salute to a different state each Friday. Idaho was scheduled early in the series, and not surprisingly they wanted Idaho's senior senator to participate. After all, Church was a ranking member of the Senate Foreign Relations Committee, an anti-war leader from the Vietnam era, chairman of the Senate Committee on Aging, a leading conservationist in a time of energy shortages, and he was in charge of the ongoing investigation of the CIA and the FBI. For good measure, he was probably going to run for president.

I wondered which of those topics they might want to cover.

"We want him to stand in a potato field and talk about potatoes," they said. "We've got this potato field near a place called Blackfoot, Idaho. Your governor has agreed to be interviewed in the potato field, and we'd like the senator to be there, too."

Potatoes are both the pride and the curse of every loyal Idahoan. On the one hand, because of a volcanic soil as favorable to potatoes as some other soils are to wine grapes, Idaho potatoes really are exceptional. Lord knows, I'm enough of an Idahoan to insist on that.

On the other hand, a loyal Idahoan can get awfully weary of his state's being known only for sexless sacks of spuds. It's the first thing anyone mentions when they hear you're from Idaho. We get as tired of hearing about potatoes as Georgians in the Jimmy Carter period must have been of hearing about peanuts.

But there had been an improvement. After all those years of, "Oh, yes, Idaho; that's where the potatoes come from," we had been hearing in recent years, "Oh, yes, Idaho; that's Frank Church's state."

But at NBC, it was back to the old potato patch.

Except Church was stuck in Washington for the intelligence hearings. The "Today" show salute to Idaho had to feed Church in from the Washington studio. There were no potatoes to talk about. They had no choice but to ask him instead about the CIA's tendency to mash our liberties and whether the rumor Church might run for president was half baked.

With such an inauspicious beginning, it shouldn't have been a surprise when the media failed to rush aboard the Church press bus. Indeed, the reporters had been overlooking most of the lesser presidential candidates most of the time, which helped keep them lesser. I think it was a hangover from Watergate-big story fever. Everyone wanted to cover a winner. So they flocked almost exclusively around Ford, Carter, and Reagan. Partly as a consequence, the reporting was a mite wide of the mark in one primary after another.

In New Hampshire, for instance, Ford transparently poor-mouthed his chances. Gee, he didn't know whether he could pull it out or not with Reagan spending so much time in the state.

When he won, Ford brandished a narrow margin as a stunning victory and as proof of Reagan's meager appeal. Much of the press bought it, writing off Reagan.

The meaning of New Hampshire was quite the opposite. Gerald Ford, though possessing all the countless political advantages of being President of the United States, barely won an election in his own party. A president should and usually does cream a primary opponent. Eight years earlier, Lyndon Johnson was compelled to leave office because he had "won" that same New Hampshire primary against Gene McCarthy by a margin similar to Ford's. New Hampshire demonstrated a basic weakness in Ford as a candidate and proved that challenger Reagan, far from being finished, was an emotional Republican force to be reckoned with.

But Reagan was quite prematurely declared out of the running after New Hampshire, and at several stops thereafter along the primary trail.

Senator Henry Jackson won the Democratic primary in Massachusetts the next week. Many reporters wrote off Carter as a flash in the pan. "The Jackson juggernaut" was on its way.

Even when they were right, many reporters made it look difficult. By the eve of the Michigan primary, Reagan was alleged to have peaked and the standard press assessment was that Ford might pull it out.

Pull it out? Ford clobbered Reagan in Michigan by two-to-one. What kind of reporting is it when you can't see a landslide of that proportion coming?

Church was written off in Nebraska. Most newspapers didn't bother to cover the state. Most said it wouldn't even be close. ABC reported on the eve of the election that the Church campaign would be little more than a little bump beneath the wheels of the Carter bandwagon.

Church won.

It was one thing after another in an election that began with a lot of scoffing about Carter's chances. How could so much of the press be wrong so often? Whatever the reason for the weak reporting, and whatever its considerable disadvantage to a candidate who is not a front-runner and is being overlooked, an inattentive press also offered one advantage: We had no trouble hiding things. Nobody was watching us. We got away with murder.

I lived in terror, for instance, that the daily explosions, the crazy abnormal factionalism inside our national headquarters would be discovered and reported.

Hardly anyone noticed.

And of course, the press never caught us in all that early groundwork for the campaign, back when non-candidate Church was supposed to be sticking strictly to his intelligence investigation. I was sure we would be discovered. But we weren't, even with rather transparent campaign appearances in several primary states long before Church announced. The political reporters were off chasing Carter, Ford, and Reagan.

Perhaps most beneficial of all was the inattention to Church just before Nebraska. Carl Burke, Church's national campaign chairman, and I had started stepping up the hype in the traditional fashion about a month before Nebraska, telling reporters that Church just might pull it off. We thought it was time to begin building a bandwagon effect.

Church, having read our comments in the papers, called us in and told us to knock it off. "When I win Nebraska, I want it to be a complete surprise. I want them to write that I won a miraculous victory against incredible odds in a state where no one had given me a chance."

Church understood that news is the unexpected. If his win wasn't expected, it would get heavier play around the country and might build him up for other wins over Carter. Frank Church didn't want the press writing that he had won Nebraska "as expected." He wanted front-page headlines.

"That's a good theory," I told him, "but it'll never work. If you're going to win Nebraska, that will become obvious to any good reporter several days before the election, and that's the way they'll write it."

"Maybe so," Church answered, "but humor me."

Thereafter, Burke and I dutifully gave reporters the line laid down by our candidate. Nebraska was just a warm-up for later primaries. If he won there, it would indicate he had more on the ball than even we imagined. If he won there, it would indicate that Carter's support had been soft all along, that he could only win in a crowded field or in the South and that he couldn't handle a one-on-one situation against a real contender. But naturally, we said, Church couldn't win his first primary in Nebraska. That would take a miracle.

By the time Nebraska rolled around, I was beginning to believe our own poor-mouth propaganda. The newspapers and networks were looking ahead to other primaries and rarely mentioned Church. Church got so little press attention I feared he might be ignored to death. It really would take a miracle to win in Nebraska.

There was only one place in the nation where Church was getting any press at all. Fortunately, that was in Nebraska, where the papers and stations covered all the candidates evenly and fully. But Nebraska voters, watching the networks and reading national newspapers and magazines, were being told, in effect, that they would be wasting their time voting for Frank Church.

And then Church won.

It was a miracle.

Church fed the headline writers that word during an interview with anchorman Walter Cronkite during the CBS election night coverage.

Cronkite let it pass and noted instead that Church had spent several thousand dollars more than Carter on campaign advertising, which was true—because Carter had kissed off Nebraska as a sure win.

Church was incredulous.

"Walter! Governor Carter has been on the network news every night for weeks. I haven't. And his face was on the cover of both *Time* and *Newsweek* as the people of Nebraska went to vote. Governor Carter has had $8 million worth of free publicity."

Nebraska launched Church, if not into the forefront, at least into the range of the media's narrow 1976 field of vision. If Church had lost it would have been over. If he had been expected to win and had merely done so, it would still have been over. But those "miracle" headlines made it possible to get a little bandwagon in gear, fuel it with fresh campaign funds, and roll on to several more victories.

But we couldn't have got away with our manufactured miracle if the reporters hadn't been off their feed in 1976 and stricken with tunnel vision.

It might have been a different story if there had been more reporters like Johnny Apple of *The New York Times*, one of the few not surprised by Nebraska. He not only went into the state and took a look, but he also didn't attach himself to Church or to Carter, the way most reporters did. You can read some of an election by watching the candidates, by noticing whether they are catching on with the crowds. Apple did that. But he also spent time talking with barbers and bartenders and farmers and precinct politicians. He didn't write that Church looked like a winner or a loser in Nebraska. He just reported what he heard—a lot of Nebraskans enthusiastic about Frank Church. A reader could figure out from Apple's stories that Frank Church had a chance in Nebraska.

So Johnny Apple and the *Times* were not surprised at the outcome. The *Times* doesn't believe in miracles. Or in the Tooth Fairy.

And it would be unfair to indicate that the networks took no interest at all in Church's Nebraska campaign. Church was to appear at a Democratic dinner in Omaha on the weekend before the election. We got word that Carter was going to crash the dinner, hoping to upstage our candidate and steal the spotlight and the coverage.

But when Carter arrived on the platform, Church presented him with a bucket of "Idaho peanuts," a pail of potatoes.

The networks were ecstatic. Rather than steal the coverage, Carter had to share it on the newscasts with Church and the potatoes.

The networks love those potato pictures.

Chapter Twelve
Idaho, the Jews, and the Mormons

I remember as a boy hearing my father laughing about still another green Easterner visiting Idaho and asking to see a Mormon bishop. As recently as World War II, some Easterners still believed a peculiar canard that Mormon bishops have horns. Naturally, they wanted to see one while they were in Mormon country.

Those greenhorns were the same gullible Easterners who were nervous about coming west because they had heard that the Indians were still as vicious as they were depicted in the movies of that era.

It was all nonsense, of course. Indians aren't vicious. And Mormon bishops don't have horns. I have known a few horny Indians and a couple of vicious bishops, but never the other way around.

Nevertheless, local comics would sometimes have a little fun with the greenhorns, leading them on. One wag in our neighborhood, telling an eastern woman that Mormon bishops not only had horns but beards as well, showed her a billy goat and told her it was a Mormon bishop.

Of course, she didn't believe him. Easterners of that era were quick about things like that. It had too many legs to be a Mormon bishop.

The Indians have also been known to tease Easterners, sometimes lapsing into Hollywood Indian talk: "Red man welcome white brother to land of mighty mountains and swift-running water where buffalo roam and sky is not cloudy all day."

That might be laying it on a little thick today, but a more subtle version of the same thing still goes on. One night at a banquet in Boise, a mischievous Nez Perce Indian from Lapwai, Idaho, was overheard enduring a patronizing non-Indian raving about his fascination with Indian customs and professing to be an expert.

"Have you ever eaten dog?" the Nez Perce asked him.

"No," the man answered in awe. "What does it taste like?"

"I don't know," the Nez Perce answered.

On another evening, that same Idaho Indian asked a waitress in a hotel restaurant to bring him a cup of "buffalo juice."

"I'm sorry, sir," she said, "I've never served an Indian before. I don't know what that means."

"You've never served an Indian?"

"No, sir. I don't know anything about you people."

"Have you ever served a Shriner?"

"Yes, we have conventions here all the time."

"Well, we're just like Shriners, only we wear funnier hats."

But for all their teasing of others about Mormons and Indians, the people of Idaho have harbored myths of their own about a religion and tribe with which they are largely unfamiliar—Jews. Back in those years when Easterners touring Idaho regarded Indians as both noble and savage, many Indians had similar contradictions about Jews. Many in the Idaho of my childhood regarded Jews as talented and tight-fisted, great comedians who were devoted to their families, would sell you a cheap suit, were tremendously religious, and might cheat you in business—the usual list. And the rare sight of someone wearing a yarmulke—usually in a newsreel—was as strange to Idaho eyes as the horns on a Mormon bishop.

But we were certain in those days that we knew more about Jews than Easterners did about Mormons and Indians. After all, we had seen Jewish comedians on the "Ed Sullivan Show." We learned about Jews the same way Easterners learned about Indians—through movies and television.

And of course, we all know who controls television in America.

That's right, the Indians and the Mormons.

Our ambivalence about Jews tended to extremes. On the one hand, most Idahoans were at least verbally bigoted; they were once rather free with expressions like "Jew him down." And Jews were sometimes blamed for the unpopular policies of a Roosevelt or a Truman. There was a lot of that kind of talk in the Idaho of my childhood.

But at another level, the few Jews in the state usually had no trouble joining service or country clubs, unlike much of the nation at the time. There was rarely any overt social or political exclusion. Indeed, Idaho was the first state in the land—in 1914—to elect a Jew (Moses Alexander) as its governor. But Idaho did not exactly have a great foundation for understanding Jews. Jews are about as numerous in Idaho as Mormons in Tel Aviv. I was asked constantly during the presidential campaign how Frank Church, an Idaho senator, had become one of the most steadfast friends of Israel in Congress.

I sometimes answered that it was fear of the Idaho Jewish vote—all 27 of them. But in reality, Church's support for Israel was no mystery. He had habitually come down on the side of underdogs. He believed American interests were directly involved in the Middle East. And he was quite comfortable tilting toward the only democracy in the region.

On the other hand, Church's position could also be regarded as politically expedient to the extent that it was quite popular among Idahoans. He was a typical Idahoan in his respect for Israel. But many Idahoans, though admirers of Israel, were thoroughly puzzled by many American Jews. The major myths about Jews withered in Idaho over the years, but the citizens of the state were sometimes baffled by what they regarded as "the Jewish personality." It might also be called the Italian, the Irish, the New York, the New Jersey, or the northeastern personality. But in Idaho and other intermountain states, that bizarre, uninhibited way so many Easterners react toward others was once considered distinctly Jewish.

It is the open emotionalism of the East versus western stoicism. Idahoans and others in the region have, until rather recently, kept a lid on their feelings. As a general rule, they don't kiss their wives—or anyone else's—in public. They are not openly sentimental. Public crying is bad form for adults. And when angry, they usually keep it contained and try not to let it show, boiling just beneath the surface.

I found it much more common in the East for people to get visibly angry. When an Easterner is offended, he will usually say so, even if the transgression is rather minor.

If you are accidentally standing on an Idahoan's toe, he may silently curse you, but he will endure the discomfort until you get around to moving. He doesn't want to create a scene. That would be embarrassing.

If you step on an Easterner's toe, he will say rather candidly, "Get off my goddam toe!"

One day in Church's office, Jerry Levinson of the senator's Multinational Subcommittee staff—a New Yorker—was disagreeing with me about something when I said rather unctuously, "Two wrongs don't make a right."

"I don't need your goddam instruction in morality," he snarled, shocking the hell out of me and receiving my quick apology.

Jerry sometimes flashed like that several times a day. It was his normal way of correcting people and he didn't mean anything by it. He had merely cleared the air and taught me where his toes were. After a time, I learned to think nothing about those little outbursts.

But if he had reacted the same way in Idaho at so slight a provocation, people would have been startled and embarrassed. Without saying anything, they would have left the room and probably avoided him in the future. You give crazy people a wide berth. In Idaho, most people don't say sharp things to each other unless the offense is extreme and they are truly furious. When an Idahoan blows, he really blows.

The eastern way is more honest, although it is a kind of honesty akin to telling a lady her dress is ugly. It takes some getting used to. Indeed, I had to learn after a time in Washington to blow back—whether I was truly angry or not. The many volcanic Easterners in Church's national campaign headquarters seemed to respect you more if you did things their way. So I blew. But it certainly seemed an odd way for people to work together.

Open anger must be an eastern habit rather than a Jewish trait because Idahoans who move to the East often become a little crazy in their personal relationships. And Idaho Jews are as impassive as anyone else in the state.

We all tend to be a lot alike in Idaho. It is the final melting pot. It has been years since we have had any substantial ethnic neighborhoods anywhere in the state. We all just sort of run together like warm cheese. There's nothing Irish about the Irish. The Italians can't speak Italian and would just as soon have potatoes as pasta. My children from my first marriage are of half Mexican extraction but they can't speak Spanish. Neither can their mother. And Idaho Jews are as easily offended by a volatile "Jewish personality" as any other Idahoan.

Yet there is no state that admires Israel more. There are reasons. Israeli Premier Yitzhak Rabin referred during a 1976 American Bicentennial message in *Time* magazine to "the instinctive kinship Israel feels toward America."

Idaho, with as few Jews as any state, has that instinctive kinship with Israel and, in many respects, has more in common with Israel than New York does. Idaho and modern Israel are young by comparison with eastern America. Idaho is four generations old and Israel about two. There are people still alive in both places who know first-hand what it means to carve an agrarian existence out of a raw beginning. Both were settled by gritty people looking for a home where they could be themselves—not what their neighborhood branded them. Both pushed some other people aside to dominate the land. Neither has been quick to make amends to the dispossessed.

Both believe in standing their ground. Idahoans, among the most jingoistic of Americans, never did dig détente with the Russians or any other form of international compromise with evil empires. They often can't understand why, when provoked by some pip-squeak nation, the United States doesn't strike back hard and fast "the way the Israelis do." The Israeli habit over the years of counterpunching is greatly admired in Idaho, and the American policy of a more measured response is not.

Idaho's many Mormons have a special feeling for Israel. There is, of course, the attraction of the Holy Land for any devout and Biblically based people. But the Mormons have also known persecution. The Idaho Constitution was written at the height of anti-Mormon feeling late in the last century. The voters of Idaho did not, until late in this century, finally do away with an embarrassing, though unenforced, article forbidding Mormons to serve on juries, vote, or hold public office. (Ironically, however, it was not until late in this century that the Mormons themselves abandoned the practice of denying church office to black people.)

The early persecution of the Mormons included the forcible eviction of whole settlements from the East. Utah was their Israel, their promised land, where they could at last practice their faith without violent harassment. Their arduous journey to their Zion taught the Mormons a tenacity and a cohesion that remains apparent today and is at the foundation of their admiration for Israel.

Westerners, Mormon and non-Mormon, also tend to identify with Yitzhak Rabin's admonition in that Bicentennial *Time* essay that, "the first condition of our individual strength and survival is our own self-will. . . . There is no outside substitute for the inner resolve demanded of a democratic society in the pursuit of its national security and the liberty of its citizens. A free nation that is not willing to mobilize all its inner resources to protect its right to live through its own self-sacrifice cannot be helped by others. . . . We alone are responsible for our own defense."

Idahoans like that kind of talk. It is the rugged individualism of the frontier, the self-reliance of pioneers who couldn't always wait for the cavalry to arrive.

So Frank Church's long support of Israel was not so surprising for a senator from Idaho. It is part of that instinctive kinship he and other Idahoans feel for Israel.

Israel has spunk.

Idahoans like spunk.

*   *   *

Jimmy Carter's early campaign for the presidency rested on two formerly incompatible pillars—white Georgians and blacks nationwide.

Frank Church's early campaign also appealed initially to two groups far more than to any others—Idahoans and Jews nationwide. Without either, the Church campaign would never have begun.

But what an unlikely combination it was at first—demonstrative Jews and reserved potato pickers. For the first few weeks of the campaign, workers neither Jewish nor from Idaho must have constituted less than 20 percent of the national headquarters staff.

When factionalism broke out in headquarters, someone—undoubtedly a Georgia Baptist—ignorantly labeled the two factions "the Idahoans" and "the Jews." It was a considerable misnomer. An Idahoan headed the "Idaho" faction and a Jew led the "Jewish" faction. But that was the extent of it. The "Jewish" faction included Idaho Christians. And the "Idaho" faction included Jews.

I was appalled at the designations, both because the labeling was potentially so destructive and because it would be murder if the press got wind of it. I raised hell, and the practice stopped, at least in my presence. But before I heard the last of it, the use of the labels had been carried to a ridiculous extreme. Mort Schwartz, a Jew from Miami and the most uncontrollable faction fighter on my staff, came running into the press room one day shouting, "Do you know what the Jews have done now?"

I had to remind him that the "Jew" he was fuming about was a Gentile from Blackfoot, Idaho.

Not surprisingly, I also heard Mort damned one day by a member of the opposing faction for having made a mistake that was typical of "those damned Idahoans." Indeed, the opposition once targeted "the Idahoans"—with Mort included—for a bloodless coup. They said we should all go back to Idaho where we came from. If they had succeeded, poor Mort would have been exiled to Idaho whether he wanted to go or not.

After the pejorative labeling finally seemed to stop and I regained sufficient composure to see some humor in what had happened, Mort and I agreed that I would declare him an honorary Idahoan and he would declare me an honorary Jew. But the agreement fell apart. Mort was on a diet and refused to eat potatoes. And I refused to let him circumcise me.

*   *   *

In February 1976 I had an experience with Church that gave me a new understanding of Jews in general and of our visceral respect, as Idahoans, for Israel.

Jewish leaders from throughout the world gathered at Brussels to focus global wrath on the stinginess with which the Soviets then granted exit visas to Jews waiting to leave Russia. Numerous Gentiles, including several politicians and Christian ministers from America, flew to Brussels to stand with the Jews in that cause. Frank Church was among them.

The Soviets were cranky as hell about it, inastutely denouncing the gathering and thereby giving it even more global attention. The Soviets were especially steamed at Church, the ranking American politician at the conference. The CIA, following its standard Washington practice, delivered a translation to Church's office of what the Soviet press was saying. The Soviets were furious at his "meddling."

But the Russians hurled nothing more than dogmatic insults at the conference—merely words—while others in the world were considered capable of darker acts. The police were everywhere and a person had the sense that week in Brussels of being part of a magnet for terrorists. There are people in the world who imagine that they can serve their cause by murdering Olympic athletes. So there was no reason to doubt they might be tempted to react with similar savagery at a gathering of Jews from throughout the world that included former Israeli Premier Golda Meir, as well as that Gentile senator from America.

Everyone at the conference, including Church, had to stop by a Brussels police station to receive a security badge, complete with colored photograph. The Churches went through the process by appointment. I joined the delegates standing in line. The police station was a madhouse. Each person surrendered his passport and waited while the police checked it against some mysterious master list. The next step was the preparation of the security badges in a room filled with typewriters and cameras. But there seemed to be no coherent system. People who had been standing in line for more than an hour had yet to be summoned to the picture room. Others waited a minute or two and went right through.

Finally, a long-neglected woman from New York standing next to me began bellowing like a taxi driver, shaking her fist at a police lieutenant who looked a lot like Peter Sellers as Inspector Clouseau.

"I have waited long enough!" she stormed. "I demand to be processed! I will not wait a moment longer for you and your pack of incompetents to get this line moving! This is an outrage!"

The lieutenant, with restrained fury, told her in a classic French accent that they were doing the very best they could, that he had been without sleep all night working on security arrangements, and that his heart didn't exactly bleed for her.

I was on his side. She was obnoxious. But as he spoke, he kept glancing at my embarrassed face there beside her, apparently assuming she was my repulsive wife. He rebuked me with his sad French eyes for having no control over her.

She continued the diatribe until he finally threw his hands in the air, turned his back, and walked away.

I was mortified. The police had their hands full processing several thousand people through a security system designed for their own protection, and here was this rude guest in Belgium— from my country—making a scene. I knew what the lieutenant was thinking: "Typical American."

I knew what I was thinking: "Typical New Yorker."

Back at the hotel, with my new security badge, I discussed another security matter with the woman in charge of public relations
for the Brussels Hilton. She was worried about Church's drive through
downtown Brussels to the conference center for his speech that afternoon. She recommended a police escort. The security arrangements already in place had left me quite paranoid. I instantly agreed.

She called the police station and three plainclothes officers
came to the Church suite. She told them in French what she wanted
and they all began jabbering and gesturing at once. I don't understand French, but it was apparent the police were not inclined to
cooperate. They were already stretched quite thin trying to protect several thousand potential targets of terrorists. Indeed, earlier
in the day they had wrestled to the floor of the hotel lobby a strange
young man with a shoe box. The box contained cookies, but it made
them realize how easily someone could slip inside the police protection. So they refused to divert the requisite half a dozen officers
to a motorcycle escort, even if the senator might be more of a target than most of the others who had come to Brussels.

But the Hilton PR woman persisted. She was angry, nose to
nose with one of the officers, shouting at him in French. He shouted
back. But she outdid him. Soon all three officers glared at me.

She stopped and asked for my government identification card.

"I've been telling them how important you are in the American government," she said. "They don't believe it."

I fished out my U.S. Senate staff card with my picture on it. Glancing at the card, she nodded her approval and then displayed it—defiantly—to the officers, pointing out the words "U.S. Senate" and a line
drawing of the famous Capitol building next to my photograph.

They kept glancing at me and at the card and I kept trying to
look like an important figure in the American government, wondering how one says in French, "My dear friend Ted Kennedy will
hear of this outrage."

The three officers chattered among themselves and then set
their jaws, stiffly handing her my identification card.

"They are not impressed with you," she said, turning to enter
the fray once more.

The four of them soon yelled and gestured again. At one point,
she paused with a clenched fist still poised in their faces, turned to

me, and said sweetly in English, "I am now flirting with them." And then she resumed her shouting.

Perhaps she meant "toying" with them. Or maybe not. I couldn't tell the flirting from the hollering. But one or the other worked. The officers left, slamming the door behind them. Frank Church would have a police escort.

That evening, some American delegates to the conference invited the Churches to dinner in the restaurant atop the Brussels Hilton. The hosts were kind enough to tell the senator to bring his press secretary along. Suffice it to say, this was no Idaho hash house. I've rarely had better food or wine. But it's not the meal I remember best from that evening. It's the conversation. I sat next to a quiet, sad-faced little man in his forties. I had been told his name like I should know what it meant, but I didn't. It turned out that he was sort of famous—far more in Jewish circles than in mine—as the writer of some sort of touching little stories. They told me he was a victim of the holocaust and sometimes wrote about that. He had survived the death camps but his family had not. No wonder he looked so sad.

Our hosts, his and mine, were clustered around the Churches, listening raptly to the senator, while we two writers were parked at the opposite end of the table to entertain each other. And we did, in the fashion of writers. That's what we talked about—writing, not the holocaust. I instantly like him, not just because we shared a passion for language, but also because he was such a civilized and gentle little man. It was hard to think of anyone ever abusing a man like that. In retrospect, I doubt he would have minded talking about his terrible experiences as a boy in the death camps. He spent the balance of his life making certain that we all knew and remembered. But it seemed to me that night that it would be out of place to start grilling him about it.

I wish now that I had entered into that topic because 10 years later my affable dinner companion—Elie Wiesel—won the Nobel Peace Prize. He has since headed the committee that brought to completion the Holocaust Memorial Museum in Washington. And since that evening over dinner, I have read his writing and admired the power of his succinctness. But the striking thing about him, in person or on television, is his lack of outward anger. Somehow he has overcome that and proven himself too civilized to become like those who brutalized the Jews. How does he manage that?

"Because I remember, I despair," he said in his Nobel lecture. "Because I remember, I have the duty to reject despair."

*   *   *

As I rode in the limousine through Brussels with the Churches—protected by a motorcycle escort—I was put in one of those no-man-is-an-island frames of mind. A generation before—partially because America and other nations reacted too slowly and too indecisively to what was happening to the Jews—my Gentile Uncle Jim from Boise, Idaho, wasn't able to ride through Brussels in an escorted limousine. He walked every footsore step across Belgium behind a U.S. Army tank and was lucky to come home with no more than a concussion. So I was glad that day that another guy from Boise—this one a presidential candidate—had come to Brussels to help the Jews of the world draw a hard line on some other mean bastards.

The World Conference on Soviet Jewry was being staged, and I do mean staged, in an ancient and ornate opera house, ringed with balconies and boxes. Jews of every description from every corner of the world filled the hall to the rafters. They wore earphones on which they heard translations of speeches in half a dozen languages. As Church stepped into the wings to make his entrance, and as I slipped through a side door into a box, a stunning young woman at the microphone read in a ringing voice the honor roll of Jews jailed in Russia. The crowd underscored each name with proud applause.

And there at the head table, simultaneously strong as a bulldog and gentle as a kitten, sat the former prime minister of Israel, the iron grandmother herself—Golda Meir. I couldn't keep my eyes off her. I've never seen a living symbol with so much impact, a person with so much historical star quality written so broadly on a face so full of character.

But there was an amusing aspect as well. With that enormous head, those sharply drawn facial lines, and her generous nose, she was a living editorial cartoon. It is true that she looked like Lyndon Johnson in drag.

But there was more. Hers was also the face of a mother and a warrior in one person. She was strong without being hard. There was comfort or terror for the beholder of that face, depending on your intentions. I would want that lady on my side in an alley fight.

Church told his favorite Golda Meir story that day: She once answered the charge of outside propagandists that Israel was a dictatorship. It is easy, she snapped (as Church paraphrased her) to tell a dictatorship from a democracy. One has only to ask whether the members of the opposition party are in parliament or in jail.

The senator also recalled a visit to her home some years before when she was still prime minister. She had inquired of her guests whether they wanted tea or orange juice, and then exited to the kitchen. Church assumed at first that she had left to instruct a maid. But hearing the rattling of dishes, it dawned on him that the leader of Israel was preparing the refreshments herself. So the senator stepped into the kitchen, as he might have done in an Idaho farmhouse, and offered to help.

She said she could manage the refreshments but that there would be other ways in years to come in which he could help.

"One of those ways is to be with you here today," Church told the throng in the Brussels opera house. "And that is why I have come."

Among native Idahoans, it is almost an article of frontier faith that you must stand your ground when seriously challenged, that bullies must not be given an inch, that there comes a time when you must draw the wagons in a circle. Idahoans will tolerate a lot of empty insults and walk away from countless outbursts by emotional Easterners. But when they have finally had enough, it is wise to get out of the way.

The same stubborn spirit was at work that day in Brussels. Indeed, the message of that gathering, though unstated, was abundantly apparent and quite elementary: After all those centuries of persecution, Adolf Hitler had put a period at the end of their patience. They simply weren't going to take any more crap off anyone ever again.

An Idahoan can understand that.

Frank Church in 1975, the year before he ran for president. *Barry Kough photo*.

Above: Church in 1975, the year in which he directed Senate investigations of intelligence agencies and of international corporations while taking the first steps toward launching a presidential campaign. *Top right:* Church shares a laugh with Governor Cecil Andrus, one of his closest allies in Idaho politics. Church worked hard for Andrus and Andrus for Church—especially during Church's 1976 presidential bid. But Andrus's fellow governor, Jimmy Carter, understood and named Andrus his Secretary of the Interior just the same. *Lower right:* Verda Barnes, the senator's long-time chief of staff and political guru, is—characteristically—the center of warm attention from Frank and Bethine Church at Barnes's retirement party in 1975. *Barry Kough photos.*

Above: The chairman of the Senate investigation of the CIA checks out press reports of the undertaking. *Top right:* Chairman Frank Church and Vice Chairman John Tower confer with Senate Minority Leader Hugh Scott, left, and Majority Leader Mike Mansfield, right, on what is expected of the new Senate intelligence investigation. *Lower right:* Church engaged in sober discussion early in 1975 with CIA Director William Colby as the intelligence committee investigation is just getting under way. *Barry Kough photos.*

Frank and Forest Church help the senator's mother out her front door on the way to the announcement of her son's candidacy for President of the United States. *Glenn Cruickshank photo.*

The crowd at Idaho City awaits the arrival of the candidate for president. *Barry Kough photo.*

Top left: Church enters the presidential race from a platform in Idaho City. To the right of the picture are national finance director Henry Kimelman, radio-television coordinator Mort Schwartz, and, just on the other side of the Idaho flag, the author. *Lower left:* Frank and Bethine Church address the crowd from the tarmac during a stop at Lewiston. *Above:* A Secret Service agent gives the senator a chuckle. *Barry Kough photos.*

Above: Mike Kopetski of Oregon, co-chairman with Larry LaRocco of Church's Oregon primary victory, advocates Church's vice presidential candidacy at the 1976 convention. In later years, both Kopetski and LaRocco were elected to House seats in Congress—Kopetski from Oregon and LaRocco from Idaho. *Top right:* Church, surrounded by Secret Service agents, is still in the running for the vice presidential nomination after meeting with Jimmy Carter at the 1976 convention. *Lower right:* Bethine, Frank, Chase, Amy and Forrest Church, flanked by Verda Barnes and Carl Burke, to the left of Bethine, along with other supporters, listen as Carter announces what he has already told Church privately: it will be a Carter-Mondale ticket. *Barry Kough photos.*

Above: Church enjoys the spotlight during the ceremonial floor rally in support of his long-since-finished candidacy at the 1976 convention. *Barry Kough photo.* *Top right:* Carl Burke, national campaign chairman and close personal Church chum since boyhood, confers with his candidate. *Glen Cruickshank photo.* *Lower right:* Henry Kimelman, national finance director of the Church campaign. *Barry Kough photo.*

Mort Schwartz, radio-television coordinator of the Church campaign. *Barry Kough photo.*

Peter Fenn, Church family friend and an aide to the senator, shares a campaign moment with the author. *Barry Kough photo.*

The author, back in the Idaho newspaper business, greets Church at Lewiston airport where Church was campaigning in late 1976 for the Carter-Mondale ticket. Hall noticed the senator was inadvertently wearing his Carter campaign button upside down. Church asked him to right it lest, he said, it be mistaken for an international distress signal. *Barry Kough photo.*

Chapter Thirteen
Firestorm

"A campaign should be fun," said national chairman Carl Burke, bubbling through the latest of his many happy-time pep talks to the department heads of the Frank Church campaign. "You should all be enjoying yourselves. We've got a great candidate and great department heads and a great group of people working in this campaign all over America. And we're going to beat Jimmy Carter because Frank Church deserves to be president. Now, we can have our little spats. That's normal in a campaign. Henry and I fight a little almost every day, but we still like each other, don't we, Henry?"

Henry Kimelman, our national finance director, nodded in good-natured agreement.

"But for all our occasional arguments," Carl Burke continued, "and for all the long hours of hard work, we can still have fun in this campaign. If you're not having fun in a political campaign, you're trying too hard."

We were trying too hard.

We didn't have any fun at all in the spring of 1976. Moreover, Carl Burke and Henry Kimelman, among others, were going well beyond friendly little spats. Frank Church's national campaign headquarters was open warfare from morning until night. Day after corrosive day, we vilified each other with sincere and heartfelt obscenities. We maneuvered and backstabbed and outflanked and threatened to tell Frank Church on each other—or, when truly provoked, threatened to tell Bethine.

But we waged one hell of a campaign that spring.

Unfortunately, we waged it against each other. We rarely laid a glove on Jimmy Carter. The enemy was us. Carl wanted us to have fun. I haven't had so much fun since the last time my feet slipped off my bicycle pedals.

Every presidential campaign has its episodes of fierce faction-alism, some worse than others. But this was more than mere fac-tionalism; this was a four-month firestorm of emotion. If we had expended half as much energy on our candidate as we did quarrel-ing with each other, Frank Church would have become president and Jimmy Carter would have become Secretary of Sincerity.

Not that his feuding staff cheated Church out of the presidency. He chose that staff. And he could never quite bring himself to tell Carl Burke or Henry Kimelman that one or the other was fully in charge at national headquarters. And so they both were.

Burke and Kimelman seemed to get along well at first. I think they respected each other in the beginning. They shared twin pas-sions—Frank Church and the game of politics. Burke had man-aged Frank Church's successful campaign for student body president at Boise High School 33 years earlier, plus Church's suc-cessful campaign for student body president at Stanford Univer-sity, as well as all four of Church's campaigns for the U.S. Senate. Indeed, the only campaign Church ever lost before 1976 was for a seat in the Idaho legislature. Burke didn't manage that campaign; he was busy that year losing his own race for the legislature.

As high school students, Church and Burke used to sit around and talk about the day when Church would run for president. It went without saying, as Church prepared to enter the race, that Carl Burke would be his national campaign manager.

And so Frank Church's friend, a big, gregarious Boise attor-ney with a booming baritone laugh that could shatter windows and warm hearts, arrived in Washington early in 1976 eager for the task before him and cheerleading all the way. Burke constantly told the staff that Church had "a real shot at it," even though he was entering late, because the senator was "the smartest man I've ever met," and because he had the greatest campaign staff ever as-sembled, most especially including Henry Kimelman.

Of course, much of that overflowing optimism was aimed at pumping up morale. But Burke was genuinely delighted as we embarked. He was thrilled to be in Washington and at the helm of the campaign he had been waiting for all his life. And in the begin-ning, he loved everything about it. He relished the long hours. He enjoyed his coworkers. He even declared our scruffy but service-able old headquarters building behind the Cannon House Office

Building the perfect place to run a campaign. Indeed, he was so delighted that he began slipping fivers to the street people living under a porch in the alley behind our building. They seemed like such nice fellows, and Burke wanted them to feel welcome. He said they would look after the place at night. And if you had asked, he would have insisted that Frank Church's campaign had the greatest street people in Washington.

Our headquarters building was the same one George McGovern had occupied in winning the 1972 nomination. Indeed, it was the same headquarters that Watergate operative G. Gordon Liddy had cased from a car across the street, trying to figure out how to crack the building's security.

Henry Kimelman, who had been aboard that campaign, laughed at Liddy. He said the McGovern headquarters was such a typical disorganized circus of volunteers and visitors that any eight-year-old could have strolled in off the street and picked up anything off any desk and never been noticed.

The same held true of the building during the Church campaign. It was a crackerbox. I returned late one night from dinner to find myself locked out. I climbed the fire escape and, using a strip of scrap steel I found in the alley, pried open an unlocked window and crawled through. Either our scruffy street watchmen in the alley were sleeping one off, or they recognized me and decided to mind their own business. But G. Gordon Liddy would have been amazed.

*   *   *

Henry Kimelman had a reputation as the man who worked miracles for George McGovern. Half a dozen of the 1976 Democratic candidates had been after Kimelman to handle their fund-raising. But Henry waited for Frank Church. The Kimelmans and the Churches had vacationed together frequently over the previous decade. And Kimelman admired Church. Kimelman also admired Kimelman.

Kimelman and Burke were as much of a contrast physically as they were temperamentally. Henry, fiftyish, was deeply tanned winter and summer from hours in the Virgin Islands sun where he managed a fortune in real estate. He wore modish casual clothes with his shirt usually unbuttoned halfway to his belt, exposing a gold chain or two. He was movie-star handsome with unruly black hair and resembled the actor Victor Mature.

Burke, a balding, round-faced man with squinty, almost-Oriental eyes, always wore square, prosperous business suits and looked something like a capitalistic Mao Tse-Tung.

Kimelman was a politics junkie. Most of us were. But he was a heavy user. Indeed, I had the impression that most of the major fund-raisers are. They are almost a separate, higher caste in politics. They all seem to know each other exceedingly well. Kimelman was constantly on the phone checking with finance chairmen for every candidate from Jimmy Carter to Ronald Reagan. When Reagan bought half an hour of time for a network fund appeal, Kimelman gave us daily reports on how much money they had raised.

Apart from his wish that his friend, Frank Church, be elected president, Kimelman seemed driven by some private competition among his fellow fund-raisers. I often wondered if they hadn't all gone to dinner a year earlier, parceled out the candidates to whom each would attach himself, and placed a few side bets on the outcome. To Henry Kimelman, there was a sporting aspect to the campaign quite apart from helping the public decide whether Frank Church or Jimmy Carter might make the better president. It was a fund-raising contest to see whether Kimelman or Morris Dees, with the Carter campaign, could raise more money—not just for the good of the republic, but just for the hell of it.

Dees and Kimelman had worked together on the 1972 McGovern campaign and their direct mail and television fund appeals had raised millions. They would send out letters to a large mailing list and the money would pour in. They would put McGovern on television, baldly begging the nation for money, and more checks would roll in. No candidate had ever done as well using either technique. So Henry Kimelman came to the Church campaign as the man who had discovered the magic formula in 1972 for shaking money out of the American political public.

Unfortunately, it was no longer 1972.

Kimelman's confidence and our initial faith in him was a classic case of old generals fighting this year's war by the last war's rules. The rules had changed. In the first place, George McGovern was essentially a one-issue candidate in a one-issue time. He was the anti-war candidate that year in a Democratic Party heartsick and angry over the government's obsession with the endless stalemate in Indochina. All McGovern had to do was touch that raw

Vietnam nerve and thousands of Americans who shared his outrage would send him money.

The 1976 campaigns, by the nature of the times, had to be far more generalized. There was no one issue anyone could monopolize. Moreover, the remodeled federal election laws transformed fund-raising. In 1972, one contributor—Stewart R. Mott—gave George McGovern $400,000. In 1976, Mott could legally have given a maximum of $1,000.

Henry Kimelman had come out of a 1972 experience in which it had been possible to raise the entire budget for one state presidential primary with a single phone call. The 1976 campaign required hundreds of phone calls to raise the same amount.

As the Church campaign began, Kimelman didn't want to fool around buttonholing individuals for a thousand dollars a throw. (Burke raised more money that way than Kimelman did.) Henry was faunching to commit large wads of our relatively meager front-end money to a massive direct mail appeal, with plans to move a little later into network television pitches—just as he had for McGovern.

The direct mail appeal brought in less money than it cost. So did the network commercials.

Henry's refusal to recognize the new reality was a principal source of the frictions that developed between Burke and Kimelman and their various partisans inside national campaign headquarters.

Church and Burke were uneasy from the very first about committing so much money to direct mail and to national television. But in a still-friendly showdown at Church's house one evening, Kimelman explained in a long discourse that it was the job of Church to campaign, the job of Burke to spend the money, and the job of Kimelman to raise the money as he saw fit. All Burke need trouble himself with, Henry said, was to tell him how much money needed to be raised for a given period. It was as simple as that.

"I'll need $500,000 by the day Frank announces," Burke quickly responded.

"You'll have it," Kimelman countered.

Church, with misgivings but concurring with Henry that there had to be some chain of command, agreed to commit most of our early money to Kimelman's magic fund-raising techniques—money spent to raise even more money. It made sense to me and I sided that night with Kimelman, a bit of an old general myself.

And so the national headquarters war began.

I was told that Kimelman had always been eccentric and difficult to work with. But he seemed to choke as the fund-raising efforts sputtered. He became increasingly hyper and rude. An engaging and intelligent man at ease, he became insensitive to all around him in the heat of battle, treating practically all of his co-workers as witless flunkies.

In his obsession with making the formula work, he became even more impulsive than usual. He would walk into headquarters in the morning, get a sudden idea that it was a simple matter of one more network commercial, and start yelling out the names of staff members at the top of his lungs.

"I've got a terrific idea," he would announce as the staff assembled. "We did a commercial for George in '72 that was almost all fund appeal and not much message. We made a killing, and that's what we need now."

Within no time, he would call a network in New York and commit us to buy five minutes. An hour later, with people scurrying about renting a television studio and preparing the script, he would suddenly remember he promised Church he would double-check such decisions with Carl Burke in the next office.

"Goddam it, I forgot to tell Carl," he would say, cursing himself for his forgetfulness.

When Carl was finally told—invariably after the fact—he would go into shock. The campaign was usually down to its last $20,000, with workers unpaid and cash needed for local advertising in an approaching primary. Even if the national commercial brought in its cost, which never happened, it would take a couple of weeks for all the checks to arrive. Meanwhile, Burke would have one hell of a cash flow problem.

"Henry," he would wail, "I've just barely got enough money for some television in Nebraska, and you've just spent that. And I haven't paid anybody. My God, I have this good, hard-working kid out in Oregon who's going to help us carry that state. He hasn't been paid in three months, his wife is pregnant, and they don't know where their next meal is coming from."

Henry just blinked. It wasn't that he was unmoved; he didn't understand. Henry was a millionaire. He simply had no idea what it's like to have a pregnant wife and no income. Besides, he assured

Carl, this next television commercial would be the one that would do the job. This next commercial would leave the campaign rolling in money—"a hundred thousand minimum"—and then Carl could give the kid in Oregon his back pay and a raise besides.

Kimelman's impulsiveness scared me because any mistake he might make was utterly unavoidable. When he got one of his terrific ideas, he didn't have time for diplomacy. He had no interest in other opinions that might have found a flaw and saved the situation. He would shout down anyone who offered an objection or an improvement. When he got rolling on a terrific idea, he would snarl at people whether they agreed with him or not.

He came running into my office one afternoon asking my help on the wording of a fund appeal at the end of the latest commercial. He had no sooner asked for my suggestions than he was struck with a thought himself and began dictating it to an underling. He got stuck. He was reaching for the right word.

I suggested one.

"Goddam it, Bill, shut up," he thundered. "This is fund-raising and none of your fucking business."

Henry had instantly forgotten that he had just entered my office asking for help. He had no idea how rough he came across. He simply meant, "Just a second until I get this thought out of my head." But he didn't have time to say it nice. Henry never had time to say it nice.

Before long, the national headquarters staff had divided into three groups—the Burkites, the Kimelmaniacs, and the majority—the latter made up of sane people who tried to stay out of the way of the warriors, do their jobs, and avoid some of the storm at the top. The noncombatants had the bizarre idea that they were working for neither Burke nor Kimelman, but for Frank Church.

I swore in the beginning to become the founding member of a fourth group—the peacemakers between the Burkites and the Kimelmaniacs. But between Kimelman's snarling at me and Burke's telling me his troubles with Kimelman, I began to get caught up in the Burke camp.

The clincher was Kimelman's tendency to characterize the Idahoans in the campaign as political incompetents. "Those goddam Idahoans don't know their ass from a hole in the ground," he confided to me one day, forgetting where I came from.

I asked if that included Frank Church. He answered that Church wasn't really an Idahoan any longer after living in the East for 20 years.

I had just been called a pariah by Henry Kimelman. I lost interest in peacemaking.

* * *

After one especially wild day I began to feel the strain and did what anyone would do in similar circumstances: I called my psychiatrist and asked her to join me for a drink.

In Idaho, my psychiatrist had been my vegetable garden and my patio. Each morning it had long been my habit to putter around the garden, checking on my tasty friends the beans, the potatoes, and the tomatoes, and then eat breakfast on the patio among the flowers, followed by a cup of coffee and some time with my favorite newspaper. My Idaho routine is similar to this day. And by the time I arrive at work, I can handle any crisis or crank call that the world might throw at me for the rest of the day. In the evening, after work, I return to the yard with a diet pop (wine in my drinking days) and listen to the song of the crickets chirping and the grass growing. (The crickets are a little louder than the grass.)

But in Washington, there was no tranquilizing back yard. When I really needed help, my psychiatrist, Doctor Sasser, would join me at a Pennsylvania Avenue restaurant for a glass of wine. Doctor Sasser was Myrna Sasser, Church's constituent services specialist. For years, she helped Idahoans with federal frustrations. I was a constituent. I was in the federal capital. I was frustrated.

I told her about Kimelman's crack against Idahoans. She just gave me an I-told-you-so look. She had warned me earlier that the Washington grapevine had it that Kimelman was explosive and impossible to work with.

"Well, I still have hope," I said. "Maybe with a little more time, we'll learn to work together."

"Maybe," said Doctor Sasser.

* * *

In the summer of 1975, a Jewish mother named Mort Schwartz adopted me against my will. Mort came to Washington to interview Church for a Miami radio station. An exuberant and impulsive man, he had been instantly dazzled by the senator. He offered to do anything he could if Church ran for president. Mort had broadcast and film production experience. I didn't. I tucked his name away for future reference.

That wasn't necessary. Thereafter, he called or wrote repeatedly to renew his offer. Finally, late in 1975, he called to say he would be moving to Washington the first of the year to help Frank Church whether we were ready for him or not. He would be in touch.

One afternoon, early in 1976, Mort and his French wife, Capucine, flew into New York from France where they had spent the holidays with her family. They immediately called Church's office, leaving a message for me to meet them that evening at the Mayflower Hotel. And then they boarded the next flight for Washington.

I entered the Mayflower lobby just as they rolled in. They were as excited as two children on Christmas morning. Capucine—or Cappy, as she was called—was half a generation younger than Mort's 46 years. She looked and dressed like a high-fashion model ready for the camera. She greeted me in what I was to learn was her usual effusive manner.

"Oh, Beelee," she bubbled. "I am so 'appy to meet you. I weel geeve you a French kees." Whereupon she pecked me on each cheek like a French general awarding the Legion of Honor. It wasn't what an American would call a French kiss. It was just her leetle joke, a joke she repeated the next day when meeting Frank Church, thereby startling another Idaho square.

I joined them in their room while they changed for dinner. Cappy emerged wearing one of her Vogue model outfits—a dark violet turban, a silk scarf around her neck, a dark violet blouse, plus lipstick and nail polish the same hue, and a pair of dark harem pants. I'm not sure of the material. That is not my field of expertise. Suffice it to say, it looked like swell material, really swell.

She topped the whole thing with a Cossack-length fur coat—dyed raccoon or something like that.

Mort changed into a crushed velvet suit the color of deep red wine. He completed his ensemble with a black velvet bow tie, his modified Jewish-Afro haircut, and an oversized leather wallet, too large to carry in a pocket and perhaps too small to be called a purse.

I was dressed that night in a light gray suit that had set me back $119.95, which might seem a little steep, but it came with two pair of pants. I also wore a baby blue Arrow shirt that I had picked up for seven bucks at a year-end sale. My hair was done in a style known as modified Kansas Gentile, swept wantonly back over a bald spot at the back, thereby exposing a daring swath of high, bare forehead. The *piece de resistance* (or is that the *coup de grace?*) was my Bicentennial tie with the dates "1776-1976" and little macho American flags all over it.

And away we went to dinner—two Guccis and a J.C. Penney.

I think that evening was the first time Mort ever kissed me. It was a strictly platonic, straight on the cheek, man to man kiss. And he did it out on the street in front of the Mayflower while we waited for a cab. Mort was a trifle manic. He alternated between being the angriest person in the world and the happiest. When he was happy, he was deliriously happy. He was so happy he couldn't contain himself. He loved everyone. He would spontaneously grab friends, male or female, and hug them and kiss them on the cheek.

"I'm so happy tonight," he said, standing there on the curb, squeezing me with an arm around my shoulders and bussing my cheek. "I just love you, Bill Hall."

"I love you, too, Beel," Cappy cooed, smooching me on the other cheek while the doorman, rolling his eyes, called a cab.

I was kissed a lot by those two over the next few weeks. It was always a little sticky for an Idahoan. We are not a demonstrative people. We don't much show physical affection in public, except occasionally toward our horses and our bird dogs. And you just wouldn't stand in front of the hotel in downtown Boise and let some fashion model and some guy in a crushed velvet suit kiss you repeatedly and still live to run for sheriff.

After a time, Mort finally sensed my discomfort. Cappy still came running toward me in national headquarters each morning, purring "Beelee, let me geeve you a good-morning kees." It was much earlier in the day than I normally even begin speaking to people, let alone necking with them. But at least Mort stopped kissing me. Thereafter, when he was especially happy, he would merely stand facing me and lightly dance his fingertips on my cheeks, saying, "Oh, Bill, I'm so happy."

I got to where I really hated that.

But I've never worked with anyone so loyal. He was so totally, so blindly, so fervently loyal to Frank Church and to me that it was sometimes frightening—such as the time he volunteered to pitch Henry Kimelman out the window for me and meant it.

Mort had been on the job only about two weeks when I first saw the trembling, infuriated half of his personality. He entered the office in a rage. A young man in headquarters had asked him how much he was being paid. Mort answered that he was volunteering his time to Frank Church until the campaign got on its financial feet.

"Well, I'm paid staff," the young man said, strutting a bit.

Mort insisted on being paid. His bank account didn't need the money, but his pride did.

"No goddam kid is going to pull that shit on me," he fumed. "I want to be paid staff, too."

So Carl Burke had to put Mort on the payroll earlier than planned and sooner than the campaign could afford.

Mort was to be our radio and television director. He had some credentials in the industry and we were going to gamble. We were going to produce our own commercials, in-house, and save the usual agency costs. I would write the commercials and Mort would produce and direct. We did produce one five-minute biographical commercial that way that we used frequently early in the campaign. Mort also produced several shorter television spots and some for radio that Henry Kimelman used infrequently and then tossed aside.

Henry, the television fund-raising specialist, had been appalled from the beginning that we were using Mort instead of an agency. Soon we were no longer using Mort. Kimelman lined up a New York agency without telling Mort or me, or even Carl Burke.

Mort was the first to find out. Years before, he had been a witness to wars for control of a Hollywood studio. He had developed a keen sense for sniffing out double-dealing. It was so keen that he frequently detected and exploded over double-dealing that wasn't going on.

"That son of a bitch Kimelman is dealing with a New York agency behind our backs," Mort said, storming into the press room. "I thought I was the television director of this campaign."

I checked with Burke. He seemed surprised but asked me to be patient while he worked things out. Translation: Kimelman had taken off on his own again, spending money on an agency without telling Carl. Carl didn't want to admit that to me at first. He wanted to talk to Church and see if the candidate had authorized the new television project and the money to pay for it.

I had a rough idea what was going on but didn't want to give Carl any more headaches, so I didn't push it. Meanwhile, I had to deal daily with an extremely impatient and terribly hurt Mort Schwartz. He would rush into the office each morning, screaming his obscene opinion of Kimelman and company. Soon he would be trembling with the veins standing out on his temples. More than once, I thought I saw a violent streak simmering beneath the surface of that sometimes ecstatically joyful man. After several days of that, he began to frighten the press room staff, including me. And it became impossible to calm him.

"But you don't know what those sonsabitches are doing down there."

"Mort! Now, goddam it, get hold of yourself."

"I'm telling you that they're screwing Frank Church and I'm going to sue their ass off."

"Mort! If you don't calm down and talk about this quietly, I won't talk to you at all."

"But you don't know what those assholes are doing to us."

"Mort! I'm going to walk out of here if you don't simmer down. If you can't talk without yelling, I don't want to hear it."

"But those bastards are down there trying to get you."

There was no stopping him, so I would turn and walk out of the office. It was the only thing I could think to do.

It sometimes worked. When I returned in a few minutes, Mort would occasionally agree to be calm and listen. I told him I was trying to get some answers out of Carl. I asked him to please be patient because I thought Carl was also in the dark. And then I would march downstairs, finally catch Carl off the phone and be told, "I don't know what to tell you, buddy. I've got to have a talk with Frank."

And then back to Mort to tell him it would take a little more time. Mort would be satisfied for the moment and leave for lunch. That afternoon, he would return, get upset all over again and the whole insane ritual would be repeated.

And twice again the next day.

And again the next.

And the next.

Mort offered to resign several times a week, providing the campaign would pay him the back money he was owed. He had paid for some of the film processing out of his own pocket. Mort's proposition was simple: he would resign if he got his money.

Burke said we couldn't afford it. He asked me to keep Mort and his daily furies for a while longer.

Occasionally, Burke would win some temporary agreement from Kimelman that we would give Mort a project, that we would put him back in charge of producing commercials. And then all would be forgiven. Mort was so happy. He said he wasn't in any rush for the money. All he had ever wanted was to feel useful.

But the mood usually lasted about 24 hours before there would be some new slight and everything would come unglued again.

Kimelman had a habit of talking openly around headquarters about how much more gifted his agency people were at producing commercials than Mort Schwartz was. Indeed, he could be scathing in his public estimates of Mort's abilities. Mort overheard more than once. A stormy confrontation ensued each time and it became necessary for someone to jump between them to prevent mayhem. One such encounter occurred just as a reporter arrived on the premises for a look at Church headquarters. Fortunately, I saw him enter and rushed to his side, grabbed him by the arm, and steered him toward the opposite end of the building with a cheery, "Let me show you our lovely paper-storage room."

The day after Church's Nebraska victory, Mort was in the middle of his daily diatribe against "those assholes" when a local television crew came around the corner filming the two of us with a long lens from down the hallway.

"Watch it," I said, talking through my teeth. "Television crews. Get it off your chest, but calmly and very quietly. They've got a microphone."

And so we stood there, nose to nose, while Mort told me for the hundredth time what a son of a bitch Henry Kimelman was. That night on the evening news, the local station carried a shot of two exceedingly somber aides to Frank Church, apparently discussing a very serious matter—undoubtedly strategy for the next primary.

Mort's father died unexpectedly one day and Mort flew to Florida for the funeral. He returned to report that his father, who had been wearing a Frank Church button before he died, was buried with one on the lapel of his suit.

Late in the campaign, Mort rushed in one day, furious as usual, to report that Kimelman was holding a meeting in his office to plan a series of television commercials. He had refused to admit Mort.

It took 10 minutes to get Mort under control and there were tears in his eyes before we were through. (By then I was having some success with, "Mort, why do you hate me so much that you would do this to me every day?") When Mort finally simmered down, I became furious myself. I slipped downstairs to Kimelman's office just as the television planning meeting ended. I marched up to Henry with fire in my eyes.

"I don't care whether you like Mort or not," I said, "but I insist you stop treating him like a piece of shit."

Kimelman was stunned.

"I didn't treat him like a piece of shit."

"Yes, you did. He's up in my office right now, crying. I don't think you realize, Henry, how goddam rough you come across to people when you get in one of your big rushes to get something done."

Henry was crestfallen. He truly didn't realize.

I returned to the press room. The phone rang. It was Kimelman wanting to see Mort. Mort went downstairs. He returned with a stunned look on his face.

"What happened?" I asked. "Did you get an apology?"

"Yeah," he shrugged with a grin. "I guess Henry's not so bad."

Within two days, they were screaming at each other again.

We had a peacemaker in the beginning. Peter P. Curtin, Jr., a New Jersey native in his early thirties who hoped to run for Congress one day, was our director of political organization. He was always shaking his head and telling me that we all had to get along.

I told him it was a little difficult to get along with Henry when he was constantly ignoring Burke and working around Mort and me.

Curtin shook his head gravely. I thought at the time that he was agreeing with me.

Meanwhile, Mort came boiling in to report that Kimelman and William Landau, our treasurer, had sent a check to a film lab Mort was working with, and then stopped payment on the check—as a way of answering the demand that the bill be paid while still keeping the money to buy more commercial time for their New

York-produced commercials. Furthermore, Mort said, he had just learned that Kimelman and Landau were secretly trying to get us both fired.

Oh, God, I thought, if it were only true. If they could only pull it off.

* * *

Television wasn't our only headache. Kimelman had hired a woman from New York to handle the direct mail campaign that was supposed to bring in the flood of money. She produced an initial draft that was adequate in a bland sort of way, but it didn't focus on what Church considered the principal themes of his campaign. The senator didn't like it and asked me to draft a new version along the lines he dictated.

Unfortunately, he ran into the direct-mail lady on an airplane about that time and she asked him how he liked her copy.

"Fine. Fine," he fibbed, leaving it to underlings to do the dirty work and tell her later that it wasn't good enough. (A politician normally delivers good news himself and leaves the bruising bad news to an aide.)

When she was told later by one of Kimelman's people that the senator had prepared a substitute draft, she didn't believe it. After all, Church had told her himself on the airplane that he was pleased with her version. She demanded to know who had written the new copy and was told I had, but on orders of the senator and following an outline he had dictated. Moreover, she was firmly told, Frank Church, as was his practice, had personally polished the words into a final draft. And he had.

She still didn't believe it. To her, it was an obvious case of some hotshot—me—who presumed to think he knew more about her business than she did, unilaterally changing the copy without the senator's knowledge. She was dealing with a budding Machiavelli and, by God, she wouldn't let him get away with it.

The Kimelman people, the Burke people, and even a couple of dispassionate people in neutral, all tried to convince her, in one telephone call after another, that the new version was, indeed, the one Frank Church wanted. For once, we were unified.

But she would have none of it. She printed half the run using her original draft before we found out about it. There was some angry negotiation and Kimelman's people finally agreed to live with the half she had already printed. But she agreed—on pain of not getting paid—that the second half of the press run would be the new version. She said she would be paying strict attention to which version brought in more money, because it was obvious that her copy, which Frank Church himself had liked so much, would do better than the one that had been slipped past him by that meathead Bill Hall.

The letters were scheduled to be mailed in time to reach households across the country just as people were reading in their papers and seeing on television that Frank Church had announced for president.

The letters went out a week late, well after the initial national chatter about this new candidate, Frank Church, had begun to fade.

And we will never know which version might have raised more money. On reflection, she was so certain that Frank Church really preferred the first that she printed them all that way. There were times when neither faction had any control over the campaign.

Frank Church was incredulous. Carl Burke was distraught. Henry Kimelman called her on the telephone and screamed at her. I was in shock.

It was obviously time for another session with Doctor Sasser. I invited her to dinner that night.

She told me that war is hell.

I felt a lot better.

*   *   *

On the morning of April 6, I awoke with a wicked hope. Mo Udall had a chance of defeating Jimmy Carter that day in Wisconsin. Udall's failure, week after week, to win a single primary was about all that was keeping the Church campaign alive during that period. As long as Udall failed to show he could win, there remained room for another "liberal alternative" to Carter. But if Udall won that night, it would probably end our chances. It would be a mercy killing. The campaign would be over, and I would be heading home to the good life, to my garden and sanity.

When television reported that Udall had, indeed, won that night, I went to bed wearing the smile of a happy traitor.

But when I awoke the next morning and learned that the television declarations of a Udall victory had been a trifle premature—that Carter had pulled it out after all—I vowed never to forgive Mo Udall. To think that a fellow Westerner would have condemned me to still more weeks in that nut factory, where the supreme indignity was that I was one of the head nuts.

*   *   *

Perhaps the most habitually snafued department in the whole operation, and in many ways the most crucial, was scheduling. Where the candidate is scheduled—what states he hits when and the events and interviews he is sent to—has a lot to do with whether he gets enough public attention to win. Church constantly had to overrule his schedulers. They were always bucking him, trying to slip him into a primary state they thought he should enter but which the senator had decided to avoid. Moreover, they were inclined to drive him harder than Bethine Church would let them. And when she put her foot down, refusing to let headquarters schedule her husband on another 16-hour day or another overnight flight, the schedulers would make acid comments about what a baby their candidate was.

As a consequence of all that tugging and pulling between the candidate and his schedulers, there were many times when we quite literally didn't know from one day to the next where Church would be. There were days when Church learned in the morning what state he would sleep in that night.

Worse, from my standpoint, were the press calls:

> *NEW YORK TIMES:* We want to follow your candidate next week and see how he's doing. We need a schedule.
>
> PRESS SECRETARY: Ah. . . . There have been some changes which we're trying to work out, so I can't give it to you in any detail.
>
> *NEW YORK TIMES*: That's fine. We just need to know what states he'll be hitting next week.
>
> PRESS SECRETARY: Ah. . . . Let me check with the schedulers and get back to you on that in a day or two.
>
> *NEW YORK TIMES*: Look, we know you're just getting started. Why don't we wait a week or two and cover him when you really get your act together.

And of course, everyone in headquarters was always asking me why so few reporters followed Frank Church. Some who asked that question worked in scheduling.

*　*　*

As the warm weather and high humidity hit Washington, our air conditioning conked out. Or so we were told. Perhaps it was only a coincidence that our landlord had been sent a rent check on which payment had been stopped. It was more than 100 degrees some days in the windowless sections of headquarters. People got sick. And of course, the mood grew even uglier.

I began huddling daily for advice and comfort with Verda Barnes, who had retired the year before as Church's administrative assistant. (Of course, she soon volunteered to work for free on Church's campaign.) Verda was a veteran campaigner. It was the measure of how long she had been around Washington and involved in high-level politics that there was a time when she used to slip in the White House and drink tea with Eleanor Roosevelt. But Verda had never seen anything quite like our campaign. An Idahoan and intensely loyal to Church, she was concerned that our Mickey Mouse operation would devastate Church's national reputation—and perhaps his personal standing in the Senate. We were both worried, along with Carl Burke, about all those campaign bills stacking up. Some of Frank Church's oldest friends could be left holding the bag. If Nebraska was a lost cause anyway, and much more money was poured into Kimelman's national television commercials, a lot of people were going to get hurt right along with Frank Church. At one point, Verda and I recommended to Carl that we bag the whole mess—before Nebraska—and cut the losses. With what we had left to spend, he was going to lose anyway. (Oh, we of little faith.)

Burke was tempted, but he was also determined to give Church at least that first, and perhaps his last, shot in Nebraska. But he was even more frantic about the finances than we were.

Carl and I occasionally ate dinner together and he began taking those occasions to tell me his troubles. It suddenly dawned on me that, just as I was routinely sharing my frustrations with Doctor Sasser, I had become Doctor Hall to patient Burke. That scared me. If a poised veteran of so many campaigns sought moral support from a greenhorn like me, then maybe we were in even worse shape than I thought.

One spring night, Carl changed his mind about wanting to go to a restaurant for another session of counseling. We picked up a couple of steaks at a supermarket and headed for the Church house in Bethesda, Maryland. Burke was staying there, and the Churches were on the road. We would have the house to ourselves for another long talk.

We cooked and ate the steaks, and then attacked Carl's liquor supply. We drank everything that sloshed. Our drinking and our talking took place on a screened sun porch looking out on the wooded backyard. It was an eerie setting because, as we examined our fate, the Secret Service agents, always on duty around the Church home, occasionally strolled by, professionally pretending there weren't two morose drunks babbling on the other side of the screen.

"Carl," I said, finally bombed enough to butt in, "get control or get out. Two people can't run a campaign. If the senator won't back you, then you can't do him any good anyway. Tell him he has to put you in charge, or Henry in charge, or somebody else in charge. But we can't go on with this two-headed monster."

"I'm going to have a talk with old Frank," Burke agreed.

As we finished the session, I realized I was in no condition to drive. I crawled into the nearest available bed. The next morning, I opened my eyes and realized I was in Church's bedroom—in the King's bed! At first, I couldn't remember how I got there. I snapped my eyes shut again and felt tentatively on either side of me in the bed, to make certain the King and Queen weren't in there with me, not realizing they had a visitor. And then, finding no one, I opened my eyes again and got the hell out of there.

The following Saturday night, Carl called in high spirits. He had had his talk with Church. And Church, in turn, had talked with Kimelman. It was all straightened out. Burke would be fully in charge of the campaign. Kimelman would stick strictly to fundraising. And Kimelman would spend no money on any project without Burke's agreement. Moreover, Church was placing a second mortgage on his home. It would provide enough money to get us through Nebraska. If Church won there, then it should give him sufficient credibility as a candidate to bring in more money for the next primary down the line. No one would be left holding the bad-debt bag, except possibly Frank and Bethine Church and their newly mortgaged house. The campaign was on an even keel at last.

Three days later, Henry Kimelman got another terrific idea and committed several thousand dollars more to network time, forgetting to check with Carl Burke to see if we had any money.

And Mort Schwartz came faunching into the press room in another purple rage. Kimelman was bringing in a New York director to oversee the taping.

And away we went again.

*   *   *

Church kept getting things confused. He thought we were all working for him and not for individual factions. He didn't know who the players were. Nobody had given him a scorecard. And so he asked me out to the house one night to help draft the script for another television appeal for funds. I would be working on that script with both Church and the television director Henry was bringing in from New York in place of Mort. Mort was not pleased, but he didn't blame me.

I wrote two drafts before I arrived—the one I thought Church wanted and the one I hoped he would use. The first was our standard appeal, a general attempt to reach the broadest possible audience. The second might have pleased Henry Kimelman, although he never saw it. That draft zeroed in on the anti-war people, McGovern style. It tried to hit that old nerve. It called for Church to note that he, like McGovern, had very early (1964) turned against the Vietnam adventure. And the thrust of the script was that, though the war was over, the policy that gave rise to it was alive and well and living in the White House. Church would say that it was an interventionist policy that could lead the United States into new Vietnams. The pitch concluded with Church's pledge that, if elected, "I will take that musty State Department and that rusty Department of Defense, turn them upside down and shake out all those lethal myths that have given our country so many heartaches, a sickened economy, and 40,000 fresh graves."

It is tempting with a national television audience of something like 20 million people to try to reach them all. It is also impossible. I was thinking that, if Church could touch a nerve, albeit an old one, reaching just one percent of that 20 million, and they each sent in a dollar, it would raise ten times the cost of the commercial. The trouble with our standard, safe, general appeal was that it wouldn't really rouse anyone enough to prompt a contribution.

Church kindly said that he liked my more sharply focused draft as an accurate statement of his foreign policy position. But he thought it was a mistake strategically. He wanted to go for the general audience.

So did the New York specialist Kimelman brought in. A brassy little man in his early thirties, dressed in chic designer jeans, he believed you sell politicians the same as toothpaste—to as many millions simultaneously as possible—a scatter-gun approach, pleasing all, offending none. He insisted on the most rudimentary words and ideas, shooing Church away from his customary poetic flourishes: "Well, Frank, 'Freedom's sentinel against the dark impulse of tyranny' has a ring to it all right, but how about, 'keeping an eye on the Russians?'"

Church bought most of the suggestions that he keep it common. But he drew the line on one extreme: "Frank," the director said, "you've got to jar them and get their attention. How does this strike you? You say, 'There's been too much blah, blah, blah in America.' And you keep riding it. You say, 'I know you're tired of all this blah, blah, blah, and when I'm your president, I'm going to give you something better than the same old blah, blah, blah.'"

It dawned on me that he wasn't just using "blah, blah, blah" as a shorthand substitute for some common complaint against government. He meant that Frank Church should quite literally use the words "blah, blah, blah," and repeat them over and over throughout the message.

There is a technique in commercials in which you deliberately irritate the audience with the infuriating repetition of a line as a way of driving the name of the product into America's subconscious. This guy was actually proposing that a candidate for president sell himself with an irritation commercial. He was recommending that we rub the audience so raw that it would never forget the name Frank Church—the name of that obnoxious, undignified son of a bitch who brayed "blah, blah, blah" at people until they were ready to climb the walls.

Church declined: "Well . . . ah . . . I think maybe that's not quite in keeping with my usual style," Church said. "I would be uncomfortable with that."

"It's revolting," I volunteered.

"Anything you say, Frank," the director said, ignoring me. "Now, let me sail another little idea by you . . ."

We recovered from the blahs only to finish the script in extremely generalized, toothpaste-vending language. The next day we all met at the studio for taping. The New York script expert was there to direct. Unfortunately, so was Mort.

Mort had arranged for a dark blue backdrop. The New York director insisted that the backdrop be changed to a pale blue.

Mort insisted on the dark blue backdrop. The studio people insisted that we decide on one director. They assured us the taping would go smoother that way.

Carl Burke said we would go with the New York director. "It's Henry's show all the way."

With the other director in charge, Mort slipped into a control room where the technicians greeted him as an old friend they had worked with over the years. Just before taping began, when he didn't think I was paying attention, Mort whispered something to the technicians. The backdrop was electronically changed to a dark blue.

I thought it looked a lot better that way.

*   *   *

Henry Kimelman had another terrific idea. We would demand to buy half an hour on all three networks simultaneously. And that was when cable TV was just a baby, when the three networks owned the airwaves. It meant reaching practically everyone watching television that night.

Of course, Henry knew we didn't stand a prayer of getting the time. The networks were enjoying a very fat year. They were virtually sold out through the fall season. To make room for Frank Church, they would have had to cancel scheduled advertising at far more lucrative rates than they were allowed to charge politicians. Henry knew that. All he wanted was the publicity he and Frank Church would receive in a pseudo-struggle with the networks.

His plan succeeded—almost too well.

We issued one press release after another, demanding Frank Church's right to explain his programs to the electorate. We stuck it to the networks pretty hard for being so mercenary, so indifferent to the noble American process of choosing a president.

Soon I started getting calls, not only from political reporters but also from broadcast industry magazines wanting to do stories on the little Church campaign doing battle with the giant networks. Henry got a little miffed at me that I didn't put the calls through to him so he would be quoted. Finally, he asked me to ghost him a piece for *The New York Times* op-edit page. I wrote him a little essay charging that the networks were obviously more interested in dog food commercials than in giving America a look at the candidates for President of the United States. We were choosing a leader, the article said, but all the networks cared about was their Gravy Train.

The *Times* declined the article. But one of their own writers did a piece making the same points, with the slight variation of talking about the network obsession with cat food commercials. Other papers and publications took up the same theme.

And then, out of the blue, two members of Congress, sitting on committees capable of making life miserable for broadcasters, spontaneously issued a press release pointing out that in most countries free time would be provided for something as important as a presidential campaign. But Frank Church couldn't even *buy* time on American television, they complained. Neither congressman was a Frank Church partisan, and we were as surprised as the networks at their action. They had read the reports in the *Times* and elsewhere and had become genuinely outraged. They sent a letter to all three networks demanding an explanation and warning that, lacking a satisfactory answer, they would begin preparing possible legislation on the subject.

That set nerves on edge in two places—in the network boardrooms and in my skinny little body. Kimelman's campaign was getting out of hand. It was beginning to look like we might get what he had been demanding—a chance to buy half an hour on all three networks.

That would present a problem.

We didn't have the money.

The confrontation finally blew over. But the networks missed a chance to retaliate in style, giving us exactly what we demanded and then relishing our tortured explanations of why we didn't really want the time after all.

*   *   *

As the headquarters war went on, the workers in the press room started to get a little flaky. Mort's daily explosions were getting worse. Cappy Schwartz, who was worried about Mort's health but had given up on talking him into leaving the campaign, stopped coming in each day. Indeed, we were all worried about Mort's health. He had recovered from a heart attack only the year before and he would sometimes turn gray when he flew into one of his many rages.

Meanwhile, I began to wonder when I might have my first heart attack. And I was worried about everyone else in the press room. They were all heartsick and their nerves were on edge—with the exception of Debbie Herbst, the assistant press secretary. Debbie was the calm in our storm. Through it all, she cracked wry jokes to relieve the tension. And she could often soothe Mort better than I. She wasn't exactly enjoying herself, but that slender young woman in her mid-twenties was our rock. She looked after the others while I was out of the office and tipped me when people were getting close to the thin edge so I could Dutch uncle them a little.

One day she reported that Cherie Coleman, my administrative assistant, had suddenly begun crying uncontrollably. Debbie had held her and talked her through it and the sobbing finally passed.

That worried me. Cherie turned out more work than any three of us. She was a large part of what functional competence the press room had left. Typical of her, one day while I was answering a reporter's questions on the phone, she whispered to me to write her a check. And I did.

As I finished that call and took the next one on the other phone, I asked her, "What the hell was that all about?"

"It's your mother's birthday," she said. "You just sent flowers."

On another occasion, I came back to the office from some meeting and she showed me a report one of the senator's committees had issued, something over a hundred pages. My heart sank.

I would have to read the whole bloody thing and write a press release on it.

"I know you're busy," she said, "so I read it and roughed out a press release for you." She wasn't much more than 20 and she was trained as a secretary. But in a page and a half press release she had summed up the report with a speed and skill most old pros couldn't have managed.

If there was ever a lull in our operation, Cherie would visit other departments in the campaign, asking if anybody needed any typing done.

"I hate not being busy," she explained.

Naturally, when somebody that crucial cracks and starts crying, it shakes everyone's confidence. When I heard about it, I immediately went to Cherie, but she just laughed, saying it was only nerves and she was sure she had it out of her system.

I wasn't so sure.

That night at dinner, I complimented Debbie for the poise and tranquillity that was keeping the press room crew as close to an even keel as possible.

As I was speaking, I noticed her upper lip was twitching. Tears appeared in her eyes. That composed face on which we had all relied was crumbling. She was feeling the pressure as much as anyone but had merely been better at concealing it.

The next day in headquarters, Debbie came apart, sobbing on Cherie's shoulder.

That did it. After another brief session with Doctor Sasser, I marched into Carl's office and told him we had to accept one of Mort's many resignations.

"I'm sorry, buddy," he said, "but we just don't have the money to pay him. Try to live with it a little longer if you can."

The next day I tried a new approach on Mort. He was as fond of the two young women as we all were. He wouldn't hurt them intentionally and he didn't know he had. I told him. I explained that his daily rages were taking their toll on everyone, that Cherie and Debbie had been reduced to tears, that we were all miserable, including him, and that it simply had to stop.

The report on Cherie and Debbie shocked him to his senses. He was ashamed of himself. He promised that if he ever felt like exploding again, he would contain it until we could both get outside the press room where he could blow as high as he liked without unnerving the whole crew.

"Don't be mad at me, Bill," he said.

"I'm not mad at you, Mort," I sighed.

"Great," he said, breaking out in a broad grin and hugging me, "then you'll let me buy you lunch." He wanted to have a happy lunch just to show me what a fun guy he could be now that he had decided to reform.

At lunch at a nearby French restaurant, he was once again ecstatically happy. Jolly Doctor Jekyll had returned.

Mort remained jubilant throughout the lunch, asking to be reassured several times that we were "still friends." Each time I reassured him, he would reach across the table and dance his fingertips on my cheeks, saying, "Oh, Bill Hall, I'm so happy."

*   *   *

One day toward the end, Henry Kimelman had another terrific idea for another terrific five-minute network fund appeal that we didn't have any terrific money for. But this time, I wasn't summoned to draft the script.

I knew something was going on when Steve Russell, an Idahoan who had attached himself to Kimelman, occasionally stopped by and asked me for a copy of something Church had said on this or that. He was taking the quotes I gave him to one of the researchers in the issues section who occasionally did some writing. The researcher (unknown to them, a friend of mine) slipped into my office and told me what was happening. Henry was preparing another commercial and was flanking me.

Late that afternoon, a red-faced Steve Russell came running into my office, saying "the senator wants you in his office right away with your draft for the taping tonight."

"What taping?" I innocently asked.

"Jesus Christ," Russell said, protesting a bit too much, "you mean nobody told you?"

Earlier in the day, Burke, Kimelman, and peacemaker Peter Curtin had met with Church. The senator agreed, at Henry's insistence, that he would try one more commercial. The taping would be at 7:30 that night, and Church said to tell me to get cracking on a draft of what he would say. Burke, who had to go over some campaign details with Church, remained behind after the meeting and asked Curtin to relay the word to me.

Instead, Curtin, Russell, and Kimelman kept me in the dark. They gave the assignment to a writer they thought would more likely follow Henry's instructions and load the script with more blatant begging for funds. I was inclined to write a script in which Church spelled out his positions on the issues, with an announcer's voice taking on the less dignified task of pleading for money. Henry wanted and usually won a script that had Frank Church looking with sad, threadbare eyes into the camera and saying, "I really need your help. Please send as much as you can, as soon as you can, to me, Frank Church, Box 1976, Boise, Idaho."

And even that wasn't enough. Henry was always after longer fund appeals, wanting Church to explain in more detail how very much he needed the money. I wouldn't have been surprised if Henry had put Church on television, down on one knee in an Al Jolson pose, singing, "Money, how I need ya, how I need ya, my dear old money."

So Kimelman, Curtin, and Russell had gone around my squeamishness to another writer. But Church didn't know that. And when he was unhappy with the draft they offered him and asked for the script he had directed me to write, Russell had no choice but to come to me. They could pass it off as a failure in communication and maybe there would still be time for me to whip up something.

"Somebody should have told you," Russell said. "You're going to have to write something pretty fast. The taping is at 7:30." It was damn near 5 o'clock.

I snarled at Russell and Curtin, and Curtin shook his head, saying it was all some misunderstanding and he didn't know why people couldn't get along. I grabbed my file of Church quotes and galloped across Capitol Hill to the senator's office.

But there was no hurry. Church had been compelled by scheduling to fly all night without sleep and then fight all day on the Senate floor for some Intelligence Committee legislation. He had been on the road seven days a week for two months. And he was due to fly out after the taping to an overnight stay in Cleveland where he would get his first sleep in two days. Carl Burke was in the office as I arrived, and he doubted there would be a taping.

Church was so exhausted and groggy that he had gone to the Senate baths, hoping a good soak would wake him up.

What he needed was a cold shower. He took a hot, oh-so-relaxing bath. Shortly after I arrived, he came shuffling into the office like a zombie. There was a silly little grin on his face, like he had just had a lobotomy and all the world was wonderful.

"Hello, Senator," I said.

He stopped and looked at me for the longest time, that strange peaceful smile on his face. He didn't recognize me at first.

"Well," he finally said in an ancient voice, "Bill Hall. How are you, Bill?" He gave me a campaign handshake, smiling even more, proud that he had remembered the name of still another constituent.

There was no taping that night, of course. Instead, our candidate got a brief nap and then rushed into still another airplane, heading for still another city somewhere out there in that country the size of a continent.

The next day in headquarters, I issued the ultimate threat to all the appropriate people: "If you ever pull anything on me like that business yesterday with the television script, I'll show you what dirty fighting really is. I'll tell Bethine."

That scared the hell out of them for several days.

But there came an evening shortly thereafter when Carl Burke, more blue than usual, wanted to barbecue a couple more steaks on the Church patio. As we settled in for the evening, Carl told me that Kimelman, campaign treasurer William Landau, and peacemaker Peter Curtin had called him into Kimelman's office that afternoon.

They informed him they had held a meeting among themselves and had voted unanimously that Carl should resign. The junta had decided that Carl was just getting in Henry's way. And naturally, they explained, when Henry took over, he would fire all the other "Idahoans," including me, Verda Barnes, and of course, the Idahoan from Miami, Mort Schwartz.

Carl was so crushed by their disapproval that he hadn't even stopped to consider the effrontery of their vote to dismiss him.

"Maybe I should go back to Idaho," he said, feeling sorry for himself. "I wonder if old Frank would like me to go home."

Carl was puzzled at my reaction. I was elated.

My God, I told him, maybe they could pull it off. They were pretty good at flanking maneuvers. Maybe they could really get us all fired and we could all go back to Idaho several weeks earlier than planned. I even offered to slip into headquarters late at night and leave some kind of damaging evidence against us on Henry's desk.

Carl finally located a few tattered threads of his once-robust sense of humor. We spent most of the evening creating scenarios on how we could get ourselves banished to Idaho where we would be condemned to sit on the patio and drink wine and watch the grass grow under a blue western sky.

We toyed with a Bre'r Rabbit plot. If members of the junta learned that we actually wanted to return to Idaho, they might just be mean enough to make us stay in Washington. So we would emulate Bre'r Rabbit and spread the word around headquarters that nothing frightened us more than the thought of being fired and thrown into the Idaho briar patch.

As the night wore on, I developed another scenario and was half serious about it. Carl and I wouldn't go into the office the next day. Instead, we would drive to Monticello and spend the day with that old faction fighter, Tom Jefferson, leaving the junta to wonder where we were and what we were up to. We wouldn't be up to anything, but our unexplained absence would make them paranoid about what we were hatching in the way of retaliation.

Carl rumbled with laughter at the thought of it. But he chose to treat the suggestion as a joke. I think it concerned him that I seemed to be perfectly serious. But I was serious. I had never seen Monticello. And I had seen all of a presidential campaign I cared to.

* * *

Any pretense I had of being a fully functioning presidential campaign press secretary had evaporated by then. The Churches were wisely running most of their own PR straight from the campaign plane with the help of two proficient young press people—Bob Kholis of California and Jan Ziska of Colorado—who had been added to the traveling staff earlier in the campaign. Except for phone calls from reporters wanting to know Church's position on given issues, I was functioning largely as a campaign chaplain, trying to pump up the morale of the emotionally exhausted people around me.

And of course, in the evenings, when need be, I had Doctor Sasser to lean on for my own underpinning. But it was strictly a social occasion and not for more counseling that I accompanied her to Verda Barnes's apartment one night for dinner. I wouldn't burden her that night.

But we got to talking about our campaign trouble. All of a sudden a wave of melancholy swept over me. Tears came into my eyes and I just let them roll for a couple of minutes. When it passed, I felt purged. I hadn't been so relaxed in weeks.

As the evening ended, Doctor Sasser and I went down the elevator together. As we descended, she began choking. She seemed to be ill and I was afraid she was going to lose her dinner right there in the elevator. When the doors opened, she made a beeline for the parking lot, still seeming to be choking on something. But as we reached her car, she began sobbing. I threw my arms around her and held on while the dam broke and ran over for a very long time.

Myrna Sasser, as a Senate staff worker, had been outside the center of the battle in national headquarters. But she could not escape the burden of what friends like Carl Burke, Bill Hall, Verda Barnes—and Frank and Bethine Church—were going through. Myrna felt the pain of her friends. So her reaction was normal. Nonetheless, it is unnerving to watch your psychiatrist fall apart like a normal person. I didn't know how much more of national headquarters I could take without Doctor Sasser to lean on.

A few nights later, Carl Burke called. He cheerfully ordered me to leave immediately for Oregon, to get out of headquarters and go do my thing with the reporters on the road.

"I wish I could go with you, buddy," he said a little less cheerfully. "But you enjoy yourself out there. Just remember that a campaign should be fun."

And in Oregon, 3,000 miles from national headquarters, it finally was.

Chapter Fourteen
Out in Oregon with Dave Broder
and What'shisname

David Broder of the *Washington Post* groped toward our table in Portland's murky Benson Hotel bar. He had called earlier in the day suggesting we meet there. I brought along Larry LaRocco, a Church organizer who was respectful that I knew the famous political writer. Larry and I were settled in with other reporters, awaiting Broder's arrival, when we spotted him coming our way. He sat down next to me. Larry was impressed.

"Dave," I said, "this is Larry LaRocco, one of our Oregon coordinators."

They shook hands and Broder turned to me.

"I don't believe we've met," he said, putting out his hand.

He was embarrassed as I reintroduced myself. Larry avoided my eyes.

"It's so damned dark in here," Broder apologized.

It wasn't that dark. It was the measure of how long I had been out of circulation, playing desk general in the press operation at national headquarters, that one of the principal political writers of America had forgotten what I looked like. So had many others. I spent most of the week before the Oregon primary regaining contact with the national press people who would or would not make Frank Church a serious national contender if he won the Oregon primary. Oregon presented an unusual opportunity. Campaigning there that week were Frank Church, Jimmy Carter, Jerry Brown, Ronald Reagan, and Gerald Ford. As a consequence, Portland's Benson Hotel bar became a nightly convention of major political reporters. Each night around 6:00, I would settle into the Benson bar and remain there until 2:00 a.m., feeding Frank Church tips to writers. A more devoted press secretary might have given his kidneys for his candidate. I declined. I was determined to keep both my kidneys and my marbles. I stretched two or three glasses of white wine over an entire evening.

As I arrived in Oregon, the polls were not encouraging. The undecided vote was still large, but Church trailed Carter by quite a bunch. He was running about even with Jerry Brown, who entered too late to get his name on the ballot and had launched a massive, heavily funded write-in campaign. We would be outspent in Oregon several times over by each of Church's opponents.

But there was something in the air. In Portland I found a Frank Church headquarters that knew what it was doing. Under Larry LaRocco and his co-coordinator, Mike Kopetski, neither one of whom was yet 30, the Oregon operation was focused, functioning with several hundred people scattered around the state working their butts off. And there was none of the constant warfare of our paralyzed national headquarters.

I asked LaRocco to join me my first day in Portland to help answer questions from Don Campbell of Gannett News Service. Campbell started by asking about our Oregon organization, and the next thing I knew, LaRocco got carried away and gave him some figures that had to be pure baloney. He told Campbell that the Church organization would reach virtually every household in Oregon, either by phone, mail, or through door-to-door canvassers. He mentioned something about 125,000 phone calls.

I was disappointed in Larry. He was laying it on dangerously thick.

"I think what Larry means," I interjected, "is that our goal is 125,000 phone calls—if we could round up the manpower and the money."

"No!" Larry said sharply. "I mean we'll make 125,000 telephone calls by election day."

I let it pass. But after the interview, I took Larry aside and lectured him on the dangers of conning the press.

"I'm not conning," he insisted in a wounded voice. And then he ticked off the phone banks, the number of people manning them, and the hours they were in operation.

"You mean those mail and door-to-door figures were also correct?"

"That's right," he said defiantly.

"And we really are going to reach everybody in Oregon by the election, one way or another?"

"Damn near everybody," he said.

"Are Carter and Brown doing the same?"

"They aren't even coming close."

"Jesus Christ," I said, contemplating the effect on the large uncommitted vote, "that makes it sound like we could win."

"I expect us to," LaRocco said, not batting an eye.

I took him back to the bar with me that night, hoping to steer the conversation with reporters toward how well the candidates were doing respectively on reaching individual voters. Broder came in shortly after we arrived.

"Hi, Larry," he said, sitting down next to LaRocco. And once again, sticking out his hand, he said to me, "I don't believe we've met."

I reminded him once more who I was, and Broder and I were both embarrassed. But Larry LaRocco, who is ordinarily a tad short, stood tall that night.

As we talked, it became plain that Broder also believed Church might have a chance in Oregon. But he wondered what it would mean if Church only narrowly defeated Brown, a write-in candidate. A write-in, Broder reminded me, is a tremendous handicap.

"Not in Oregon," I countered truthfully. "This is a well-educated, high-turnout, populist state. They all know how to write in a name. There isn't a voter in Oregon over 30 who hasn't written in a name at least once in an election. They do it all the time. Being a write-in certainly doesn't help, but unless he comes within a point or two, it will be Frank Church, not the write-in procedure, that beats Jerry Brown."

Broder remained skeptical. I could see it coming. Church would win the Oregon primary, but the press would write that the real winner was Jerry Brown:

> PORTLAND—Jerry Brown came within 50,000 votes of carrying the Oregon primary Tuesday despite the crushing handicap of a write-in candidacy.
>
> Frank Church of Idaho may have received more votes but the real winner was the remarkable young governor of California . . .

*   *   *

One day in Oregon I encountered one of those tricky press decisions that influence so strongly the selection of the next leader of the free world. The question was whether to put Frank Church on a bicycle for the first few blocks of an environmental bike ride. The question, in short, was whether to stage a media event. Church had prepared a fresh and thoughtful speech for the same day. But television was up to its rabbit ears in thoughtful speeches and the resulting pictures of little talking heads. The enthusiastic young man who thought up the publicity idea advised me that Frank Church would have his best shot at making the network news that evening if we could get his distinguished fanny on a bicycle seat and let him pump a few blocks. The young man was right, of course, but conscience demanded that I fight the idea for a time:

"My God, there's a lot of quality in this man," I preached, more at the television age than at the young man, who patiently waited for me to get it off my chest. "Frank Church would make a damn good president, but he's a lousy bike rider. I'm not even sure he still knows how to ride a bicycle. Surely we aren't going to choose our president again this year on the basis of who can think up more media events. Surely we have gone beyond that as a nation. Surely we are more mature now."

The young man said that we surely should be, but that we surely would make the network news that night if we could get Frank Church on a bicycle.

I capitulated, but I made him promise, before scheduling Church, that he would check with the senator to see if he had been on a bicycle lately.

The young man said he would check if it made me feel better, but it didn't really matter whether Church could manage a bicycle or not. Footage of the senator falling off a bike would be certain to make not only the evening news but the morning news as well. It was plain the young man almost hoped Church had forgotten how to ride.

Church thought the idea sounded like fun. He was getting as bored as the networks with his being a little talking television head, giving one speech after another.

And the scheme worked. The networks passed over the profound speech Church delivered that day. But there he was, coast to coast, wobbling along on a borrowed bicycle.

Thereafter, we took that lesson to heart: None of that idea crap; we concentrated on pictures. One day we sent him to the Portland Zoo where he conferred with a gigantic tortoise, the creature Church had adopted as the mascot of his campaign and the symbol of his late, late entry into the race. Not only did Church and the tortoise make the networks, but also front pages all over the country. In place of the talking head, we had given the networks the green, scaly, beady-eyed head, and they anointed our campaign with coverage.

The bike-riding event reminded me of an expression from my youth when I spent two summers working in a carnival as a pitchman for a fun house (part of my early preparation for presidential press work). The carnies I worked with would pull into a dusty little town somewhere in the Midwest, look around, and then swear: "God damn! The people in this town are so cheap they wouldn't pay a nickel to see Christ ride a bicycle."

The networks would—and a lot more. But Christ could skip all that Sermon on the Mount stuff. Who needs another talking head?

*   *   *

I was surprised one day in Portland to run into Warren Manshell and his wife. They were wealthy friends of the Churches from New York. I asked Warren what the hell he was doing way out in Portland, Oregon.

He was vague about it, so vague, in fact, that it suddenly dawned on me what the hell he was doing way out in Portland, Oregon. And though he and his wife are two of the most charming people you could meet, I quickly terminated the conversation and got away from them.

The Supreme Court had ruled earlier that year that it was an abridgment of free speech to forbid an individual to spend as much as he pleased on saying who he thought our next president should be. The court held that the law could require candidates to accept no more than $1,000 from each contributor because that was a matter under the candidate's control. If a candidate wanted to cash in on federal matching funds, then that candidate could be expected to abide by federal rules which set the $1,000 minimum. But the same law could not override the First Amendment and deny an individual the right to spend whatever he pleased, strictly by himself, on uttering his political opinion on the presidential campaign. The court held, in effect, that the law could no more restrict an individual to $1,000 worth of speaking his mind in television commercials than it could restrict a citizen to only 1,000 minutes that year of telling his neighbors who he thought our next president should be. As long as a wealthy individual acted on his own, without any collusion with the candidate, the First Amendment would permit him to spend as much as he wished toward furthering the cause of any candidate he admired. In short, it was a loophole in the law—if a candidate had an admirer with the imagination and generosity to figure out on his own that some substantial surprise expenditures would be most appreciated.

I had heard that Warren Manshell had been as generous as he was imaginative in buying television time for Frank Church in Nebraska. If he was inclined to be equally generous in Oregon on behalf of the same cause, I didn't want to know anything about it. That might be collusion and a violation of the law.

I had an even closer call the next day. Someone with the Oregon environmental movement had been spreading the fib (on behalf of which Church opponent we never did learn) that Church had voted against legislation to preserve scenic Hells Canyon on the Oregon-Idaho border. The truth was that Church not only voted in favor of the legislation, but was its prime sponsor. So it was a pretty big fib. But some of the environmental leaders of Oregon, not doing their homework, bought the story wholesale.

Church, who was proud of the legislation, was furious—and concerned that the story would cost him votes he felt he had earned. He asked me to contact Ted Trueblood, an Idaho outdoors writer with something of a national following among environmentalists. Church wanted Ted to prepare and sign a newspaper advertisement attesting to Church's early and persistent devotion to Hells Canyon and other conservation causes.

I called Ted. He was willing, but puzzled.

"I'm coming to Portland tonight to make some television commercials for Frank," he said.

"You are?"

"Yes, some gentleman named Warren Manshell wants me to tape some conservation commercials. I don't understand why you don't know about it."

"I think maybe now I do, Ted," I answered, "but we better not talk about it. I'll explain why after the election is over." And then I quickly hung up.

That night, as I prepared to board the press bus with the reporters to follow Church to a speech, Ted Trueblood popped out of a cab right in front of the bus.

"Well, hello, Bill," he said. "Have you learned any more about my commercials?"

"No, Ted," I said, grabbing him by the arm, steering him out of earshot of the reporters and asking if he didn't agree it was a lovely evening. He was puzzled as I excused myself and boarded the bus.

Later that same evening, I was having dinner in the Benson Hotel with a reporter from Idaho and a reporter from *The New York Times*. Ted Trueblood strolled in with the Manshells. They sat down at the next table without noticing me. Complaining about the light in my eyes, I scooted my chair to a position that kept my back toward the adjoining table.

*   *   *

I know my severe limitations in the television world, so it was not like me to take over a Portland television station. Church was doing another half-hour call-in show. He would go on live answering questions called in from throughout the viewing area.

Mort Schwartz, our sometimes television director from Washington, had flown in to produce. For all his usual emotionalism, Mort was all business while in charge of a show. Just before we went on the air he did flare briefly, telling a man wearing a Jerry Brown button to leave, "because I don't want bastards like you in my control room." But that was the only outburst.

It was tempting to offer Mort a few suggestions, but I knew how unwelcome amateur opinion would be. I had learned, accompanying Church to many television interviews, to keep my place. A live television program is a nerve-wracking business for the crew. They have neither the time nor the tolerance for any interference. A control room can get hectic enough without some yo yo bothering you.

And so I stood silently against the back wall of the booth, out of everyone's way, as the show went on the air. Church began well.

He fielded a broad range of rather controversial questions smoothly and without hesitation, coming across as strong and well-informed, showing a flair for the format—much as Bill Clinton would do in his campaign for president a generation later. The clincher on Church's appearance would be his two-minute, well-rehearsed, but seemingly spontaneous pitch directly to the Oregon voters at the close of the program.

"Keep an eye on the clock," Mort said near the end of the broadcast, "and let the floor man know when we're down to two minutes."

Misunderstanding, the director leaned forward to the mike—with six minutes to go—and said crisply to the floor man, "Signal two minutes."

"No!" Mort moaned. "It's six minutes."

"Oh, Jesus!" someone else said.

"Tell the floor man, 'Not yet!'" Mort said quickly but evenly. But it was too late.

"Well, senator," the moderator said over the control room speaker, "we have only a couple of minutes left. I wonder if you might have some final word for the people of Oregon."

And Church, thinking he had two minutes rather than six, launched into his closer.

"Have the floor man tell him they'll have to go back to a few more questions at the end," Mort snapped.

But that was wrong. It would be plain to anyone watching that Church was wrapping up the broadcast. If he went back to questions and then tried to come up with still another closer, it would be too obvious that the program was all screwed up. Who would want someone running a country who couldn't even handle a half-hour television show?

"No!" I called out in a crisp command voice I didn't know I had. "That won't work. Just let the senator know how much time he really has left. He's a pro. He'll fill."

No one stopped to question what the hell I was doing barking orders in a television control room. They just did as I said. And Church, who was indeed a pro, filled the time almost effortlessly, sweating only on the inside.

As the program finally ended, a feeling swept over me of great relief—and also of great power.

*   *   *

I had another drink with Dave Broder in the Benson Hotel bar a couple days before the election. This time he actually recognized me. Moreover, he acknowledged the accuracy of my theory that the write-in status of Jerry Brown was not that great a handicap in Oregon. He had checked it out. Typical of Broder's thoroughness, he had spent all day Sunday going door to door, interviewing the residents of an entire precinct in a Portland suburb. He encountered numerous Church voters. More important, every time he found someone who planned to vote for Brown, he asked them how a person writes in the name of a candidate.

"They all knew," he said.

And so, when Frank Church won Oregon, defeating not only Carter but also Brown by a wide margin, Brown supporters tried to make excuses. The Brown people tried to feed the notion to the press that the write-in procedure, rather than Frank Church, had beaten their candidate, that it was a moral victory.

But most of the press, with the respected Dave Broder leading the way, wouldn't buy it. They wrote that Frank Church won. Indeed, Broder wrote after Oregon that Church was the most underestimated candidate of the year.

*   *   *

Church flew to California the day after his Oregon victory. He wanted me to rejoin the campaign plane and follow along rather than return to national headquarters. He didn't have to ask twice. As we flew south from Portland that morning, Church's son, Forrest, slipped into the seat next to mine. His father wanted me to "do what you did in Oregon." I had learned in Oregon that I could be most effective when I stayed away from Church. Carl Burke, Forrest Church, Bethine, and I were the only ones authorized to speak for the senator to the press. When Church was around, no reporter wanted to talk to a press secretary; they clustered around the candidate himself. But when Church wasn't around, they would take what they could get. I could then feed stories about Church to the reporters. He would get more exposure if I worked where he wasn't. With few exceptions, that's what I did the remaining two weeks of the campaign. When Church was in Los Angeles, I would go to San Francisco, and vice versa.

On that morning after the Oregon victory we had been scheduled to hit Los Angeles, where Church addressed the UCLA student body, and then fly on to San Diego for a dinner of Church supporters. Church overruled that plan on the way to L.A. He wanted to go on to Ohio. He figured Brown would take California anyway, and Church had a lot of catching up to do in Ohio where he might, he reasoned, stand a better chance.

But some of the network television equipment was by then already checked through to San Diego. The television correspondents were not pleased. One of them gave me a tight-lipped little lecture:

"Look," he said, "this isn't the first time your campaign has fucked up, not by a long shot. For you guys, it's just standard operating procedure. And we've been patient. We know you've been operating on a shoestring. And we know your scheduling is a disaster and you've got World War III in your national headquarters. What the hell difference did it make until now? But now your candidate has won two primaries in a row. He's become a real candidate. If you don't get your act together pretty damned fast, we're all going to start reporting how really fucked up the Church campaign is."

That seemed clear enough.

But I had some good news for him on that same subject. The reporters had asked me more than once why we didn't place Cherie Coleman in charge of press logistics. Cherie was a born travel agent, a genius at working out impossible airline schedules and hotel reservations. The reporters had no faith in our scheduling department and had frequently leaned on Cherie by telephone to make certain they went where the senator went and had a place to sleep when they got there. I told the television correspondent whose gear was on the way to San Diego that Church had agreed that morning to bring Cherie aboard the campaign plane the next day and place her in charge of their travel and accommodations. And thanks to Cherie, we did get our act together. Thereafter, life contained fewer surprises for the reporters covering the Church campaign.

But Cherie's personal sacrifice was great. She was terrified of flying. She would work like a driven woman right up to the time the plane took off. And then she would quietly settle into the seat next to one of the reporters and bury her head in his chest while he held her until the plane was aloft.

*   *   *

Los Angeles, despite its frenetic reputation, was like being on vacation after the preceding months. The Los Angeles Church headquarters functioned in an exceedingly leisurely fashion. Oregon had been frantic, people racing about from morning until night. In Los Angeles, campaign workers sat quietly at desks, speaking softly on the telephone. Others gathered casually to discuss budgets or scheduling—without raising their voices. Most of the workers rolled into headquarters around 10:00 in the morning. And yet they seemed to get as much done as we had in Oregon—and certainly more than in national headquarters.

Some evenings I was invited to sit around a pool or stroll by the ocean. Campaign workers told me about their psychiatrists and boasted especially about their answering services. I gathered it was a terribly trendy thing at the time.

Working with reporters in L.A. was also something new. The local press seemed bored with the election. And there was nothing equal to Portland's Benson Hotel bar with its nightly congregation of national writers. But many of the national reporters dropped by the Church headquarters. The easy pace seemed to affect them as well. We would go next door for coffee and a sandwich, and hyper reporters would visibly relax. Jovial banter was the rule rather than the usual tough questioning. It was always too nice a day in sunny Los Angeles to play hardball.

After national headquarters, the oddest aspect of Church's Los Angeles headquarters was that the workers were kind to each other— and to me. Four of them in particular—Barbara Brown, Barry Rice, Mimi Adams, and Mike Novelli—became my benevolent keepers, feeding me corned beef, pouring me wine as I sat by the pool, driving me to newspapers so I wouldn't get lost in that sprawling city, and pretending that they hadn't been functioning well without me.

After all those weeks of racing and quarreling in national headquarters, I began to heal—and to yawn. I felt like I had been committed to the Los Angeles Home for the Politically Sane.

In San Francisco the next week, it was more of the same. The press was exceedingly civilized and listened patiently to my fairy tale about how I wouldn't be surprised if Frank Church did a lot better in California than everyone expected.

One local television commentator, Rollin Post, had been scheduled to have lunch with me. But something came up and he kindly pawned me off on Carolyn Craven, the station's reporter in charge of researching Frank Church. Witty, intelligent, and attractive, she insisted on having lunch in the sun on a dock overlooking the bay. After nearly four months of being held captive inside a seething, claustrophobic political headquarters, I was relaxing over lunch with an engaging companion, sipping a gentle white wine, and letting the sea breeze blow the cobwebs from my psyche.

Carl Burke would have approved. The campaign had become fun.

*   *   *

As election day drew near, it was obvious we would get waxed in both California and Ohio. It was time to head east, pick up my belongings, and prepare to return to Idaho. Church was campaigning in Ohio. I hopped a plane to Cleveland the day before the election to be in on the end of it all with my candidate.

Larry LaRocco, who had gone on to Ohio after the Oregon win, met me at the Cleveland airport to give me a lift into the city. He mentioned that one of Henry Kimelman's people, also in Ohio for the finish, had scolded him for wasting his time picking me up. "Why can't he take the airport bus?" he had asked Larry.

That final night in Cleveland, a dozen members of Church's personal staff gathered with the candidate and his wife for a private dinner in a secluded section of a seafood restaurant. The Churches knew what the next day would bring, so it no longer mattered. With the pressure off we were all in high spirits.

Frank and Bethine Church went to bed early, but the staff gathered in the hotel bar. We sat around a large table—Cherie Coleman, Mort and Capucine Schwartz, Mike Wetherell, Larry LaRocco, and a couple of off-duty Secret Service agents. We had a party.

It was the night before the ignominious end, but all was right with the world. After all, we had been part of an American presidential campaign. It wasn't the greatest campaign in the history of the republic, and it had frequently been wrenching. But we had been deep inside a ritual. We had courted the affections of the American people. We had loved and we had lost and now it was over. And that was cause for celebration.

Chapter Fifteen
Oh, Give Me a Home
Where the Pundits Don't Roam

On June 8 of 1976, Frank Church was mashed like a small potato in the Ohio and California primaries.

On June 9, the Democratic Party stampeded to Georgia and Jimmy Carter.

On June 11, Frank Church's press secretary climbed into the saddle of his little automobile and headed west at a full gallop. The campaign was over. It was time to go home.

Home, in Lewiston, Idaho, was a continent away. It is as far from London, England, to Moscow, Russia, as it is from Washington to Lewiston. But I found the pull of Idaho unusually strong that first day on the road. I covered a third of the continent, more than 700 miles, not stopping for rest until 3:00 in the morning 80 miles west of Chicago.

West. That was the word. I would not sleep well until I was once again home in the West. Home is a compulsion among those who have never managed to become rootless. An attachment to the land is an almost metaphysical tie. Perhaps it is only an emotional apron string, but it is almost as though, as a life-long parasite on a benevolent host, my chemistry and my heartbeat were synchronized with the land. And so I wasted no time putting Washington behind me—Maryland, Pennsylvania, Ohio, Indiana, and Illinois in a single day. Wisconsin, Minnesota, and South Dakota the next. Sprawling Wyoming and massive Montana the third day. And then, over the Continental Divide into Idaho. A three-and-a-half-day dash from one side of the country to the other.

And home.

I encountered people along the way strikingly different from those who labor in Washington. Politically, there are two Americas—

Washington and the rest of the country. Frank Church used to scoff at attempts by some of the more misanthropic Washington reporters to take sophisticated little digs at him and other western and southern politicians. Jimmy Carter was an especially popular target early in the campaign. Washington reporters snorted at Carter's rustic and unconventional ways, thereby endearing him to the electorate. But a Washington veteran like Church also got the treatment on occasion. One *Newsweek* article characterized the senator as a puritan, a goody-two-shoes, a stuffed shirt. "Frank Cathedral," they dubbed him. "An Eagle Scout," they tittered, printing the article with a picture of Church at a national jamboree wearing a Boy Scout uniform.

Church chuckled when he saw it. He recognized that the article was intended as a put-down. But he also recognized the effect outside Washington of a magazine story accusing him of being too sincere, too pure, too overbearingly honest. Outside Washington, the common estimate of politicians—including candidates for president—is best summed up in the hyperbolic folk judgment, "They're all a bunch of crooks." In that climate, there is worse publicity for a candidate entering primaries in places like Nebraska, Oregon, and Montana than being labeled an Eagle Scout.

And so some in the Washington inner circle laugh cynically at the rest of the country. But the rest of the country also laughs at Washington. And they're both a bit over the edge in their estimates. Not everybody in Washington is an arrogant twit and not everybody in outer America is a selfless genius. Nonetheless, much of America has the rather vain view of itself that ordinary people outside the capital have a pure perspective on those issues that confuse Washington. That is part of the reason outlanders like Jimmy Carter and Bill Clinton get elected. Most people outside Washington believe that they, unlike the occupants of the capital, can see straight to the heart of a matter.

As a matter of fact, some of them can. There is a grain of truth to the folk faith in unclouded provincial wisdom. But for every perceptive, open-minded rustic brimming over with greater sense than the government, there are dozens of dour provincials who carry to extremes the belief that there is a superior, bedrock wisdom outside Washington. There is an abiding hatred of the federal government in the provinces, a populist conviction that we would all be better off without that overbearing government. Idaho is at the forefront of such thinking. But as I neared Idaho on the drive home, my progress was slowed by one truck after another pulling massive mobile homes. For once, I didn't mind. Two weeks earlier, the Teton Dam had burst in eastern Idaho, sweeping away hundreds of houses. Those mobile homes, on loan from the Department of Housing and Urban Development, would be the only protection from the elements many of my fellow Idahoans would have for more than a year. Ironically, eastern Idaho, scene of the dam failure, is a hotbed of hatred for the federal government. Except for that incompetent dam—which they begged the federal government to build—they view most of the government's domestic functions with suspicion. And they resent their share of the cost.

But they accepted the free mobile homes and all other assistance they received from their government in the wake of the disaster. They were soon back on their feet—and back to damning Washington.

Such inconsistencies are nothing new in Idaho or elsewhere in the interior of the country. Some years ago, Idaho congressman (and later senator) James McClure voted against an appropriation to combat rats in the slums of large cities.

"In Idaho, we kill our own rats," he sniffed.

"In New York City," replied Idaho journalist Perry Swisher, "they fight their own forest fires."

I discovered on the trip across the country that other proud populists had been chastened by events. As I drove past Rapid City, South Dakota, on a Sunday morning, I listened to the live radio broadcast of a church service in that community—a community devastated by a flood of its own four years before.

"Many of you have asked," the minister said, "if we could take a collection this morning for the victims of the Teton Dam disaster in Idaho. You will find an envelope for that purpose at your seat—so that you might help as we were helped four years ago."

But of course, communities that have not yet experienced extreme misfortune are less quick to come forward with assistance. There is rarely enough help volunteered in these situations. So we have formed a federal government, as a way of pulling—somewhat involuntarily—together.

*   *   *

Anyone who has driven the 200 miles of Highway 12 from Missoula, Montana, to Lewiston, Idaho, will know that it was not entirely a homesick boast to believe that the most stunning portion of my drive across country was the last. Highway 12 follows the approximate route of the Lewis and Clark expedition through the wilderness those two explorers labeled "the green hell" because it was so nearly impenetrable. But that forest was skillfully penetrated in the 1950s by a new federal highway, a highway that winds through the country that welcomed me home. The road follows the Lochsa River, a mountain stream that tumbles through rock rapids for several hundred yards at a stretch, and then relaxes in deep green pools where plump little rainbow trout wait for the current to wash them food—and an occasional well-placed dry fly. Along the banks and climbing up the massive mountains on either side is the same wilderness that Lewis and Clark saw when Tom Jefferson sent them west to look over the new country. That was, of course, a federal expedition. And without the protection of the government today, those federal forests would be nude in no time.

Strange creatures traveled through the forest on the day of my return. I passed dozens of red-faced young bicycle riders going the other way, straining at the pedals, fighting the steep grade into Montana. I learned later from their Idaho press clippings that they were from the East, on an American Bicentennial bike ride across the nation—and that they suffered from diarrhea from drinking polluted water. The expression on their faces made it plain that there are better ways to climb that mountain than placing your tattered fanny on a little bicycle seat and pumping the pedals until the veins stand out on your temples. They were not having a good time.

I was. Coasting downhill through the same scenery in my car, I thought how glad I was to be home in Eden and away from that godforsaken city in the East.

The cyclists, straining up an endless incline, oblivious to the scenery and wondering whether they could make it to the next biffy, must have wished they were home in the gentle East and away from that godforsaken mountain. One person's Eden is another person's hell.

I returned that day to my Eden, my odyssey ended. Sixteen months after I had left for Washington to determine whether Jody Powell or I would become press secretary to the next leader of the free world, Jody was forsaking the gentle Georgia way of life and I was settling into my backyard in Idaho.

Not long after my return, I received a message to call an assistant to Powell in the Carter press operation in Plains, Georgia. I knew what it was. They were gleaning troops from other campaigns, offering them jobs to beef up the Carter staff for the fall election—and also, thereby, offering a salve for any wounds suffered in the primary wars. I was certain they were going to offer Frank Church's press secretary a job.

But they didn't. They were considering a job for Jack Calderon, a member of the Church press staff who had applied with them and had listed me as a reference.

I gave Jack the strong recommendation he deserved and then chatted a few minutes with the Carter press person about the fall campaign and what I would do in their shoes.

"I don't suppose," he interjected at one point, "that we could tempt you to leave those beautiful Idaho mountains again so soon and come to work for Governor Carter?"

No, I said, thanking him for the gesture, I didn't suppose they could. One presidential campaign would be sufficient.

That night, feeling even more liberated from all that, I put on my old orange tennis shoes, poured a glass of white wine and strolled through the garden. I was inspecting the rows of vegetables when I spotted something new: A precocious little green bean plant had become the first that summer to pop into bloom.

I raised my glass in kinship. That made two of us who had our feet in soil that suited us well.

Epilogue
Ashes to Ashes

One day early in May of 1980, Tom Wicker of *The New York Times* called to say he was flying into Lewiston the next week to take a first-hand look at the attempt by Idaho's reactionary Republican congressman Steve Symms to remove Frank Church from the Senate after 24 years in that office. Wicker asked if I would help him find local sources and let him buy me dinner while he was in Lewiston.

I immediately agreed, of course, and not just because I am always glad to touch the *Times* for a free dinner. I had met and dined with Wicker on several occasions over the years when his work as a columnist had brought him to Idaho and, of all the roaming heavyweights of American journalism, he has always been among the most affable. I told him I would pick him up at Lewiston Airport the following week.

Nature made a change in our plans that Sunday. On May 18, 1980, Mount Saint Helens in western Washington blew away the top 1,312 feet of its original 9,677 feet, killing 65 persons, leveling trees for miles, sending a plume of volcano innards 11 miles into the air, and making the Church-Symms race seem suddenly insignificant.

For good measure, the volcano dumped several inches of dense volcanic ash in a long, fan-shaped swath through Washington, northern Idaho, and even western Montana, paralyzing life in the region in ways worse than the snowdrifts it somewhat resembled. School classes were canceled. Offices were closed. Some of the more powerful automobile engines sucked too much of the stuff in through the carburetor air intake and choked to a halt. And many Northwest residents who ventured outside those first few hours wore filter masks or handkerchiefs over their own air intakes, not certain at first how harmful the dust might be.

Lewiston was on the southern edge of the swath of ash and received only a light dusting. But some of the communities of northern Idaho that Wicker wanted to visit were deep in ash. I knew that because, when the mountain blew, I was in Sandpoint, a city on the northern edge of the ash belt. I drove back to Lewiston straight through the volcano's deepest drifts.

Talk about eerie. The evergreens, the shrubs, and the grass of northern Idaho were covered with what looked like moon dust. The pale ash swirled about as you drove, creating a blizzard of powdered rock. The forest was uncharacteristically silent and outwardly lifeless.

Wicker called the first of the week to say he was coming to Lewiston anyway. A person could always cover a political race. But it isn't every day that he gets a look at the consequences of a volcano.

I drove with him 80 miles north of Lewiston, back into the heart of the region buried in volcanic ash. Driving through the afflicted region was an adventure. Volcanic ash is more like face powder than like snow. And being rock, it is absolutely opaque. As we drove into the region with the deepest ash, trucks would occasionally pass us going the other way, throwing clouds of dust in the air and obscuring all light for several seconds. You don't know the meaning of the term "zero visibility" until you have experienced that. I had learned on my first trip through the ash belt that you must slow to a crawl every time you see a truck coming so you don't lose your bearings during the brief blackout and drive off the road.

Our search for the deepest ash took us to Plummer, Idaho, a small strip of stores, gas stations, and cafes on the Coeur d'Alene Indian Reservation. We had a lunch there that was unavoidably gritty. The ash was sifting into everything, including our sandwiches, giving us nourishment and polishing our teeth at the same time. But it wouldn't hurt a person; it had been sterilized in a volcano.

We asked some reporter-type questions of the friendly locals who, after several days of nature's nonsense, had done the only thing that you could do in a situation like that—find your sense of humor and laugh your way through it. They were in pretty good spirits for dusty people with their crevices full of ash.

We completed our interviews. But before we headed back to Lewiston, we stopped at a grocery store and bought a box of plastic sandwich bags. And then, on a hill just south of Plummer, we pulled into a turnout where the ash was about six inches deep. We got out and, using our bare hands as shovels, scooped the ash into several sandwich bags and sealed them shut. They made marvelous souvenirs for friends and relatives around the country, especially children.

But those first few days with the ash were worrisome to those covered with it. They had never been through anything like that. Suddenly they saw their green land go gray—a durable gray at that, made of rock. Some said it would be years before the ash stopped fouling car engines, interfering with agriculture, and seeping into sandwiches in Plummer cafes. Some said it could blight life in the afflicted parts of the Northwest for years to come.

We were all new to the phenomenon of such far-reaching volcanic ash. Most of us had never heard of such a thing. I had followed the stories earlier that year of a swelling mountain getting ready to rouse itself and blow, but I assumed it would be like volcanoes in the movies. In the movies, a volcano rains rocks and dust on a region a few miles around, crushing straw huts and causing Hollywood extras to run screaming toward the camera.

But when Mount Saint Helens blew, we were suddenly standing there blinking through the ash 300 miles from that rude mountain. Where did that come from?

The Northwest news media finally started to catch up. Stories came out quoting scientists who said it was ever thus with mighty volcanoes of the Saint Helens sort. The scientists called our attention to the construction cuts along Northwest highways where it has always been possible to see the grayish white layer of ash from volcanoes that erupted hundreds of miles away thousands of years before.

Indeed, the house in which I now sit is built on land that is at least a few inches higher than it would be were it not for past volcanoes. I have those volcanoes to thank for my higher perch in life and my better vantage.

The troubling part was that those long-buried layers, exposed by excavations, didn't look much different from the one freshly on the ground at Plummer. That meant the stuff was as durable as it looked and the Lord alone knew when we would ever see green again in the freshly plastered parts of the Northwest. How many years or decades would it take nature to bury the new layer of volcanic ash put down in our time? How long would it be before life in the Northwest returned to normal?

*   *   *

Before that year was out, another cataclysm occurred for friends and admirers of Frank Church. Ronald Reagan's first landslide swept the Idaho senator from office. The years of Frank Church in the Senate had ended.

One winter night, early in 1984, a little more than three years later, I lay in bed reading a novel—*Facing the Lions,* by none other than Tom Wicker. I was reading a scene in which a former candidate for president has died. All the people who worked on his campaign are gathering for his funeral, encountering each other for the first time in years. As I read that part, I was thinking that Frank Church would die one day and we would all be gathering for a wake-reunion of our own.

If you're superstitious, the next part gets a little spooky because, moments after that thought popped into my mind, the phone rang. It was Larry LaRocco, Church's coordinator from Oregon, telling me that Frank Church was dying. The former senator had just been diagnosed with pancreatic cancer.

Three months later, at 59, he was gone and we were all gathering in Boise for the funeral and, as in Wicker's novel, for a chance to see each other again.

Actually, there wasn't much of that for me. I had driven the 270 miles from Lewiston to the Boise funeral in a van load of Church partisans. We had to turn right around and head back to Lewiston immediately after the service if we wanted to get home at a reasonable hour. There was no time that day for reunions. And perhaps it was not the right time for a reunion anyway. We were all a little raw from the senator's defeat, followed so quickly and at such a premature age by his death. And in truth, my wounds from the great war of national headquarters still throbbed a little. I shook a hand or two outside the church and then gladly left for Lewiston.

The reunion would come 10 years later, in early April of 1994, on the anniversary of his death. The occasion was the release of what will probably always be the definitive book on Frank Church.

Washington State University historian LeRoy Ashby and Boise news-man Rod Gramer were bringing out their Frank Church biogra-phy, *Fighting the Odds*. And Bethine Church, who had long since moved back to Boise, decided to use the occasion for a reunion. She sent out the word, inviting anyone who had ever worked for Frank Church to the gathering.

I have to admit amazement at how well Bethine handled his death. Theirs was an uncommonly close marriage. They had blended into a single, compounded personality, not just talking to each other but thinking to each other as well, finishing each other's sentences, enlarging upon each other's ideas, accurately express-ing the thoughts of their unified mind on the rare occasions when they were apart.

And yet when he was torn from her, she not only went on—after a normal amount of grief—but regained her bubbly personal-ity, her rich store of mirth, and her infectious optimism.

I suspect it has something to do with the fact her care helped save his life during his first bout with cancer those many years before. I think she made a bargain then that, from that day for-ward, she would value every day of her husband's life that they were given. And part of such a bargain is that you must accept the end when it does come, being grateful for what you did receive rather than resentful over what you might have had. She was lucky not to lose him the first time and she knew it. They had 35 years more together than the doctors said they would. And Bethine Church is no ingrate. She kept the bargain. She went on cheerfully after his death, back in Idaho, meddling usefully in politics and bouncing grandchildren on her knee.

So the 1994 reunion was truly a happy occasion, and only a tad bittersweet. I attended, of course, but it appeared at first that there was a startling development: No one from the presidential cam-paign showed up. Only their parents did.

Or so it seemed at first. All the campaign kids I worked with were two decades older. They had all come to resemble their par-ents. I hadn't seen so much gray since Mount Saint Helens painted the Northwest with ash.

Many could not attend, of course. But it was a chance to catch up on where time had taken everyone. I already knew some of it:

Larry LaRocco had been elected to Congress, from Idaho.

So had Mike Kopetski, LaRocco's co-coordinator of the Church victory in the Oregon primary. Kopetski won his seat from Oregon.

So had Tom Lantos, the early Church supporter and fund-raiser, winning a seat in the House from California.

Cherie Coleman (now Slayton), my organizational brains, went to work in a similar capacity for LaRocco in his Washington office. Myrna Sasser—Doctor Sasser, who heard my campaign troubles—became the seasoned senior staff member in LaRocco's Boise office.

Verda Barnes, probably the most savvy politician in Idaho history and Church's long-time chief of staff, had gone on ahead to the final reunion. So had Don Watkins, my assistant press secretary, political guru, and eternal friend.

Debbie Herbst, whose comic banter kept the people in the national headquarters press room semi-sane, was still in Washington, where she had worked for Daniel Schorr of CBS and, later, as a writer and business manager for Christophe, the celebrated hair stylist.

Mike Wetherell, who succeeded Verda Barnes as the senator's administrative assistant, was practicing law in Boise where he was a member of the city council.

And Carl Burke was still practicing law in Boise. He had found his booming laugh again. But he still missed his boyhood chum. I saw it in his eyes.

I have lost track of Henry Kimelman and Mort Schwartz. I think I'll keep it that way.

And Mount St. Helens still simmers over there in western Washington, apparently on a low burner once more, not likely to trouble us again until some future century.

And me?

I still write editorials for the *Lewiston Morning Tribune.* And the humor column I started after the campaign is lightly syndicated in a couple dozen papers across the country.

I still prowl my vegetable garden almost daily, this time with Sharon, the linguist and sculptor who married me in 1985, giving me the kind of marriage Frank and Bethine always had.

One recent weekend, Sharon and I were driving through the northern part of Idaho when we passed that point near Plummer where Tom Wicker and I knelt down that day in 1980 and scooped volcanic ash into sandwich bags with our bare hands. There is no sign of the ash from Mount Saint Helens today. Indeed, most of it was gone within a year or two. And long before it vanished, it quickly settled down and began to behave itself, blending with the pine needles, the leaves, and the new dust and dirt that drifted down upon it.

Some of that ash is probably blowing in the wind. But the rest of it is still there, just beneath the surface now, a permanent layer in the Northwest soil, just like all the other layers from all the other volcanoes that have helped build this soil from which Frank Church sprang and to which we must all return. The law says ashes to ashes, whether you're a volcano or a person.

And just as the once-deep ash near Plummer has vanished, similarly, there are few visible signs of Frank Church left in this part of the country only a few years later. It is amazing how something once so large, whether man or mountain top, can vanish like that.

And how quickly people forget. There are children today in Idaho who do not know Frank Church's name. There are children today in Idaho who do not know they stand on the ashes of great mountains—and of great leaders.

We all stand on ashes. And if we should manage to rise higher and see farther than those who came before us, it because we stand on what they have done.

Some day, some little Idaho boy or girl will grow up to become President of the United States because the children of this state now stand taller than they did before a man named Frank Church put down his part of their foundation.

Acknowledgments

If there is any gratitude in the world, I suppose the acknowledgments for a book called *Frank Church, D.C., and Me* should begin with profuse thanks to Frank Church's mom, to my mom, and to Pierre Charles L'Enfant. Pierre designed Washington, D.C. Our moms designed the senator and me.

Nonetheless, for all my gratitude to Pierre and to those two dear ladies, others have also contributed substantially to this book—and in more practical ways. Chief among them has been the book's editor, Keith Petersen, and his colleagues at Washington State University Press. Journalists are especially prone to equate "editing" with impulsively whacking away, trying to make the words fit the space and the deadline. But "editing" is not quite the word with book editors. "Nurturing" would be a better word when speaking of Petersen. He has a gentle way of respecting pride of authorship and a diplomatic tendency to refer to a glaring error or a windy passage as a possible opportunity for improvement. Thanks to Keith Petersen, this is a leaner, better book than it began. Also at the Press I would like to thank Tom Sanders, Mary Read, Beth DeWeese, Wes Patterson, Dave Hoyt, Arline Lyons, and Jean Taylor.

I am honored that Dr. LeRoy Ashby, the WSU historian, called the manuscript to the attention of the WSU Press and now provides the foreword for the book. I am an admirer of Ashby, both for his work as a historian and for his star status as the professor who packs them in when it comes time to breathe life into the story of significant American figures.

My thanks to Barry Kough, the veteran photo journalist of the *Lewiston Morning Tribune* whose photographs are included in this book. Kough enjoys and understands politicians. It shows in his pictures.

Thanks also to Sharon Taylor, my wife, and to Jim Fisher, my fellow editorial writer for the *Lewiston Morning Tribune*. They peered through fresh eyes at the manuscript, saving me from several stumbles.

On second thought, Pierre Charles L'Enfant didn't have much to do with this book. But *merci* to those who did.

About the Author

Bill Hall has been editorial page editor of the *Lewiston Morning Tribune* in Lewiston, Idaho, since 1965, with a year and a half away from that job to work as chief speech writer and national press secretary to former Idaho Senator Frank Church during Church's 1976 presidential campaign.

Hall, born in 1937, is a native of Idaho. A graduate of Boise High School, he studied journalism at Idaho State University in Pocatello. He was a reporter and political writer for the *Idaho State Journal* at Pocatello for eight years.

Hall is married to Dr. Sharon Taylor, author of linguistics textbooks and director of the Intensive English Institute for international students at Lewis-Clark State College. Taylor is also known as a sculptor, both in bronze and in reshaping the uncivilized tendencies of a middle-aged newspaper writer.

Hall wrote a political column for 15 years before favorable reader response to occasional outbursts of humor caused him to shift into that gear permanently. Hall's humor column, syndicated by Extra Newspaper Features, is currently carried by 24 papers across America.

Three collections of his columns have been published as books: *Killer Chicken*, *Son of Killer Chicken*, and his latest, *The Sandwich Man*, a look at life in "the sandwich generation," those mid-life Americans stuck between the youngest and the oldest members of their families.

Index